Tips and Tricks

of

the Stagehand

[THIS PAGE INTENTIONALLY BLANK]

Tips and Tricks of the Stagehand

by
B.T. Clark

Illustrations by
Michael Hsu

Copyright © 2020 B.T. Clark
All Rights Reserved

Published by Debrouillard Ventures LLC
New Haven, CT

This book may not be reproduced, duplicated, or transmitted, in whole or in part, without the prior written consent of the publisher.

No reference in this text to a particular product or business is intended to be an endorsement of that particular product or business. The contents of this book are believed to be accurate. However, this book and its contents are being provided on an "as is" basis. The publisher and the author do not make, and each specifically disclaims, any representations and warranties of any kind whatsoever, whether express or implied, with respect to the information in this book, including, without limitation, any warranty as to accuracy or completeness, merchantability, or fitness for a particular purpose. In no event will the publisher or the author be liable for any damages of any kind whatsoever arising out of, resulting from, or in connection with your use of the information in this book, including, without limitation, any lost profits or revenues, direct, indirect, special, consequential, incidental, compensatory, punitive, or other damages.

By using the information presented in this book, you are assuming all risks and liabilities arising out of, resulting from, or in connection with such use.

ISBN: 978-1-7363657-0-0

Library of Congress Control Number: 2021902034

1.02.02

To Diana
You and me against the world.

For my better half, Steph
*My favorite travel
companion, dinner date, and board game foe,
for whom I will always save my last bite of uni.*

[THIS PAGE INTENTIONALLY BLANK]

Contents

List of Tips and Tricks	viii
Preface	xiii
A Challenge to the Reader	xvii
How This Book is Organized	xix
Part 1 Mounting a Show	1
Part 2 The Shop & The Road	79
Part 3 Fundamentals & Trivia	111
Part 4 Useful Info	159
Part 5 Computers & Calculators	191
Acknowledgments	253
References	255
Index	268

List of Tips and Tricks

PART 1

The In   3

Who's driving the forklift?	4
Low Profile Courtesy Tab	5
Wet Chalk	6
Burning a Foot?	6
Two Tape Layout	7
Adding a Setting Line	12
Make "On Center" Easy	16
Cable Label Law	17
Non-Uniform Standard Length of Tie Line	17
The Shoelace Knot	18
The Stagehand's Timber Hitch	20
Threading Sheaves	23
Monster Walk	25
Mirror Matching Hands	26
The Physics of Stacking Flats	27
The Physics of Footing a Flat	30
More Footing Physics	33
Leave them loose, make them all...	36
The Hammer Trick	37
Barn Dooring Tight Fits	39
Poker Chip PAR Lens	41
Chip Brush Door Hold	42
Hacksaw Window Hold	43
Check the Truck	44

The Run   45

Blind Pickup Follow Spot Target	46
Lock Rail Muffler	47
Ribbon Trim Fid	48
Tire Repair Tool Fid	49
Spike Tape Dog Collar	50

Spike Mark Protection	50
Sweeping the Stage	51
Sweep Top Down	52
Wet ≠ Dripping	52
Tying Up Legs	53
Tennis Ball Buffers	54
Worn Screw Holes	55
Etiquette	56
Protect the Mic	57
Four Thoughts on Scene Shifts	58
The Lonely Clove Hitch	59
Swing on a Line Set	60
The Show Stop Out	62
Hot Glue Quick Fix	62
Vodka and Condoms	63

The Out	**65**
Pull the Tape before the Cable	66
You don't coil a cable…	67
Self-Releasing Knot for Lowering Lights	68
Sweeping for Nails	70
Last Bolt!	71
Start with the Hard One	72
Remove a Bent Screw	72
On the Diamond (Getting Over Bumps)	73
Tip the Dolly	74
Super Secret Glitter Removal Formula	74
Arbor Spreader Plates	75
Stacking Stage Weights	76
Load Bars at the Tail	77

PART 2

Shop Work	**81**
A Note on Drawing Notes	82
Trash Bag Drop Cloth	82
Quick Figure 8	83

Bolt Length Rule	84
Bolt versus Screw	86
Quick Tips on Buying Hardware	87
Burning in Screws	88
Grommet Punch Jig	90
Can we just agree?	92
An Inch a Yard (Fleet Angle Rule)	93
Fleet Angle Equation	94
Swaging Tool Identification	95
Paint Pen Inlay	97
Impact Tapping	98
Stagger Casters	98
Grounding versus Grounded	99
Rot$\underline{a}$ Lock or Rot$\underline{o}$ Lock?	99
Fail Safe	100
Chasing Air Leaks	101
Pneumatic Muffler	102
Right to Work ≠ At-Will Employment	103
Travel	**107**
Luggage Carousel Tool Sale	108
Trade Show Name Tag	109
Hotel Advice	109

PART 3

Fundamentals	**113**
Bring tools.	114
Being early is on time. On time is late.	114
Stage Directions	116
A Proposal on Stage Directions	119
Electrical Overcurrent Protection	121
Bridle Tension	125
Power Transmission by Rotation	128
Power Transmission by Purchase	130
Orthographic Projection	135
Don't Run in the House	147

Trivia	**149**
Did you know...	150
If you want to learn more...	154

PART 4

Wrench Charts	**161**
Hex Head Bolts	163
Socket Head Screws	165
Rigging & Theatrical Hardware	166
Fastener Info	**169**
Drill & Tap	169
4′ × 8′ Sheet Good Fastener Schedule	170
Drywall Screw Dimensions	172
Estimating Fasteners Example	173
Stage Weights and Arbors	**175**
The Seesaw Analogy	177
Inches of Steel Weight for a Given Load	178
Total Load by Inches of Steel Weights	180
Arbor Weight	182
Pipe Weight Chart	183
Cable Weight Chart (Lift Lines)	183
Cable Weight Chart (Cable Swag)	184
Swaging	**185**
Swage Sizes	186
Swage Economics	189

PART 5

An explanation...	193
Typing Symbols	**195**
Shortcut Chart	196
AutoCAD Control Codes	198

Advanced Two Tape Layout — **199**
   Layout Flowchart — 200
Bridle Geometry — **218**
Will it fit in the elevator? — **233**
   Equation Road Map — 240
   Common Door Opening Sizes — 245

Preface

If you've been working backstage you already know some of these tips and tricks. Good advice has been passed down by stagehands in different venues for a lot of generations. Very little of it has been written down. This book tries to capture a bit of this wisdom and make it available to everyone doing the work. There are also some ideas developed specifically for this book, so even the most veteran among us should find something new to chew on.

Stagecraft has moved well beyond the traditional stage. The same techniques and technicians that started out in theaters are now at work in film and television, in sports arenas and convention centers, on corporate communication gigs and in retail displays, on cruise ships and at theme parks – just about anywhere that imagination has to be made into physical reality for an audience. You can find stagehands working gigs in the most unexpected spots, but in this book we are going to focus on where a lot of modern stagecraft began – the proscenium theater. At root, this theater is a stage in front of an audience, with hidden wings from which the performers enter and exit. We can find theaters like this all over the world. What works on this stage can, with some resourcefulness, be applied anywhere.

This is not a soup-to-nuts manual for how to be a stagehand. Even if it were, no trade can be learned solely by reading a book. Rather, this book is a collection of material that can help folks work together better by sharing some insight and answering some old questions. A lot of it has to do with the "I wish I'd known that sooner" sentiment. And while we aim to have some fun in this book, the goal is more than idle amusement.

A young stagehand takes a panel off a truck, in thru the loading door, and leans it against the back wall of the theater, just as instructed. An older stagehand that happens to be near the back wall growls at the young stagehand to give the panel more foot. *More foot?* As the younger stagehand is wondering what "foot" means – should they kick the panel with their foot? – the older stagehand walks over and pulls the bottom of the panel away from the wall so that it leans at more of an angle. "Give it more foot", the stagehand says, walking away. The young stagehand goes off to get the next panel, returns with it, and leans it against the first panel, but is sure to give it more foot this time. Another veteran stagehand is walking by, takes one look at what the youngster is doing, moves the youngster aside, and kicks the panel so that this second panel is tighter to the first panel. "Don't give it so much foot". Walking back to the truck, the youngster is wondering what to do with the third panel. *More foot, less foot, is there some perfect angle of foot that will appease these two old timers?* One response is to ask a question and risk looking stupid to the old timers who act too busy to explain things. Another response is to play dumb and just lean the panel up without care, basically using apathy as body armor from these ridiculous old stagehands that will yell at you for doing it the way the other one told you to do it. If you're getting yelled at either way, why care?

Veteran stagehands know what is going on with the panels. The first one against the wall gets a good foot, then the remaining panels are leaned tight against the first one. This gets you a pile that is both neat and won't fall over. But the young stagehand only knows that, apparently, they're getting yelled at however they do it. We see this way too often with way too many everyday tasks. These should be learning moments – no one should be feeling stupid or made to play dumb – but a myopic focus on "getting the job done" often rules. Especially with the smaller lessons, too often a stagehand is expected to learn by doing it wrong, getting corrected by someone moving too quickly to explain why, and hopefully – eventually – just figuring it out. One goal of this book is to capture our language and techniques for up-and-coming stagehands to learn faster. Another goal is to remind experienced stagehands that this job is not obvious to the uninitiated, and that there are better and worse ways to teach it.

We can all stand to learn a new thing or two. Becoming the local authority on stagecraft can happen fast with stagehands. One day you're on a call with new faces and suddenly realize that you're the one that best understands how to do the work. We have to take charge and get the work done. That's the job. But even though we've become the authority, we'd be fools to not maybe learn something new when something worthwhile comes along. This is particularly true in our business where, outside of a few hub cities, full-time professional stagehands are often isolated in relatively small groups: a union local here, a regional theater there, a production company doing gigs on its own, a school with a theater far from anything else. This book, like a stagehand on a tour, hopes to be a link between these disparate venues, spreading some good ideas picked up along the way.

There is also some information that just cannot be looked up on our phones or in the common reference books. Often these are little things, like how many screws to buy to lay a sub-deck. And there are the things we just forget and need a way to jog our memories. We remember that the orchestra pit platform's leveling feet use regular 3/4" nuts, but what size wrench fits that nut again? Is it spelled Rot<u>a</u> lock or Rot<u>o</u> lock?

Finally, if you find yourself in the role of teacher or trainer, you may find this book of some use. In particular, the fundamentals section covers some important concepts in terms of mechanical aptitude, etiquette, and navigating a stage or a drawing. Many of the lessons we teach young stagehands will find concrete form in these tips and tricks. Subjects that are treated with a rather dry, technical language in other books are explored here with practical examples in small bites.

Because this book owes its origins to many different stagehands, living and dead, who have come up with and passed on these ideas, for every copy purchased a portion of the proceeds will go to the **Behind the Scenes** charity. These good folks have made it their mission to help out those of us who find themselves facing some truly hard times. In the old days, when a stagehand was injured on the job, we passed the hat during coffee break for donations to support their recovery and their family. These days, we do the same thing on crowd funding sites, turning entrepreneurial tools into charity. It is a beautiful spirit that motivates this giving, one that we celebrate here.

Finally, on a personal note, there have been a lot of people that have been responsible in shaping what I know about stagecraft. The mistakes and the opinions in these pages are my own, but a great deal of thanks is owed to all of the folks I've had the opportunity to work with. This includes the folks who have different names for what they do, such as technical director, truck driver, scenic fabricator, purchaser, technician, machinist, projections programmer, business owner, lighting supervisor, production manager, and on and on…

By their grit and their sweat, they all make the work on the stage happen. What are we all, then, but stagehands at root?

B.T. Clark
December 2020

A Challenge to the Reader

We all use gaff tape and tie line, push things around on wheels, and have to deal with the consequences when glitter is used in a show. And so a lot of this book focuses on general skills, and is meant to be useful to everyone. But a big portion is specific to scenery and rigging. The reader will probably figure out that most of the author's time has been spent working as a carpenter and a technical designer.

Hopefully, even if this is not your department, it gives you some useful insight into my slice of the work. Now, **how about you share your own tips and tricks**, or just share your thoughts on what you see here? With enough interest – and enough material – we can push out future editions that reflect the work of stagehands more broadly, rather than this one author's time backstage.

I've never met a stagehand who had it easy. The public at large doesn't understand our work. The media only seems to mention us when there's an accident or for an op-ed that says we get paid too much. Our work day is long hours at awkward times, doing unusual things at high speed.

This book is born from a genuine admiration and respect for all hands that work on stage, and a desire to elevate the best professional standards of that work. More than that, it aims to make these standards broadly available. Traditionally, ours can be a tough business to break into because it is hard to know what is expected of you unless someone goes out of their way to show you. It doesn't help that most folks have no idea our world exists. Who can seek out a job that they don't know about?

Let's just face the facts: while none of us have it made, some of us – in addition to the standard headaches of the job – face very real, career-destroying obstacles born from old assumptions about race, sex, and class. We don't need to agree with any particular political party – or any self-proclaimed pundit or activist – to know that there is work to be done. Let the talking heads argue with each other. We'll get it done if we put our minds to it.

The simple fact is people of all types born anywhere on this earth can do the work of the stagehand.

If you think the folks backstage should match the diversity of their community, then I hope you'll join me in trying to make our work more accessible. If you think old assumptions are dividing us, then I hope you'll join me in the effort to use our work to unite us. If you think it's important that we work with each other even when we don't agree about everything – *because how else are we going to survive as a community?* – then I hope you'll join me. Let's reach out and bring each other in and bring each other up.

To Submit a Tip, a Trick, or a Comment:

Visit: modernstagecraft.com

How This Book is Organized

You did not sign any contract when you bought this book. You do not need to, nor does anyone expect you to read it cover-to-cover. Go ahead and dive in and jump around. Dog ear it, write in it, tear a page out and pin it to the callboard if you like. The goal is to make your life easier, so get there however you want.

The book begins with the phases of a show: load-in, run, strike. (These phases are also known as "the in", "the run", and "the out".) Then, in *Part 2*, the book heads back to the shop. Chronologically, shows begin life in the shop before getting on stage. But the focus ought to be on **the show on stage**. When we go to do shop work, we should always be thinking first about how the show will work on stage. So that's how it is written.

In *Part 3*, there are some fundamentals. These aren't so much tips and tricks as lessons that we pick up over time. Like most lessons, the concepts can be baffling before they are learned and obvious afterwards. I remember being confused by many of these ideas at the time I was learning them, but cannot for the life of me understand *now* how I didn't get them *then*.

The fundamentals are an important but heavy section of the book, so we have some trivia right after to lighten the mood. Then, in *Part 4*, we present tables of information. Even in the age of the smartphone-in-the-pocket, there are still things tough to find with an internet search. *Part 5* goes into computers and calculators. If you do not care how to type Ω quickly, no sweat – that is why that stuff is at the end. Think about the calculators as tools. If you don't need these particular tools in your work box, then don't bother with them. But if you face the problems they solve, maybe give them a look.

And, as mentioned before, if there's anything you'd like to see but don't, drop us a line.

[THIS PAGE INTENTIONALLY BLANK]

PART 1

Mounting a Show

[THIS PAGE INTENTIONALLY BLANK]

The In

Who's driving the forklift?

Forklifts, frankly, are a necessary evil. It would be better to roll-on/roll-off directly from the truck. But many, many venues do not have truck-height loading docks, and so forklifts are essential for getting shows off the truck and onto the ground so they can be rolled into the theater. The jurisdiction over the forklift can become a nasty problem because it varies from region to region, even from theater to theater on the same street. In some towns, the teamsters operate the forklift; in other towns, the stagehands are driving. But when it's the stagehands, is it the carpenters or the electricians? Is it one person's job and they take the key with them when they go to the bathroom?

So let's ask the question and make sure we figure this out before the day of the load-in, and let's not act like the way one house does it is the way every house does it. And, folks at the shop, please don't load the truck by driving the forklift into the trailer and stacking items. If you need a forklift in the trailer to stack it, how are the folks at the theater (who won't be able to get a forklift in the trailer) supposed to unstack it and get it out?

One more point: to a stagehand, "bring it in" means to lower an object, as in "bring in the main rag". To a teamster driving a forklift, "bring it in" means drive the forklift forward. This is one vocabulary lesson the author learned the hard way so you don't have to. Keep it safe and make sure everyone is talking the same language.

Worth Remembering…

Dock Height = ≈ **48 inches** from the road = a beautiful thing

PART 1 - The In

Low Profile Courtesy Tab

Whenever laying down tape, remember the prime directive of production work: **it's all about the out**. A courtesy tab is a good way to make tape easy to remove later, but the tab can be an annoyance. It can also snag and cause premature removal. A low-profile way to add a courtesy tab is to fold over a corner of the tape before smoothing it down. Now the tape lays flat but the corner is still easily found and lifted.

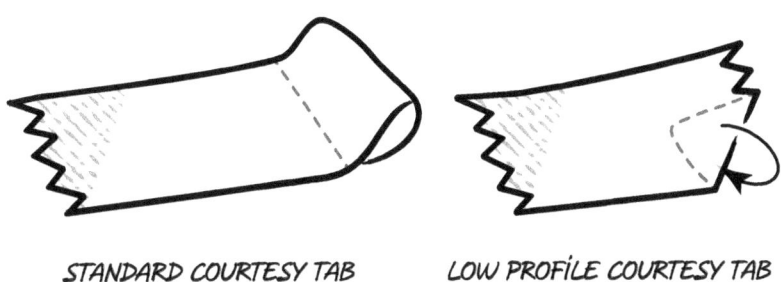

STANDARD COURTESY TAB   LOW PROFILE COURTESY TAB

"Killing" Tape

Gaff tape is great, and its glue is meant to be low tack and residue-free, but it can still take the paint off a surface. This is especially true of anything freshly painted – like new scenery – or anything that's been repainted over and over – like an old stage floor. If stagehands need to tape down a cable but want to protect the surface, they'll rip a length of tape and "kill" it by sticking it on their shirts before running it along the cable. The fuzz from the shirt buffers the tape adhesive, leaving enough tack to hold but reducing the chance of pulling up paint or sealer or anything else when the tape is removed.

Wet Chalk

Want to make a chalk mark a bit more prominent when laying out a stage? Dipping the chalk in some water will soften it up a bit and let it flow into the surface to be marked. There are industrial wet chalk markers that use the same idea with a built-in reservoir, which leave the stagehand free to hold a cup of coffee while laying out rather than a cup of chalky water.

Burning a Foot?

When laying out points with a tape measure, folks will very often "burn a foot" and start their measurements from the one-foot mark on the tape. Why? In theory, the argument is made that the hook end might be bent or otherwise not precisely aligned. Hooks on long tape measures have multiple parts to them and can take a minute to figure out. In practice, it seems that burning a foot is often done more out of habit than any legitimate need. Here's the trouble: lots of people have screwed up layout by adding a foot in the wrong direction, forgetting to add the foot, or adding ten inches to a measurement instead of twelve. A lot more grief has probably come out of burning a foot than we have ever gained in precision by avoiding the hook on the tape.

There are times when it is appropriate and necessary to burn a foot. For example, if you need to measure perpendicularly off of a taut string, you may really need to burn a foot. (This sort of measurement is common in residential construction, see the *References* at the end of the book or search the web for "batter boards" and "string lines" to learn more.) So do it as required, but only as required.

Two Tape Layout

This is a tip on how to lay out a show on a stage with two tape measures and three stagehands.

Where things are placed on stage gets laid out the same way points get drawn on a graph in math class. Each individual point is plotted from two reference lines that run at right angles to each other. In math class, these are the axes of the graph, usually called the x-axis and the y-axis. In a proscenium theater, we call these lines Center Line and Plaster Line.

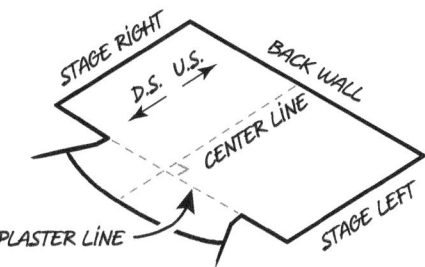

Center Line runs from the back wall of the stage, through the center of the proscenium opening directly towards the audience. The Plaster Line is perpendicular to Center Line. It connects the up stage left (USL) corner of the proscenium opening to the up stage right (USR) corner.[*]

Some shows may use a different line to set the show's location. This line is known as a Setting Line and it is usually, though not always, parallel to Plaster Line. Whether a show uses it to set the show or not, the Plaster Line is always the Plaster Line: it is the back of the proscenium arch, and it never moves. Confusion over Plaster Line and Setting Line has gotten many, many productions in trouble. To learn more about Setting Line, see the next tip. For now, we are going to ignore it.

---

[*] We are going to be using a lot of stage directions in this tip. To learn more about stage directions, check out the *Fundamentals* section in *Part 4*.

We need to establish Plaster Line first. Then we can find the Center Line of the theater. Here's how to do that with a chalk box*, two tape measures and three stagehands. (A stagehand *can* do this solo, but it involves a lot of walking back and forth.)

First, define the USL and USR corners of the proscenium. The actual architecture is often crumbling plaster or loose baseboard, so it is useful to define a specific point and mark it with a paint pen. Now snap a line between these two points with the chalk box. This is the Plaster Line.

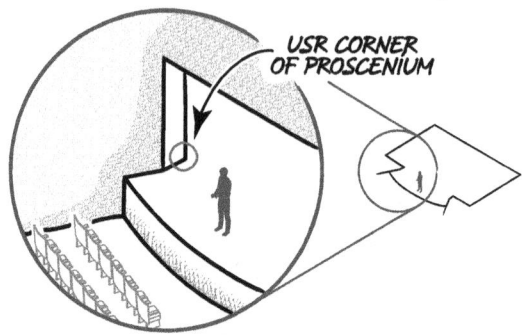

Now we find the center of Plaster Line. One stagehand stays at each corner of the proscenium, holding the hook of a tape measure on their point. That is their only job – keeping the hook at the end of Plaster Line. The third stagehand pulls the other end of each tape measures along the chalked line, running one past the other. This stagehand then finds the point where the tape measures read the same number: this is the center of the proscenium opening. Mark this point well. It is best to use a crow's foot – a vee mark, as shown in the drawing – right on the chalked line.

Now is a good time to double check the work. Use one tape measure by itself and measure from the USL corner of the proscenium to the crow's foot. Then measure from USR to the crow's foot. These two measurements should be the same. Mistakes caught while laying out are fixed by scrubbing out the old mark and making a new one; mistakes found *after* laying out are fixed with saws and hammers.

---

* Chalk boxes are also known as chalk lines and chalk reels. At root, they are just a box of chalk that a line (string) runs through. So perhaps we should be calling them "chalk line boxes"? We'll stick with "chalk box" to avoid overusing the word "line".

PART 1 - The In

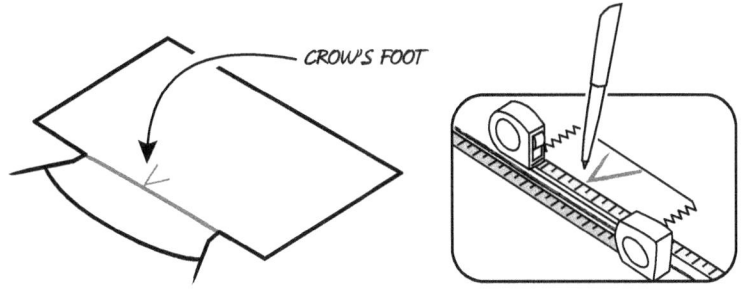

To find Center Line, the stagehand at center walks straight towards the back wall, running out both tape measures while the other two stagehands stay at the corners of the proscenium opening. The stagehand walking up stage will either run out of tape measure or will run into the back wall. At this point, the third stagehand again brings the two tape measures together and again finds the point where they read the same. A tape measure has marks along both sides of its blade. Make sure to use the edges closer to the center of the theater on both tape measures. This means the stagehand will be reading off the top of one tape measure and off the bottom of the other.

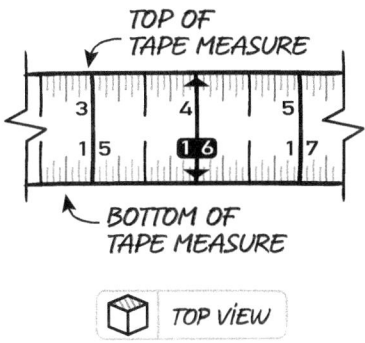

After double checking that the tapes are laying flat and straight on the floor, the third stagehand makes a mark at the point where both tapes read the same. The line defined by this point and the center point of Plaster Line is the Center Line. In geometric terms, the three stagehands have defined an isosceles triangle between each other. The apex of two sides of equal length will be centered over the third side.

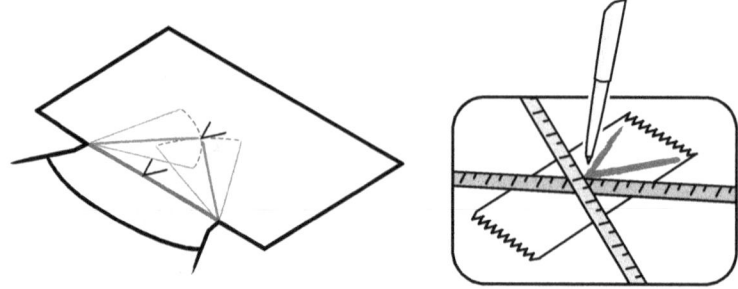

When snapping Center Line with the chalk box, it is a good idea to extend the line as far down stage (DS) and as far up stage (US) as possible. To do this, all three stagehands are needed. One stagehand anchors the end of the string from the chalk box at the DS point (the center of Plaster Line). Another stagehand runs the chalk box to the back wall. The third stagehand stands at the US point and tells the back wall stagehand how to move the line to make sure it falls perfectly over the mark. Once the line is snapped, it is a good idea to mark the back wall where Center Line ends. If the chalk line gets erased, this will make re-snapping it easy.

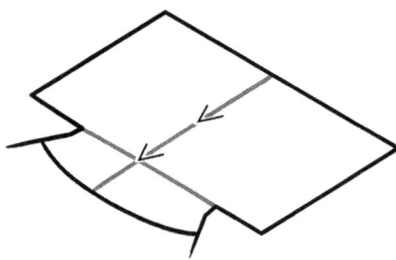

To extend Center Line all the way DS, reverse this operation with the end of the chalk box anchored to the US point to extend the line DS across the apron. This time, once the line is centered on Plaster Line, the third stagehand presses a finger down on it and only snaps the DS portion of the line. This prevents a double line from being snapped US.

The intersection of Center Line and Plaster Line is called 0,0. (This is said "zero zero".) 0,0 is the starting point for all the lay out that happens in putting a show on stage. All critical measurements should be made from 0,0. Get the layout right, and the load-in will be off to a good start.

One last point is worth making: CL is often used as an abbreviation for Center Line and PL can be used for Plaster Line. There is even a special way to write CL and PL. These symbols often show up on drawings. (If you want to type these symbols, see the Shortcut Chart in Part 5.)

CENTER LINE SYMBOL
(VERY COMMONLY USED)

PLASTER LINE SYMBOL
(LESS COMMONLY USED)

Laying out is an important skill. To learn more, check out the next tip, "Adding a Setting Line", which builds on what we've done so far. There is also a spreadsheet calculator dedicated to the subject in *Part 5*.

Adding a Setting Line

This tip builds off of the last one, where we found Center Line and Plaster Line. Sometimes, in addition to Plaster Line, we also have to lay out a Setting Line. If we have to find Plaster Line in order to find Center Line, why bother adding another line to the mix? Doesn't this just add more work and the potential for confusion? The answer is yes, but it's worth it. The problem with Plaster Line is that, by definition, it only goes as far as the proscenium opening. How do we lay out points that are further off stage, such as for lighting booms or masking? We can try to use the back wall, which in a perfect world would follow Plaster Line, but the back walls of theaters are almost always covered in equipment and junk, and usually not that flat of a reference plane.

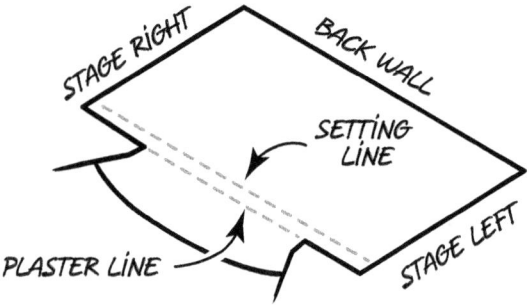

The Setting Line can be anything the folks doing a show agree to use. If the whole set is on an angle to the proscenium, it might make sense to use a Setting Line on that same angle. A very useful and common place for a Setting Line is to use a line parallel and up stage of Plaster Line that marks **the first clear line across the stage**, from wing to wing. Imagine rolling out carpet on the stage. Wherever you can kick out the first roll such that it doesn't hit any obstructions on the back of the proscenium wall, the DS edge of the carpet is the first clear line. It makes a pretty useful Setting Line.

PART 1 - The In

The most typical obstruction on the back of the proscenium are the smoke pockets for the fire curtain. These are the steel angles that house a track for the ends of the fire curtain.* It is common to use "the back of the steel", meaning the US edges of the smoke pocket, to establish the Setting Line. Because the steelwork may vary – it often does by a surprising amount – it is best to measure both the SL and the SR smoke pockets, pick an appropriate offset distance, then develop the Setting Line from Plaster Line.

Here is how to develop a Setting Line from Plaster Line. First step is to pick an offset distance. Round numbers are easier to remember. Ideally, the offset is chosen long before the day it is to be laid out. Ideally, all departments are on board and using the same offset. Measure from the Plaster Line along the Center Line and mark the offset distance. This is 0,0 – which is said "zero zero" and is the basis for the entire show. **All departments should work from the same 0,0.** Layout lasers are popular but they are not absolutely necessary. We'll continue with squares, tape measures and chalk boxes.

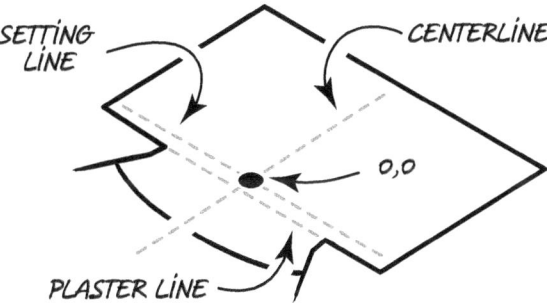

If the offset is two feet or less, a framing square can be used to simply transfer a point US from Plaster Line. For an offset up to four feet, a sheet of plywood or similar material can be laid along Plaster Line and used as a big square (just measure the diagonals and make sure the sheet is actually square first).

---

* If the fire curtain was not locked in a track, the heat and air movement of a fire would cause the curtain to just billow out of the way.

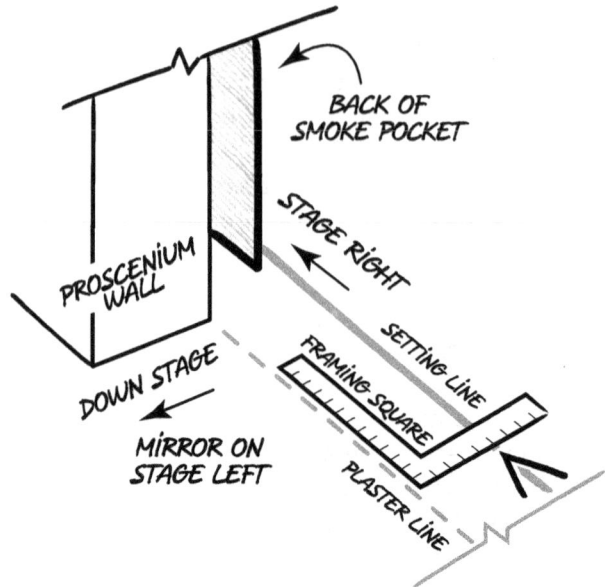

SETTING LINE CLOSE TO PLASTER LINE

For a Setting Line that is very far up stage, we need the offset distance from Plaster Line and another number: the half-width of the proscenium. The half-width of the proscenium is simply the distance from the USL corner of the proscenium opening to Center Line (which should be the same as the USR corner to Center Line). Knowing this distance and the offset distance, all we need are three stagehands and two tape measures.

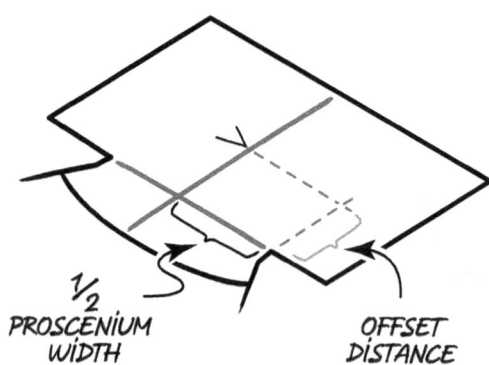

SETTING LINE FAR FROM PLASTER LINE

PART 1 - The In

First, the offset is measured from Plaster Line straight up the Center Line and marked with a crow's foot on the line. One stagehand will stay at this point. Another will go to the USL corner of the proscenium opening. The third will pull a tape measure, one from each of the other two. Now it is a simple matter of finding where the offset distance on the US/DS tape measure overlaps with the half-width distance on the SL/SR tape measure. There is a gotcha here: make sure that everyone is reading off the same side of the blade for each tape measure.

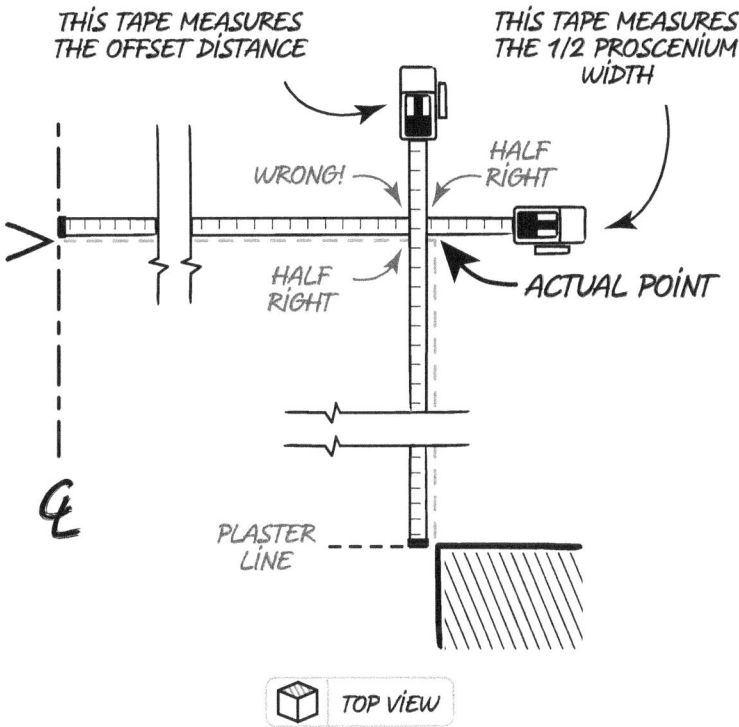

Using both the half proscenium width and the offset distance ensures accuracy. With points marked out on both sides of Center Line, it is a simple matter to stretch out the chalk box and snap the Setting Line.

Make "On Center" Easy

"On center" is a quick way to say all of these things are the same distance apart. When uniform objects are laid out with a uniform measurement, it's useful to remember that the edge-to-edge distance is the same as the center-to-center distance. Say you have a line of lights 18" on center (which we abbreviate "O.C.") and have to add one more to the end with the same spacing. Once you get the new light on the pipe with the clamp loosely made, rather than bothering with the center of anything, just hook a tape measure on the clamp of the existing light and slide the new light so that the same edge of the clamp is at 18" on the tape measure. As long as they are the same type of light, edge-to-edge is the same as center-to-center.

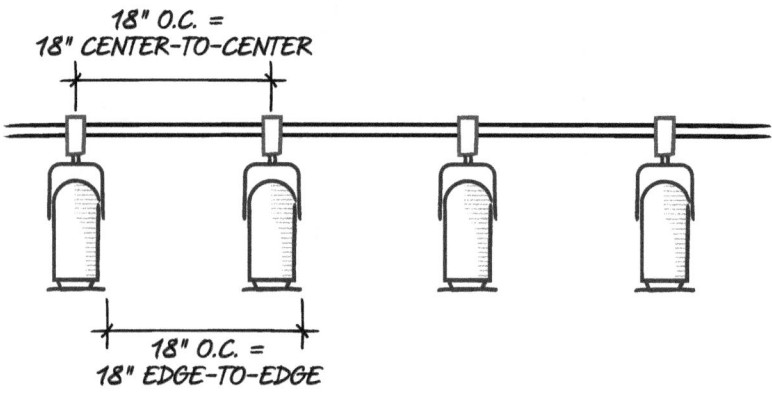

PART 1 - The In

Cable Label Law

Do the future you a favor and label both ends of the cable before running them. Stage pin, chain motor, fiber, winch motor/brake, XLR – it doesn't matter whose cable it is – stagehands who make this a habit save a lot more time when patching and troubleshooting than they ever spend on the labeling.

Non-Uniform Standard Length of Tie Line

The industry standard for tie line used to secure cables: pulling from the spool, the stagehand wraps their arm from palm to elbow with tie line. Each wrap will equal one tie. The length of the tie will vary from stagehand to stagehand (thus the "non-uniform" part of the name) but will usually be just under three feet long. When they have enough wraps, remembering that one wrap equals one tie, **the stagehand cuts the bundle <u>once</u>**, right next to where they are holding it. Make sure to cut the loop at this one point and only at this one point.

It is worth noting that cutting tie line and dealing with Christmas tree lights are pretty much the only two times it is acceptable to wrap the arm in cable or rope.*

---

* Wrapping the arm can cause kinks to form in cable or rope. This doesn't matter with the tie line because we are cutting it. Christmas tree lights are so unruly, wrapping them around something – such as an arm or a cardboard tube – is often the only way to deal with them. See the "You don't coil a cable..." tip to learn more.

The Shoelace Knot

The trouble with the shoelace knot is that the person who taught us usually wasn't a rigger. It is usually the only knot they know, other than the half-hitch.* If they were a rigger, they likely skipped the bit about bunny ears or the bunny around a tree, and they knew that the shoelace knot is really nothing more than a double-slipped square knot. (Reef knot is another common name for the square knot.) Slipping a knot just means pushing a loop of the line through rather than the end of the line. Slipping a knot like this makes it faster to untie, which is the reason we do it with our shoes. It also makes the knot less secure, which is why we don't slip every knot we use on stage.

SQUARE KNOT *DOUBLE SLIPPED SQUARE KNOT*

So the shoelace knot is a double-slipped square knot. Why does this matter? The problem is that the square knot has an evil twin: the granny knot. The real problem is when folks don't tie a square knot but a granny knot and the knot comes apart as the scrim is getting stretched on the pipe and suddenly there is a big wrinkle right at the top corner that's above the set piece so we can't get to it with the lift and now rehearsal is delayed because the designer just has to have this fixed... You get the idea.

---

* There are actually only two knots in this world: one is the half-hitch and the other is a whole lot of half-hitches. (Hey you, the stagehand that jumped all over this joke, I could hear you making it as I wrote the sentence in the text above, so I thought I'd just take a moment and say hello in this footnote.)

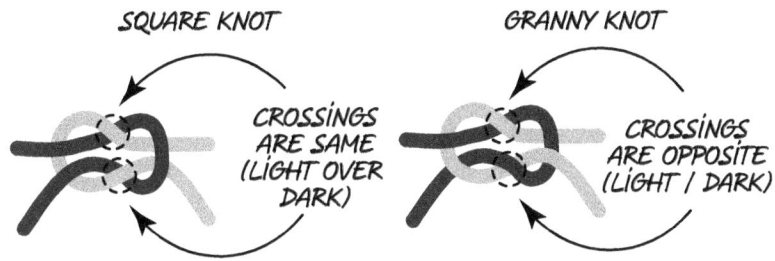

The granny knot is infamous among the knot-tying crowd for being the failure-prone result of a square knot tied wrong. It's an easy mistake to make, as easy as going left-over-right then left-over-right again. (The correct formula is to alternate: as in, left-over-right then right-over-left.) Fortunately, the mistake is easy to spot. When a stagehand ties a drape on a pipe, if the loops are running along parallel to the pipe, the stagehand has just tied a double-slipped granny knot. And slipping a granny is a way of making one of the world's least secure knots even less secure.

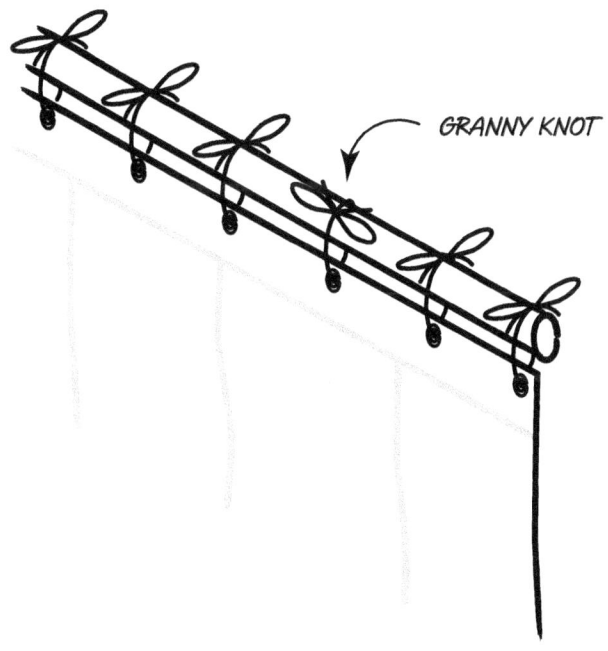

The Stagehand's Timber Hitch

To raise a pipe for a boom, or for similar applications, the stagehand uses a version of the timber hitch and half-hitch. The traditional timber hitch may be useful for dragging logs around a forest, but there are a number of downsides to the traditional timber hitch that make it unsuitable to use on the stage.* The stagehand's timber hitch is a variation that starts with a clove hitch. It works well with the objects we have to handle, such as pipe.

CLOVE HITCH WITH TWO HALF-HITCHES

To raise a pipe, the stagehand ties a clove hitch at one end and finishes it with a couple of half-hitches. Next, moving to the other end of the pipe, a half-hitch is looped onto the pipe such that it will bite when pulled.

KNOT CINCHES ON PIPE AS IT TAKES WEIGHT

This half-hitch is slid down on the pipe and cinched in place. Another half-hitch is added toward the top. Make sure there is no slack between the clove hitch, the first half-hitch, or the second half-hitch. More half-hitches can be added for extra security but two are usually enough. Avoid putting the half-hitch too close to the end: if the pipe bangs into an obstruction, the line will stretch and the

---

* The traditional timber hitch starts with a very long knot. For there to be enough room for this knot, the timber hitch can only be used on an object significantly larger than the rope's diameter, like a log.

hitch might get pulled over the end. (If only one half-hitch is used and this happens, the pipe would suddenly swing to the ground, pivoting on the clove hitch.)

Some riggers would argue that the rolling hitch rather than the clove hitch is a technically superior way to start the knot. But, in truth, the two half-hitches are generating most of the friction and doing most of the work. A significant advantage of the stagehand's timber hitch is that it is built from knots that the stagehand already knows. Knowing a small number of knots with unhesitating accuracy and speed is more useful on the job than having half of *Ashley's Book of Knots* memorized. In other words, all else being equal, the stagehand who learns to tie a bowline above their head in three seconds flat is probably going to get more work than if they spent the time to learn the Spanish and French/Portuguese versions of the bowline.*

The stagehand's timber hitch can also be used when pulling wire rope. In a typical arrangement, a spool of 1/4" 7×19 wire rope is on deck and the sheaves are up in the grid. (Another name for 7×19 wire rope is Aircraft Cable or Specialty Cord.) To get the end of the wire rope up, all the folks in the grid need to do is to drop in a 1/4" line with a cotton sheath and a nylon core. The person on deck ties the wire rope to the 1/4" cotton line with the stagehand's timber hitch and out goes the line. The cotton sheath and the narrow diameter of the pull line is key. Synthetic ropes can be too slippery. Too large a diameter of pull line will not bend tightly enough to grab. As a corollary, too small a diameter of wire rope cannot be

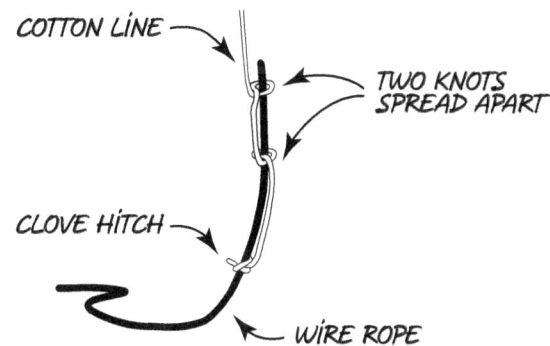

---

* Of course, all stagehands should learn the dragon bowline...

pulled in the same manner. And some wire rope constructions, such as 19×7 Rotation Resistant, may be too smooth.

100 feet of 1/4" 7×19 wire rope weighs 11 pounds and that is about the maximum load that should be lifted with this technique. If pulling from a spool, it has to be free spinning and easy to get the line off of it. The best approach is to use a reel stand or reel rollers. If the spool does not spin well for any reason, then simply flake out enough wire rope in a figure 8 pattern for the lift. This also works well when the wire rope comes in coils.

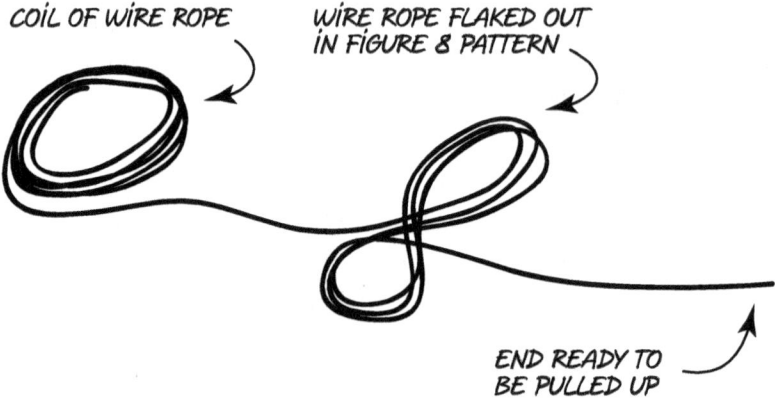

COIL OF WIRE ROPE

WIRE ROPE FLAKED OUT IN FIGURE 8 PATTERN

END READY TO BE PULLED UP

Also, just as when the hook is getting pulled up to hang a chain motor, part of the job for the stagehand on deck is keeping folks on stage clear of the line as it goes out. No one should ever walk under or close to under anything getting hoisted up during a load-in. The fact is that the wire rope can slip out and fall back to the stage deck if it hits anything on its way up. It can also slip and fall if the line snags on the deck, such as if the spool gets stopped from spinning or someone steps on the line.* This won't hurt anyone if the area underneath the line is actively kept clear by the stagehand on deck.

---

* Some riggers will prefer a wire rope grip such as Klein Tool's Haven's® Grip for pulling on wire rope. These work fine. They are generally useful tools but they can also release the wire rope if they strike anything. It remains essential to keep the area under any lifting operation clear.

PART 1 - The In

Threading Sheaves

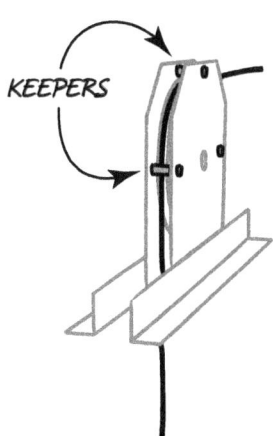

There is a necessary evil when inserting wire rope thru a sheave: the keepers. We need keepers to prevent the line from jumping off the sheave and wedging itself between the sheave and the cheek plate. This can happen if the line goes slack for a moment. So we add keepers that keep the line in the groove. All good, except that the tight clearance between the keeper and sheave makes it harder to thread the wire rope correctly. Usually there are multiple keepers and usually the first one is easy enough to clear. The next ones as the line goes around the sheave are often the troublesome keepers.

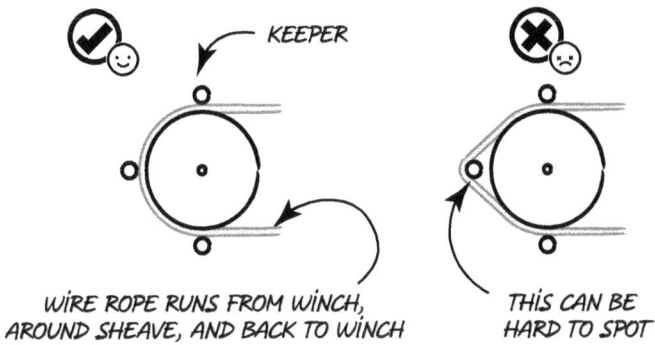

A COMMON PROBLEM WITH DECK SHEAVES

Threading the sheave will be easier if the wire rope follows the curvature of the sheave more closely. We can accomplish this by snapping a kink into the line on purpose. Make a tight loop, as if starting the bowline knot, then yank on either side away from the loop. This will kink the wire rope, giving it a bend that can be used to follow the sheave. Trimming the line tighter to the bend or snapping in a second bend can both help with really tricky sheaves.

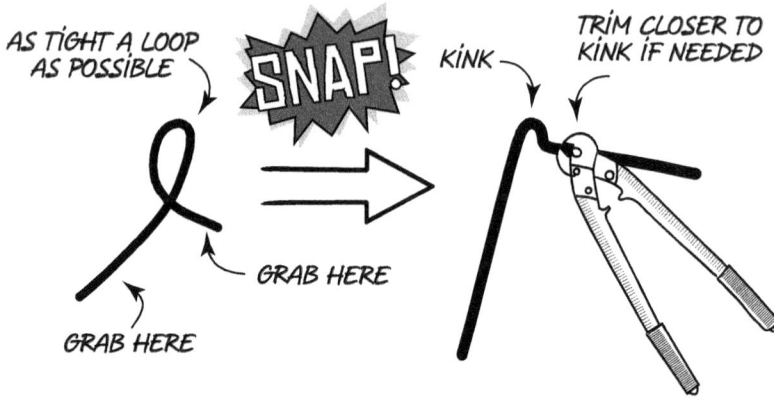

Once the wire rope has gotten through the system, these **kinks have to be cut off**. This technique is also a nice demonstration of why the wire rope needs to be treated with care: we don't want these kinks forming in the middle of a working line.

PART 1 - The In

Monster Walk

There is an old motto attributed to stagehands: "Never lift what you can drag, never drag what you can roll, never roll what you can leave".* The Monster Walk is a corollary to this motto. When it comes to objects that are wider than you, taller than you, and weigh more than you, never lift the object completely. But with something this big, dragging it for long distances isn't much better; it'll lean over too much and the stagehands will have to fight to keep it from falling. With stagehands on both ends of the piece, the trick is to take turns lifting and swinging the piece. First one side picks and starts moving the piece, rotating it on the opposite corner. When they set the piece down, the stagehands at the other side go through the same process. And the piece is walked across the stage.

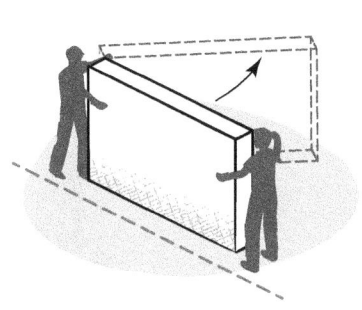 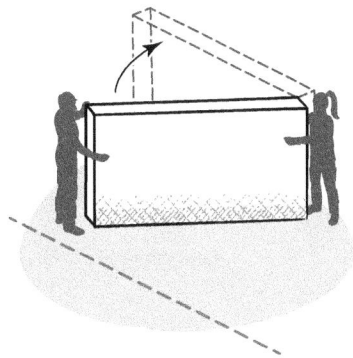

Walking a piece works well because while one half of the team is lifting, the other half is doing the work of stabilizing the piece from falling over. If everyone was lifting, everyone would also have to stabilize. Taking turns allows for more control and less fatigue.

---

* One source is Jan Adkins' wonderful book, *Moving Heavy Things*, but the idea and the saying are much older than that.

Mirror Matching Hands

When two stagehands get on either end of a flat, a screen, or any sort of panel — and if it's light enough for the two of them to carry it — the job is easier if they mirror match their hands. As they face each other across the panel, one puts their left hand low and the other one puts their right hand low. They know they have it when looking across the panel at each other is like looking at a mirror, at least so far as hand orientation goes.

HANDS MIRRORED

PART 1 - The In

The Physics of Stacking Flats

The first flat leaning against a wall needs a good bit of foot. Here's a way to test if a flat has enough foot: with the first flat leaning against the wall, give it a shove towards the wall; if it starts to move or fall over, it needs more foot. Every other flat that leans against the first one needs no foot at all. If there is air between flats as they are stacked, eventually they will begin sliding out. If you lean a book against a wall, there is an angle at which it will stay leaning and an angle at which it will slide down. Go ahead and test it out, you happen to have a book – or a digital equivalent – in your hands. As it leans against a wall, it is the friction of the wall and the floor that keeps a flat or a book from sliding down. Interestingly, the critical angle is solely a function of the friction between materials – the higher the friction*, the more lean is possible. For the same material on the same wall and floor, changing the weight or size of the material will not change the critical angle.

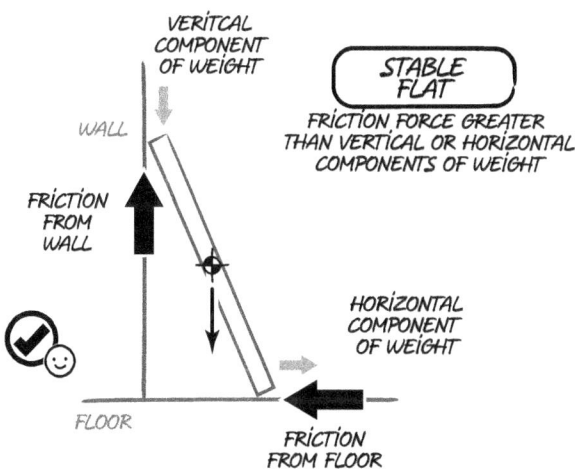

---

* This is called the "coefficient of friction". Wood on rubber has a high coefficient of friction; steel on ice has a low coefficient of friction.

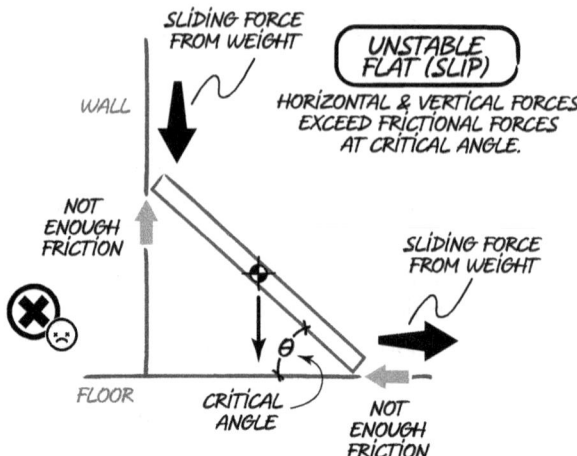

When flats get stacked poorly, they will eventually reach the critical angle at which they slide out. At the theoretical optimal, they will be perfectly parallel and never reach the critical angle. Realistically, if they get stacked neatly and professionally, the stagehands will probably run out of flats before they get close to the critical angle.

The idea of the critical angle applies to anything that gets leaned against a wall. Ladders are another pertinent example. In fact, in textbooks about statics – the study of how things stay standing up – "the ladder problem" is a common way to present this material. See the *References* for more information.

PART 1 - The In

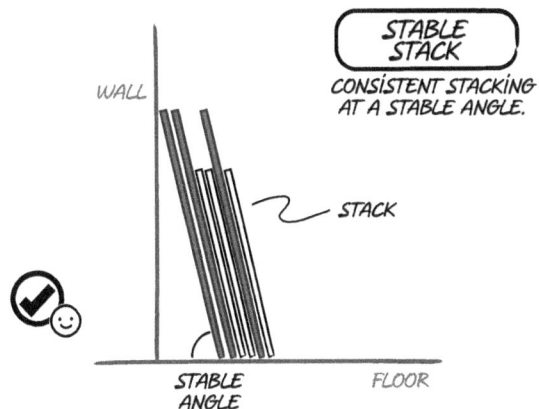

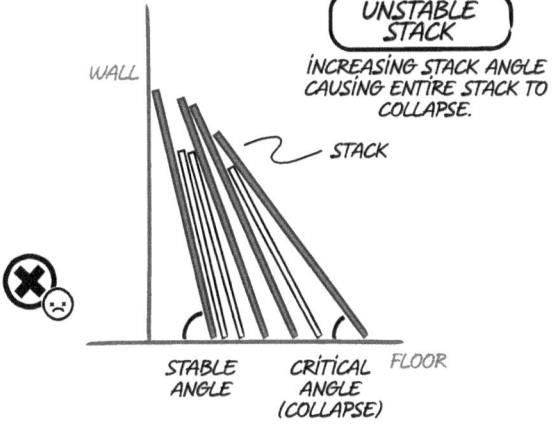

The Physics of Footing a Flat

Laying decks and picking up flats are a stagehand's lot in life. Professionals do their job well and good stagehands know that when picking up any object that is taller than the stagehand can reach – whether it is a flat or a lighting boom or anything else – not only do folks need to be lifting, some folks need to be footing.

Imagine a simple rectangular flat with consistent framing and sheathing. This flat is tall and the stagehands need to walk it up. One stagehand foots and one stagehand lifts. The stagehand footing has two jobs over the course of the lift. In the first stage, with the flat still close to the ground, footing helps keep the flat from sliding away horizontally. But actually, until the lifters get the flat above head height, the footer really isn't doing much at all. The lifters should have complete control of the piece. When they get one end higher than their hands, then the lifters are really starting to walk the flat up, and now the footer has work to do.

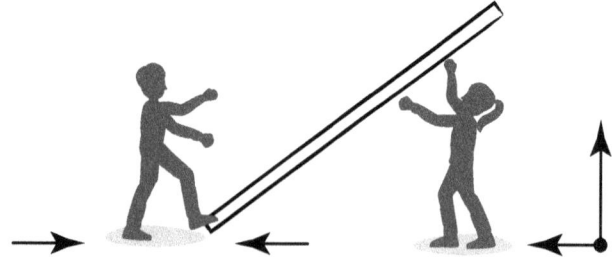

When walking up a flat, the lifter is both pushing up and pushing forward. They need the footer to resist the forward push and act as a hinge, so that the flat rotates up. The footer is a hinge, but there are two different phases to this job. Right now, with the lifter just getting

PART 1 - The In

started, the footer just keeps the wall from sliding.

Something very important happens when the lifter gets past the center of the wall. Right before they reach center, most of the weight is still in front of them, on the ground. After they pass center, most of the weight is behind the lifters, in the air. If the footer were to suddenly step away, the lifter would become the pivot point of a very uncomfortable and dangerous seesaw.

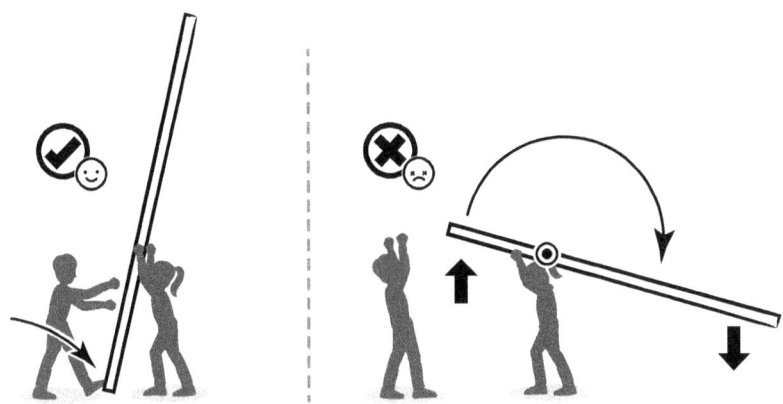

So, as the lifters reach the center of the flat, the footer begins their second job: **preventing uplift**. The longer the object, the more important this second job becomes. In a physics classroom, we would call the lifter a moving fulcrum and the flat a lever arm. Only the footer is able to resist the lever's increasing forces.

LONGER FLATS CREATE MORE FORCES

The taller the piece being lifted (and also the shorter the stagehands), the higher the forces involved. It is important that both the lifters and the footers can handle the load. But don't forget about the flat either: the most stress a flat ever sees is often when it is walked up.

Many a piece of scenery that would have been structurally sound in either a horizontal or a vertical position has failed in the transition from the one to the other. (Mirrors and molding seem particularly vulnerable to this sort of bending.) Travel braces or other stiffeners can help a wall deal with the stresses involved. Another common practice is to get a rope tied off to the top and have some folks pull the flat up, either from a position above (like the grid) or by using a pulley. By lifting from the end of the piece, the bending force on the flat is significantly reduced.

It is important for the stagehands footing to know the two distinct jobs: preventing <u>sliding</u> and preventing <u>uplift</u>. While we call it "footing", for certain lifts, the footer needs to have both hands on the piece, making sure they have all their weight on it to keep it from flipping over.

More Footing Physics

There are some realities of footing that deserve a closer look. We know that footing long objects can generate uplift. Resisting the uplift force is one of the footer's most important jobs when walking up a long object. **The length of the object is a critical factor.** In fact, an object that is lighter-but-longer can generate more uplift than an object that is heavier-and-shorter.

Here's an example: a couple of stagehands are going to start walking up truss columns. One truss is twenty feet of 20.5" box truss, the other truss is thirty feet of 12" box truss. To make the difference in weight more pronounced, we'll use the heavy-wall version of the 20.5" truss. Per the catalog, the 20.5" truss weighs 204 pounds and the 12" truss weighs 183 pounds. How does the uplift change as the stagehand doing the lifting approaches the stagehand doing the footing?

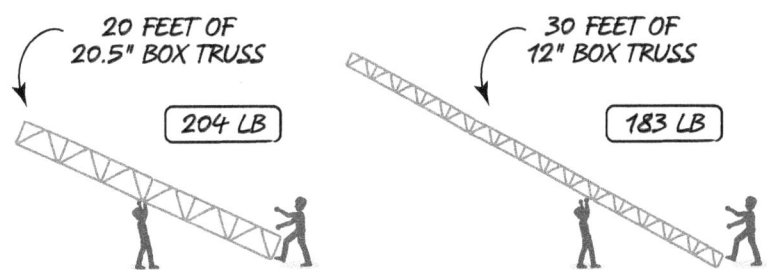

UPLIFT FORCE (lb)
AS DISTANCE BETWEEN STAGEHANDS DECREASES

	8 ft	7 ft	6 ft	5 ft	4 ft	3 ft	2 ft	1 ft
20.5" Truss	no uplift	1	16	30	43	48	36	no uplift
12" Truss	85	106	130	154	179	199	**208**	178

These figures based on the lifter pushing at a height of six feet

See the *References* for more information

The 20.5" truss, *even though it is more than 20 pounds heavier,* is far more manageable because it is only 2/3 the length of the 12" truss. The uplift never gets more than about 50 pounds. On the other hand, because the 12" truss is so long, it exerts an uplift that could pick a smaller stagehand up off the ground. Like any good pry bar, it is able to exert a force in excess of its self-weight.

Note also how the uplift first increases then, at the end, decreases as the truss approaches vertical. This happens because the center of gravity (CG) of the truss begins to fall over the base of the object. Once the CG is past the pivot point - the edge of the truss that is pushed into the ground by the footer - it will start pulling the truss more vertical. This happens sooner with a wide object than a thin object of the same length and weight. Height also matters. The higher the stagehand can push while walking up an object, the lower the forces involved.

One last thought: we have been focusing on the uplift that the footer faces. The lifters also see this force. In fact, once they get past the CG of the truss as they walk it up, they have become the pivot point of a seesaw. The have to balance both the uplift at one end and the weight at the other end. If the footers get just the uplift and the lifters get both the uplift and the weight, why have we been focusing on the footer? **Aren't the lifters doing more work? Yes, they are.** But we expect them to. All too often, with a big flat or other object, we will gather around six or eight people to walk up the flat, and only have one or two people foot the flat. Whoever is leading the lift needs to realize that forces will end up at both ends. And, it is worth remembering, that while there are some very fit people who can lift amazing loads when using their whole body to push *up*, no one can push *down* with more force than what they weigh.

Want another example?

When thinking about forces, how we pick up an object can matter as much as the object's weight. Consider a 21 foot stick of 1 1/2 inch Schedule 40 pipe.

On your own, try picking up the pipe at center and holding it level.

Now, still by yourself, try picking it up and holding it level from the end of the pipe.

Leave them loose, make them all...

... then use the wrench. **When connecting anything with multiple bolt holes, get a bolt thru every hole before tightening up any of them.** Regardless of whether it is a blind or thru connection, make all of the connections loosely before tightening down any of them. (Blind holes have the threads built into the structure, such as tee nuts or weld nuts, while thru holes use a washer and a nut.) With a blind hole, get a bite, enough to make sure the bolt will thread correctly, but leave some air. Same thing with a thru bolt: make the nut but only finger tight (or a bit less). Leaving the connections loose allows the parts to be adjusted so that all holes can be brought into alignment. Tightening any bolts before making them all can lock the parts out of alignment.

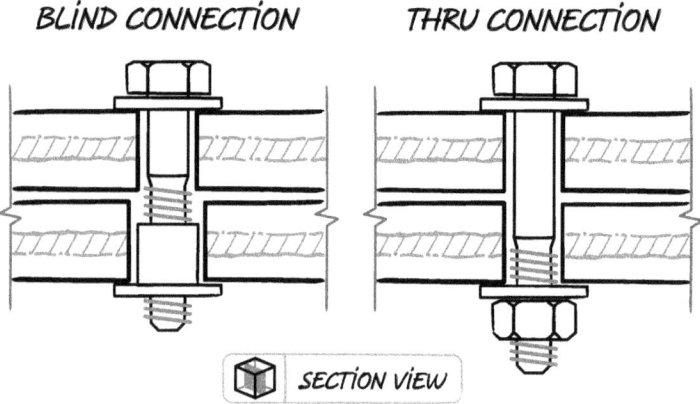

Another name for this tip could be "The Circle Truss Rule". Anyone who has had to assemble a multi-segment circle truss – or truss with other complex geometry – quickly learns how important it is to leave all the bolts loose until every single bolt has been made.

PART 1 - The In

The Hammer Trick

The flats are on stage, stood up, and bolted or screwed or clamped together. They're held up by jacks or stage braces, or perhaps they are rigged to fly. Here's the problem: the seams between flats do not line up. The bolts/screws/clamps are squeezing the frames together but the seam between flats is bumpy or uneven. (This is what video folks call a "Z-axis problem" when aligning LED tiles: an issue that is not up/down nor left/right but towards/away from the audience.) Here's one method to flatten out the wall.

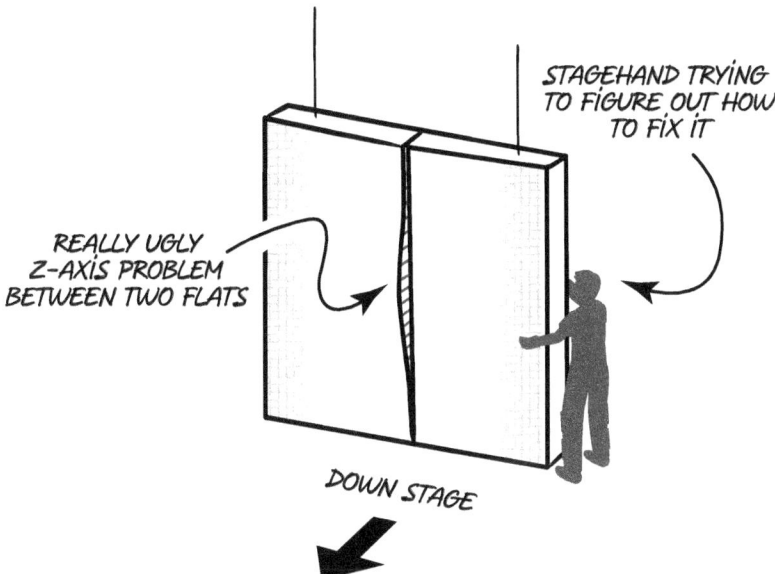

This requires one stagehand on the down stage (DS) side of the flats to call out when the seam looks good, and one stagehand on the up stage (US) side to do the work. The US stagehand will need a claw hammer, a screw gun, and a screw (a drywall screw for a wooden flat or a Tek® screw for a metal flat). We are going to call this the "alignment screw". Loosen up the bolts/screws/clamps holding the flats together. How much of the seam that needs to be loosened will depend on how much of the seam is out of whack. Find where the seam looks the worse. Starting at the center of this misalignment, the US stagehand drives the alignment screw into the frame of whichever flat is further DS. The goal is to leave the head of the alignment screw sticking out of the back of the frame. Then, with the claw hammer, the stagehand grabs the exposed head of the alignment screw and pries it US, using the other flat as the fulcrum. The US stagehand keeps prying until the DS stagehands calls it good. Then, while holding the flats in alignment with the hammer, the bolts/screws/clamps are tightened again. (It helps to have a third hand or a buddy for this part.) The work continues away from the center point as necessary, keeping the center connection tight.

Note: remove any alignment screws once completed. Also, a pry bar can be substituted for the hammer, but it is still called the hammer trick.

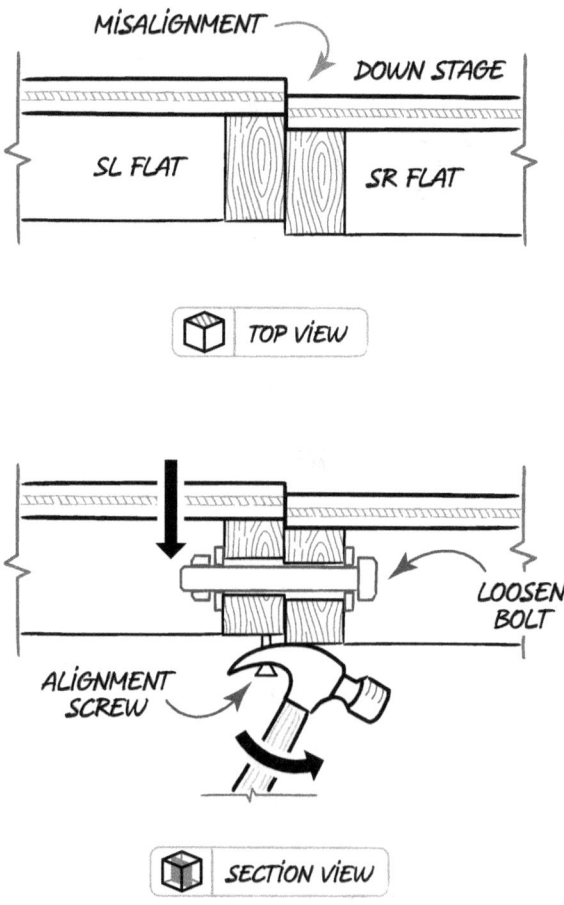

Barn Dooring Tight Fits

On old barns with sagging frames, if the big doors at the main entrance are closed one at a time, the second door will tend to run into the first and the barn won't be able to be locked up. The trick is to close the two doors together so that their edges meet and push together, forcing the frame to straighten up as the doors swing shut. Stagehands use the same trick.

Say two trap plugs need to go back into the stage floor. The first lands no problem. The second goes in most of the way but hangs up on the first plug. If it's really close, jumping on the plug might get it in. Or it might cause some damage, such as when the top layer of flooring gets hung up and ends up being ripped off. And jumping on it might just not work at all.

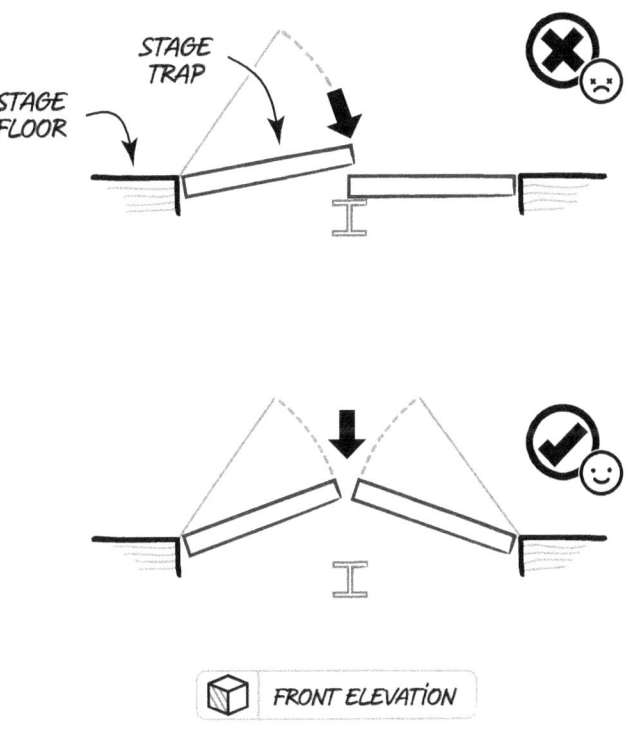

FRONT ELEVATION

1 Using pry bars to force the second plug in might work but it requires a gap the thickness of the pry bar between the plugs when done. Try this instead: with the second plug sitting on top, push or pry the first plug up. As the first plug rises, the second plug slides off the top and the edges of the two plugs wedge together. Get the two plugs nice and even, then pull the pry bars out. At this point, the weight of the plugs may well drop them in together. If not, give it a jump. **Make sure fingers, toes, and other body parts stay out from under the plugs while doing this work.**

Barn dooring works just as well when fitting vertical panels into an opening. Whichever orientation the panels are, just make sure they will actually fit in the space intended. If the frame is just too small, barn dooring may stretch it until it ruptures.

Poker Chip PAR Lens

PAR lights are heavily used for lighting a stage and modern fixtures can accept a range of lenses to change the beam spread. Because these instruments are so common and each one can use multiple lenses, there are often a whole lot of lenses on hand. Sizes vary between model and manufacturer, but they are generally somewhere between the size of a dinner plate and a salad plate. One tried and true way to keep the lenses protected and organized is to borrow a piece of equipment from the catering and restaurant world: the poker chip dish dolly. Dollies with adjustable dividers allow for the best fit. Keep a square of packing foam between each lens for even more protection but beware of very rough handling or trucking. Only flight cases with individual foam slots can allow a PAR lens to survive a drop off the back of a trailer.

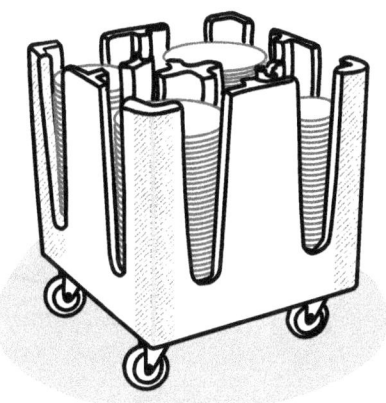

Chip Brush Door Hold

Need a door to swing to a position and stay there? No time to fiddle with leveling the stage jacks or shimming the hinges? If the back of the door won't be seen from the audience, just screw a chip brush to the bottom corner with the bristles firmly pressed into the floor. This creates enough resistance to hold the door but not so much that it keeps the door from functioning normally.

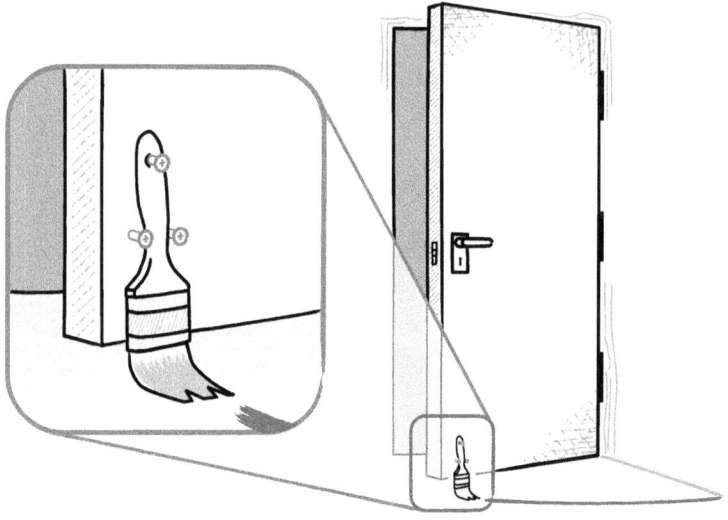

Hacksaw Window Hold

Old windows use a counterweight arrangement of sash weights and sash cord to hold the movable part of the window – known as the sash – in place when raised. Modern windows tend to be factory fabricated and use tight tolerances and friction to hold the sash up when raised. Both approaches are used in the scene shop. Sometimes, regardless of technique, a quick fix is needed. One way to improvise a window hold is to screw a hacksaw blade inside the window frame with a slight bow. The sash gets raised and flattens the blade, which springs back against the sash frame and holds it in place.

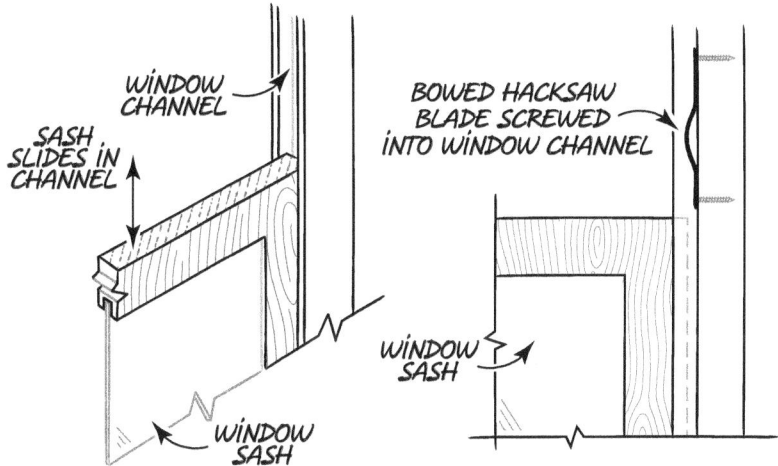

Check the Truck

Before the doors close on the trailer, someone who is responsible to the production should have a last look. Anything from bags of hardware to envelopes of drawings are easily lost in the mess of ratchet straps, packing blankets and load bars that are left over in an "empty" truck. The piece of crown molding that got knocked off in transit looks a lot like garbage and only someone who knows the show will know to grab it and bring it in. Even with trucks that are just delivering cases, how often does the shop throw something on top to service a last-minute request from the theater? How often does that "something on top" end up on the ground and kicked behind the broken laundry basket of straps? Make sure you check the truck before it leaves you alone on the desert island that is a theater in production.

The Run

Blind Pickup Follow Spot Target

If you're running a follow spot and don't have a sight, scope, or other aiming device on hand, here's a way to still make smooth pickups.* And, no, the trick is not to open the shutter a bit and let a little light out to ghost the position ahead of time. (This is called "ghosting" and is widely considered to be very unprofessional.) To make a blind pickup without a sight and without ghosting, all you need is a small hole in the top of the follow spot that lets out a concentrated bit of light. This will create a small pilot beam that will splash against the ceiling of the spot booth. Line up the follow spot for where the pickup comes, grab some gaff tape and mark the ceiling where the pilot light falls. Make sure the mark includes the cue number.

For this method to work, the position and adjustments on the spotlight can't change between shows. Spike the floor around the base and matchmark the height adjustment knobs on the yoke. Not all follow spots will work for this trick. It is a very bad idea to start drilling holes in rental or touring equipment. However, many spots have some amount of light leak that can be used to advantage.

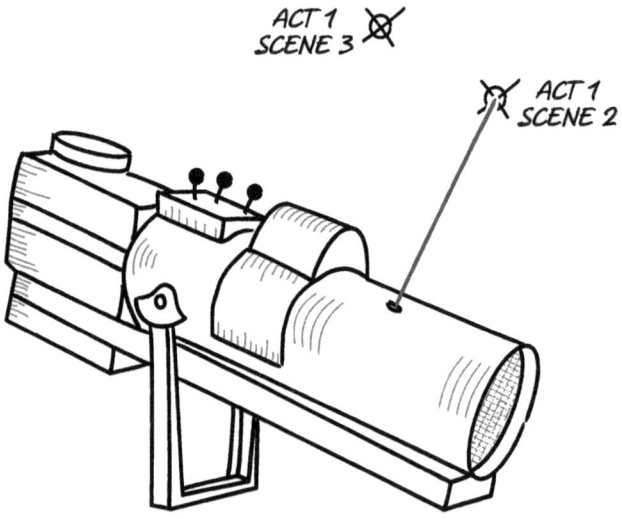

---

* The word "pickup" means when the operator "picks up" the performer by shining the follow spot on them. A "blind pickup" is when the operator cannot see the performer. The performer walks on stage and their spotlight is just there waiting for them. Theater magic!

Lock Rail Muffler

To keep the rope lock handles from clanging against the lock rail when they are released, secure a rope along the rail to act as a bumper. An old hand line is a good choice. Make sure that the rope does not prevent the lock from fully releasing: with the handle down, the hand line should be free to wiggle between the cams of the lock.

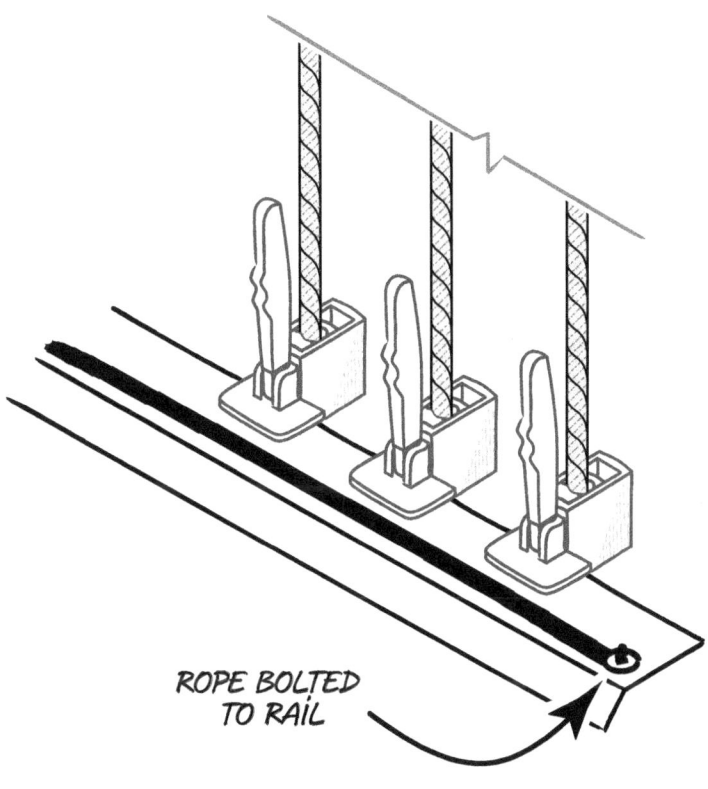

ROPE BOLTED TO RAIL

Ribbon Trim Fid

Ribbon and yarn are both popular options for marking the trim on the hand line of counterweight line sets. A fid is a tool used for opening up a rope, usually as part of making a splice. There are many different types of fids for all sorts of ropework. The stagehand at the rail, however, only needs to accomplish one task: get a ribbon or yarn thru the line quickly, accurately, and without damaging the rope. Stagehands have used lots of different tools for this job, including crochet hooks, marlin spikes, modified screwdrivers, and tire repair tools. Here's a design that does the job for three strand hand line (the most common type) and won't break the bank.

Start with a size 17 aluminum knitting needle, which is 10" long with an outside diameter of 1/2" (12.5 mm). These come in pairs and are inexpensive at most craft stores. Drill a 9/32" hole about 2" from the point. To protect the hand line, this hole needs to be deburred and sanded down. A pencil wrapped in a medium-fine grit sandpaper is a good way to get to a smooth finish. Some type of lanyard loop is essential if the fid is to be used at height. A foam rubber grip is a nice finishing touch, but anything that gives the hand more grip, such as hockey stick tape, will be useful.

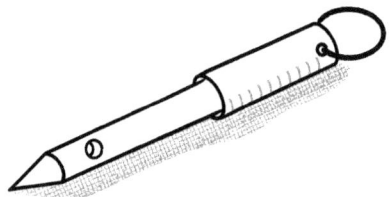

To use the fid, start by getting the line set where it wants to be, then locking it off. Grab the hand line and twist with the direction of the rope lay. This will loosen up the three strands. Send the fid thru, angling it between the strands. Now simply thread the ribbon or yarn thru the fid's hole, hold onto one end of the ribbon or yarn, and pull the rest back thru the rope with the fid.

PART 1- The Run   49

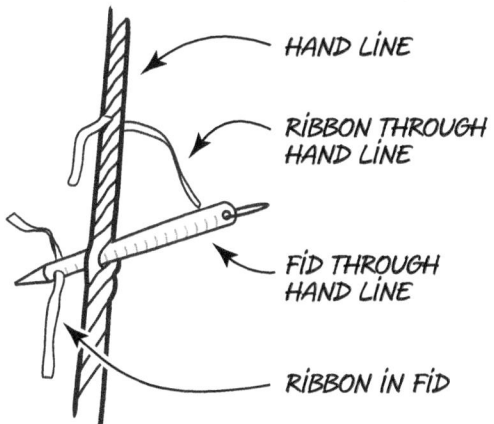

Tire Repair Tool Fid

Tire repair tools are among the popular options for lacing ribbon (but not yarn) thru hand lines. A simple improvement to the off-the-shelf item is to solder the end of the tool shut. The end is designed with a slot that releases the tire patch once pushed into the tire. We do not need this function. The two ends can be brazed or TIG welded together, but a typical soldering iron and run-of-the-mill solder from the audio or electrics shop will work as well. (Use a solder that will be safe to handle when done.) Make sure to file and sand the tip smooth. Closing the end helps retain the ribbon and protect the tool from snagging and damaging rope fibers.

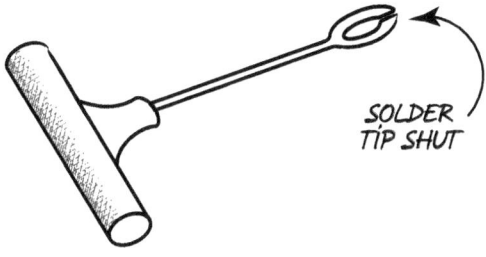

Spike Tape Dog Collar

A quick and inexpensive way to store lots of rolls of spike tape is to loop a dog collar thru them. Add a carabiner to where the leash normally clips and the collar, tape and all, can be hung on a hook or off of a belt. Dog collars are durable and easy to find, with lots of options for custom colors and patterns if you already have too many black accessories in your life.

Spike Mark Protection

There are a lot of ways to protect spike marks on a show deck from heavy traffic. Layering clear packing tape or clear dance floor tape over spike tape is a tried and true technique. When the action of a show has been frozen, and there are spikes that keep coming up, consider moving away from tape altogether. Multicolor paint markers can mimic the color of the tape so no one has to learn anything new. Glow-in-the-dark markers can mimic glow tape. Spray on sealers add extra protection. In a pinch, hair spray works ok. But be warned that adding sealers may screw up the finish of the floor. Whoever painted and finished the floor is the best source on how a particular floor should be treated. Checking in with them early may save a lot of grief later on.

PART 1- The Run　　　　　　　　　　　　　　　　　　　　51

Sweeping the Stage

There are a lot of opinions when it comes to sweeping, and not just among the stagehands. Everyone from Stage Managers to Janitors are happy to jump in and argue the point. But the care of the stage belongs to the stagehands and experience dictates there really is one correct idea about sweeping the stage: **be methodical**. Have a pattern and stick to it. Amateurs on stage will each sweep randomly into their own little piles; this is inefficient and error prone.

One popular approach is for everyone to sweep to Center Line. There are two schools of thought on how to reach Center Line: either the stagehand does one column at a time or moves up and down stage advancing the whole line. Both paths are shown in the drawing, with the stage left (SL) stagehand using the column method and the stage right (SR) stagehand advancing the line. Which is correct? Well, the long answer is that the SL stagehand is being visibly deliberate, setting an example of how the work is to be done, while the SR stagehand is following the technically more efficient path. The short answer is that both are sweeping methodically and will leave a clean stage ready for performers, so **they are both correct**.

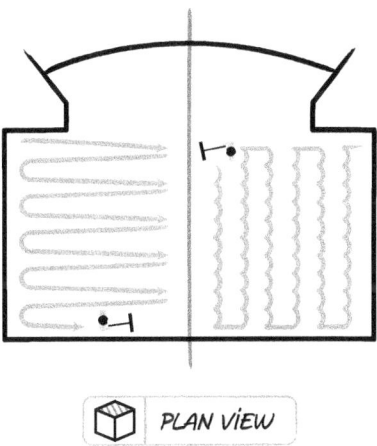

PLAN VIEW

Pick a method and stick to it. In any event, the path for sweeping versus wet mopping versus dust mopping are likely to be different. Be methodical and, for the love of your automation folks: please avoid sweeping into the gap around a lift or turntable. And never, ever sweep into the groove of a deck track.

Sweep Top Down

1

Always start at the highest point when sweeping. Dirt only falls in one direction. Even if we try to keep it all contained when sweeping on top of a two-story set, some of it is going to come over the side and land below. This is also an important rule in the shop: start by sweeping the tables, the stationary tools, and the benches before the floor.

Wet ≠ Dripping

Other than with obnoxious shows (stage blood baths, food fights, any use of glitter) wet mopping the stage is really more like damp mopping the stage. The wringer on the mop bucket is the stagehand's friend here. To get even more water out, twist the mop head a few times in the wringer before pressing down on the handle.

Tying Up Legs

To get soft good masking legs out of the way, which both protects the legs and makes moving around on stage easier, stagehands often tie up the legs. As with all soft good tasks, this is done with the preservation of the drapery the foremost consideration. The basic idea is to twist the leg, then dump it into itself.

First, from behind the leg, bring the on stage and the off stage edges of the leg together. Now begin twisting the leg by holding the two edges together at chest height and wrapping everything below that around itself. This is done tightly, but without crushing the fabric. Once fully twisted, the bottom of the leg is dumped into the pocket that has been formed just at chest height of the leg. The weight of the leg has to be enough to bind the twist from unravelling where it began. Fluff and tuck as required. The size of the leg, the type of fabric, and the bottom finish – chain or no chain – will all cause variation.

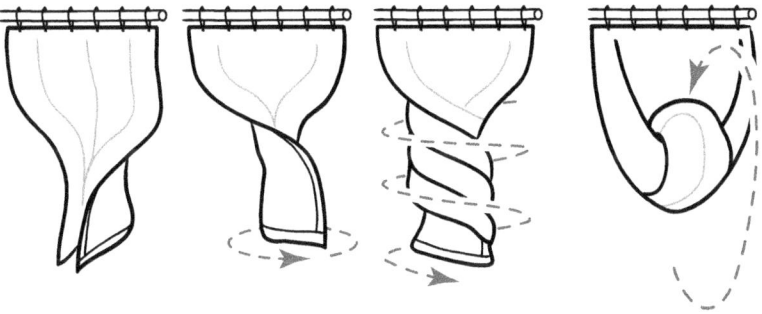

If we are tying up the legs to avoid wet paint, take the extra step and bag the legs. Trash bags are best; large legs may require the jumbo 96 gallon size trash bag. The bag can be secured with rope, clips or tape. With tape, avoid taping directly to the fabric, and just make a semi-tight girdle on the bag itself. Bagging prevents the leg from dumping out of itself if it gets bumped. It also provides protection from a carelessly wielded paint brush.

Tennis Ball Buffers

High gloss floors look great but they sure get scuffed easily. A quick and affordable way to buff out scuffs is to use a tennis ball. Stagehands can make it easier on their backs by attaching the tennis balls to broom sticks by simply slitting the ball and forcing the threaded end of the stick in.

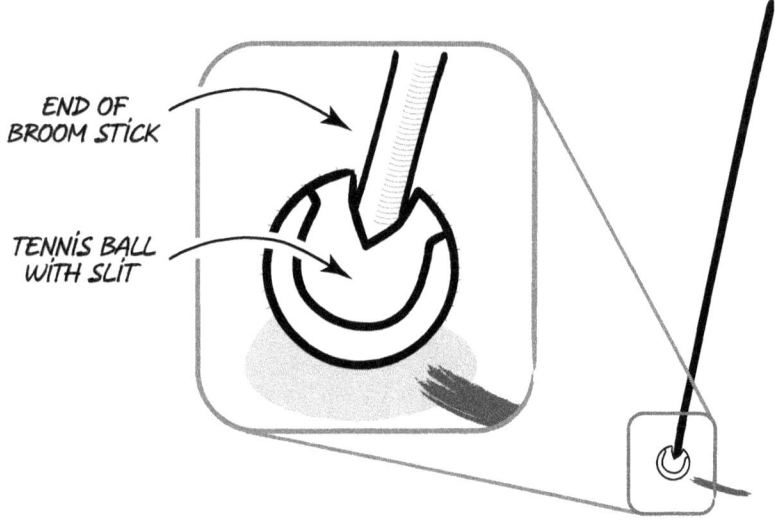

Remember: not every ding on a show deck can be buffed out. If a stagehand really goes for it, they can burn a hole thru the sealer and paint treatment, permanently damaging the deck. As always with scenic finishes, if there is a doubt, consult the charge artist first.

Worn Screw Holes

For anything held together with drywall or sheet metal screws, pulling it apart and putting it back together will cause the screw threads to wear out. This is particularly true for screws in soft wood. Here's a trick a stagehand can use to make sure the screw hole functions thru closing night: add some toothpicks to the hole before putting the screw back in. Make sure to trim the ends of the toothpicks flush to the hole. The extra material will help the screw grab.

Adding some wood glue with the toothpick will help them hold even more, but when even that is not enough, try wood epoxy putty. Typically available as a tube where a length is cut off and kneaded by hand, wood epoxy putty is good for any number of fast fixes. When cured, the putty can be cut, sanded, and even stained just like wood. (With paint or stain, the epoxy will never match the wood exactly, but it will be a lot closer of a match than a hole.) When fixing screw holes, first, make sure to really pack it into the screw hole and, second, make sure it is dry before reinstalling the screw. The screw will have little trouble cutting new holes in the dried epoxy.

Etiquette

Yeah, a lot of stagehands are not going to agree on these, but there are some common rules of etiquette out there. Who follows what varies from house to house and from show to show. (Some rules even directly contradict each other.) It's good to know what rules a house or show might follow, and we should all do our best to respect them. Of course, there's not much to be done about the inevitable conflict that arises when a show comes to a house and each has very different rules of etiquette...

- Keep drinks off the show deck.
- Don't sit on the props. Not even the one that's just a beat up old chair.
- No tape on soft goods. Ever. For any reason.
- Black clothes for running a show (often called "show blacks") includes black shoes and black socks.
- The shirt for show blacks should be long-sleeved and have a collar.
- No tape on the hand line of a line set: use ribbon or yarn for marking trim.
- Don't poke holes in the hand line of a line set: use tape for marking trim.

When in doubt, ask. When asked, explain politely.

Protect the Mic

You don't need to be a full-blown audio tech to be able to offer some basic mic etiquette: Don't blow on the mic. Don't tap on the mic. Definitely don't drop the mic, no matter how good you think you are. Yes, the mic is on, please don't fiddle with the switch (and in the thousand-to-one chance it is off, you – person speaking on stage – you're not the one to do the fiddling). If they're a rock star with a full band, let them eat the mic, otherwise ask them to keep a hand's width between mic and mouth. At very least, try and get them to pick a distance and stick with it. All of this will help the show sound a bit better because mixing it will be a bit easier.

Four Thoughts on Scene Shifts

1. Always walk the scene shift the first time it is attempted.

2. Leave some work lights on: never run the first attempt in a blackout.

3. Once the crew has walked the shift, try it in show conditions, at speed. Took too long? Don't panic. With practice, the crew will get the shift done twice as fast.

4. On the debate between scheduling dry-and-wet-tech versus wet-tech-only*, your opinion should vary by the amount of scenic automation in the show.

---

* "Dry Tech" is running a technical rehearsal without performers, just the technical elements such as lights, sound, projections, and scenery. "Wet Tech" is with performers. Some folks think dry tech is a waste of time because everything will change once the performers are on the stage.

To make this author's opinion very clear: when there are machines moving physical things around the stage, the show will look better and be safer if the automation operators get time to practice show moves without the risk of hitting performers. When performers do get on stage, the operators will be better able to focus on keeping them safe because they will already know how the machinery is working in a global sense. They can only tell how well the machinery is working if it is run in show conditions: that is, with all of the other technical elements. Does the sound cue drown out the "clear" – the verbal signal that it is safe to move – given by the carpenter on deck? Does that one moving light spin and wash out the IR camera feed just as the wagon starts moving? Only a dry tech will find these problems before performers are on stage.

PART 1- The Run   59

The Lonely Clove Hitch

> Question: What is a Lonely Clove Hitch?
> Answer: A Clove Hitch by itself.

Why should we never let a clove hitch be lonely? The best way to demonstrate is to find some tie line and a pole we can walk completely around. (A lighting boom works well.) Tie a clove hitch tight on the pole with an inch or two of tail, grab the other end with some force, and start walking around the pole, pulling the end of the rope into the knot. As the clove hitch spins, the tail will start to work its way into the knot until the whole assembly collapses and the tie line comes free. The clove hitch is a great knot but there is this major risk of it coming undone.*

In the stagehand's world, rather than the rope circling the pipe, it is more likely that the rope stays where it is and the pipe gets rotated, as in a hemp-rigged batten, but the failure mode is the same. To prevent this, simply take the tail and tie a couple of half-hitches back to the working end of the rope.

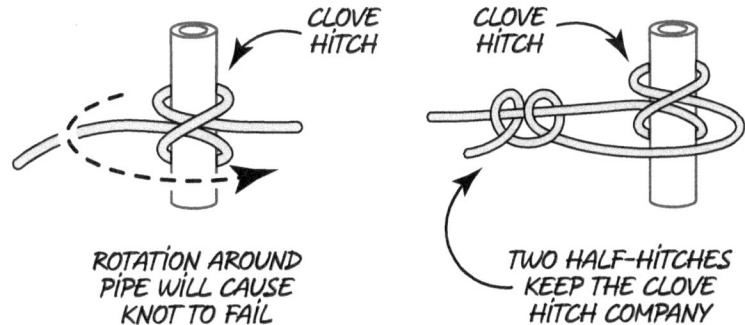

---

* This is a classic demonstration of how the clove hitch fails. Clifford Ashley even suggests its use as a parlor trick (*Ashley Book of Knots* #2578, page 415). Philippe Petit also gives the example in his engaging book *Why Knot?* (page 111).

Swing on a Line Set

Putting a swing on the batten of a manual counterweight line set is not as simple as it sounds. If the swing goes up and down with a performer on it, the performer needs to be protected from the risk of falling off. This is eminently possible to be done safely, but needs to be treated with a heightened level of planning and care. Performer flying is beyond the scope of this book. But this is not the only type of swing effect. Another common request is to have an empty swing flown in on a batten, then a performer gets on it and starts swinging.

There are two major problems we will consider. The first sounds like a riddle: does the performer swing on the batten or does the batten swing on the performer? Depending largely on the relative weights of the batten and the performer, a performer can sit on the swing and cause the batten to move above them and not move much at all themselves. The other major problem is that the person getting onto and off of the swing changes the weight of the system. This is an important challenge with counterweight systems that has to be addressed.

Here's one solution: tail down sandbags on the off stage ends of the batten. These sandbags should be close to the lift lines, out of sight of the audience, as heavy as is practicable to be counterweighted at the arbor, and just almost kiss the deck when the swing is at its lower trim. The additional weight of the bags add to the inertia of the batten: it is harder for the performer to swing the batten and therefore easier to swing on the batten. Tailing down the sandbags close to the deck reduces the risk of an out-of-weight situation. If adding the person becomes too much for whatever appropriate method is locking off the line set, all that will happen is the sandbags will drift in and touch down. When the person gets off, the sandbags drift out again until floating and the system is in balance again.

The sandbags ought to be out of sightlines. This means they will probably be flying in and out of the wings. People like to stand in the wings. Lights and monitor speakers often get installed in the wings. Make sure the sandbags don't hit any of these.

PART 1- The Run

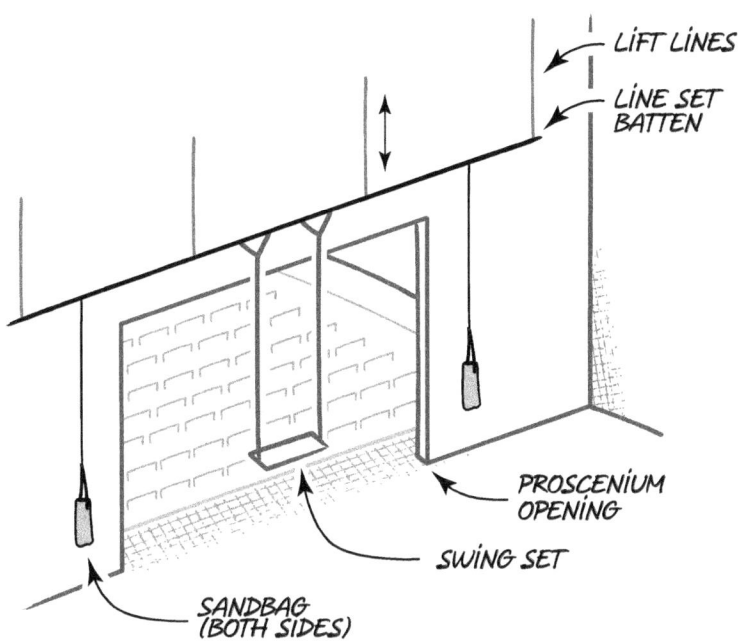

This tip is about a general approach to a common problem. The details of implementing the solution in a particular case are both critical to success and also up to the individual user. These details, at a minimum, include using appropriate hardware and design factors. How the line set will be locked off while the swing is in use is a critical question, and the answer will depend on the specific circumstances. Additionally, it may be important to add wire guides to the ends of the batten. It may be important to build enclosures for the sandbags to insure they will not hit anything as they fly in and out. (Large diameter PVC pipe can be a useful starting point for such an enclosure.) Know the risks and how to reduce them when implementing this – or any – rigging system.

One last point is worth making: we have been saying "swing" but the same principles apply to any type of apparatus that is flown in and a performer gets on it. Acrobatic effects using lyras, silks, and other equipment seem to be getting exponentially more popular. This is one approach to implement them into existing rigging systems.

The Show Stop Out

Things go wrong. This is true everywhere on earth, but it can be a particular issue when things go wrong on stage during a show. We call these "show stoppers" and there is probably an infinite variety of them, so we won't bother trying to list them all. One truth is worth pointing out: for all sorts of problems, the stagehands are going to have to go on stage to fix them. Only performers like to work with a massive audience watching them. So here's the tip: always have a way to bring in a divider between the stage and the audience. In a traditional proscenium theater, the main rag is commonly used. If there is no main rag, the fire curtain can be a viable option. For some shows, forward thinking stagehands will hang a full stage black out curtain just to have the option.* It is not always possible of course. But it is nice to have an out when you have to go on stage and fix a thing in front of a thousand people who just had their show interrupted.

Hot Glue Quick Fix

Does a costume piece or prop need a quick repair? Grab a hot glue gun and a can of spray duster. Spray dusters use a liquid that evaporates rapidly into clean, water-free, high-pressure gas. As the liquid evaporates into gas, the spray becomes quite cold and will cure hot glue rapidly. A word of warning: if held sideways or inverted, the duster will emit liquid rather than gas, which can cause frostbite. It can also damage finishes on fabrics and other material. The normal spray on its own does the job fine, so follow the manufacturer's instructions. Some, mostly older formulations can be flammable. A hot glue gun is not much of an ignition source, but take appropriate care. The can should say whether the spray is flammable. Regardless, it's a good practice to keep the can and the hot glue gun well separated.

---

* These are also useful for when there is a talk-back or other event at the end of the show. Rather than having to wait, the crew can clean the stage quietly without disrupting the post-show event.

Vodka and Condoms

A good 50/50 mixture of vodka and water in a spray bottle solves a lot of odor issues for the wardrobe folks. Unlubricated condoms are just about the best mic pack protection available in terms of size, cost, and availability. Both are staples of running shows and need to be restocked regularly, but do your purchasing folks a favor — especially if you're working in the context of a larger organization like a school — and **don't submit the receipts for the vodka and condoms at the same time without an explanation**. We wouldn't want anyone on the other side of stage door getting the wrong idea about show business, after all.

[THIS PAGE INTENTIONALLY BLANK]

The Out

Pull the Tape before the Cable

1

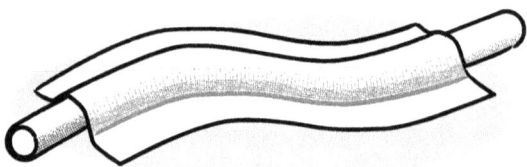

This might sound familiar: we have spent days laying cable and taping it down neatly. Then the show happens and now we have just hours to strike it all. The temptation on the out is to move fast and yank the cable up, tape and all. When this happens, the tape ends up curling around the cable and adhering to itself. Now the cable is fully encased, and all of that tape has to be stripped before the cable can be coiled and stored. Gaff tape is gentle with most materials, but it really knows how to form a strong bond to itself. Save some time, keep it neat, and pull the tape first.

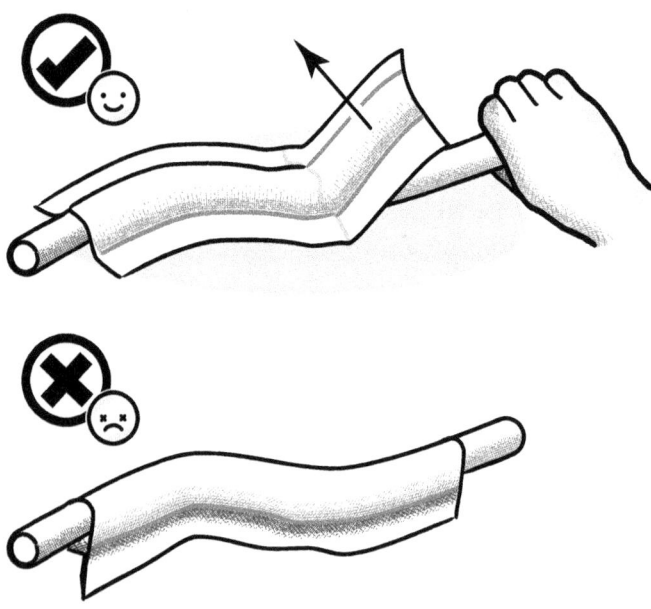

You don't coil a cable...

... a cable coils itself. Stagehands coil or otherwise store a lot of different things. Electrical cables, fiber optic lines, rope, and hose are all in a day's work. Each type has its own peccadillos. The over-under* approach is used for the majority of cables and ropes, but it is not the only technique. Many riggers prefer to either stuff a rope bag or flake out rope in a figure 8 pattern for cleaner deployment. (See the "Stagehand's Timber Hitch" tip in the first section for a picture of wire rope flaked out.) Feeder cable also gets laid out in a figure 8, but for different reasons. And it is easier and better to roll hoses rather than try an over-under coil. Here's a quick trick with big hoses such as hydraulic lines: make one loop, then tie the end of the hose to the loop, now keep rolling.

The adage of **you don't coil a cable, a cable coils itself** teaches us that we should respect the natural tendencies of the cable. If the stagehand follows the cable, they can get it back into a neat, professional coil. If they fight the cable's memory, they'll struggle more while they kink and potentially damage it. Those old extension cords that look like giant squiggles? No one was respecting how those cords wanted to be coiled.

---

* Over-under is a coiling method that alternates overhand and underhand loops. There are a lot of books with pictures and descriptions, but this is definitely better learned by just searching "over under coil" and finding a video on the internet.

Self-Releasing Knot for Lowering Lights

By wrapping a long bowline around a lighting instrument's c-clamp the right way, a stagehand can hook a light and lower it to the ground, then release the light and pull the rope back up. Use the bolt of the clamp to anchor the loop of the bowline, then wrap the rest of the knot around the body of the clamp as shown in the drawing. By definition, this knot holds when the light is supported by the rope and can release when the weight of the light is off the rope. This means **there is a risk in using this technique**. If the light strikes or hangs up on anything on the way down, it may get released and fall the rest of the way down. Always call out when lowering in an object. (This is true for lowering any object, not just a light using this knot.) Never use this approach if there is a chance of anyone or anything of value coming under or near the light as it comes in.

This approach is much safer than the all-too-common practice of just hooking the top jaw of the c-clamp with the loop of a bowline. It is also safer than just hooking the bolt. By wrapping around the clamp, the rope centers itself on the clamp, which is balanced on the instrument's center of gravity by the yoke. (If the clamp is off-balance of the light, find another way to lower the light in.) Wrapping the rope around the c-clamp also creates friction between rope and clamp that reduces the force on the bolt.

This is a one-way knot: it can only be used for lowering and self-releasing. It is dangerous to go fishing for lights.

PART 1 - The Out

END OF
A BOWLINE

Sweeping for Nails

Pulling up a show deck that was tacked down directly to the stage can leave a lot of nails behind. **Best practice is to remove the nails as each sheet is pulled up**, rather than pulling up all the sheets and trying to do the whole deck at once. It's easier to find the nails one sheet at a time, and doesn't leave swaths of stage with exposed nails to tear up boot soles and cart casters. But even working one sheet at a time, some nails are bound to be missed. A quick way stagehands check a stage for any exposed fasteners is to sweep the stage, but with the push broom flipped over so that the head of the broom – and not the bristles – runs across the stage. The head will snag on any exposed fasteners, which can then be removed. If there is a lot of stage to cover and not enough brooms, stagehands can push sheet goods (usually a chunk of show deck that just got pulled) along the floor to the same effect.

PUSH BROOM
FLIPPED OVER

SHEET GOOD
ALONG FLOOR

Last Bolt!

Verbal warnings and notifications are part of life. Most folks know what it means when someone shouts "Heads!" (Unlike most everyone else, stagehands know not to look up.) We have other calls that are standard to the work on stage. Loading and unloading counterweight line sets are each a critical call-and-response process. Focusing lights is another well-rehearsed verbal dance between designer and electrician.

One call that a lot of us use – and the rest of us ought to – is the call of "Last Bolt". When taking apart anything with multiple connections, from flats bolted together, to dance tower sections hanging on a motor pick, as the final connection between parts is removed, loads can shift in unexpected ways. **Often, a lot of tension ends up resting on this last connection.** (Which is something important to remember, if you're the person designing the connections.) Before pulling this last connection, calling "Last Bolt" lets the folks in the area know something might shift or drop. If they're supposed to be holding it, it lets them know to get ready to take the weight. If they're in another department and just standing in the vicinity flapping gums at each other, it lets them know they should move elsewhere to finish their conversation.

Start with the Hard One

It is in our nature to start with the low hanging fruit. But, for a stagehand, it is often better to start with the hard to reach parts of the problem. When unbolting two flats from each other, start with the bolts that need a ladder for access. If we start with the bolts that are easy to reach, we'll be up on the ladder when the walls are coming apart. And we know that the last bolt can end up with a lot of load on it, which makes it difficult to remove. (See the "Last Bolt!" tip for more.) Better to tackle that one at ground level.

This is also good advice on bigger picture questions, such as where the crew should start working. When striking gear from Front of House (FOH) positions, that gear tends to pile up around the seats and fill the aisles. If we know there are tough places to get to FOH, let's start with them so we are fighting less stuff on the way.

Remove a Bent Screw

A screwdriver is not much good with a bent screw and of no use with a screw that has been stripped out or lost its head. Locking pliers — popularly known as Vice-Grips® — are a good solution in these cases: lock the pliers on the screw and just twist it out. A fast alternative is to use a cordless drill: insert what's left of the screw in the chuck, tighten the chuck down on it and set the drill to reverse, and back it out. A word of warning: the drill's chuck may get damaged if this is done too often or with too much force.

PART 1 - The Out

On the Diamond (Getting Over Bumps)

Road boxes. Hampers. Meat racks. Dollies. Scenery carts and deck carts. Cable trunks. Sheet goods carts. Wardrobe gondolas. Z-racks. Flight cases.*

Stagehands push around a lot of things on wheels. When they hit an obstruction like a threshold of a doorway or a lip in the flooring, they know to pull back, give it a bit of an angle then hit it again. By turning the wheelbase — taking it on the diamond — only one wheel hits the obstruction at a time. Consider an even load on four wheels. Rather than forcing two wheels carrying half the weight over the hump, when taking it on the diamond, only one wheel carrying a quarter of the weight goes at a time, and the stagehand can keep on rolling.†

Taking a hump on the diamond has another advantage: it can prevent the wheelbase from bottoming out on the obstruction (also called high-centering) by reducing the distance between wheels relative to the obstruction. To work, the distance between wheels has to become less than the width of the obstruction.

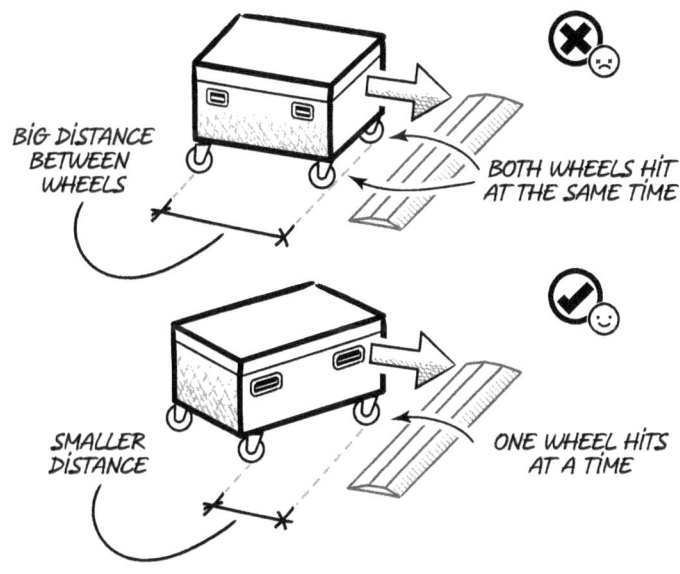

---

* Did we miss any? Send in your suggestions if you think of one.

† This assumes the wheelbase flexes as the wheels hit the hump, which is pretty common when heavily loaded.

Tip the Dolly

When tipping something over onto a dolly, it's often easier to first bring the dolly up to the piece, then tip both the dolly and the piece together to the ground. This prevents the dolly from being knocked out of the way by the load as it is coming in.

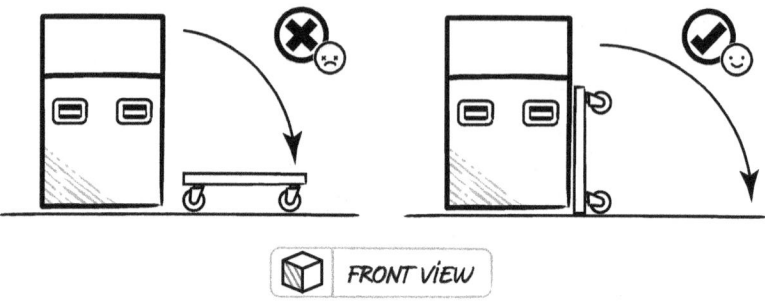

FRONT VIEW

Super Secret Glitter Removal Formula

There are few things more despised by stagehands than the use of glitter in a show. It just gets everywhere, on everything, and will stay around long after the show is gone. Once upon a time, the stage deck of a black box theater had to be replaced. After sweeping, mopping, and vacuuming, the top layer of hardboard was removed. (This hardboard had been painted and sealed before any shows had been mounted in the space.) After the hardboard, there were two layers of plywood. All layers were cross-lapped. When they reached the concrete sub-deck, what did the carpenters find? A solid layer of glitter from shows past that had – somehow – worked its way thru the stage deck.

If there is glitter in a show, there is only one way to clean the stage deck: paint it. There is no super secret way to remove glitter. The best that can be done is to encapsulate it to the floor. Even with paint, every so often, some glitter will work free and continue to turn up.

PART 1 - The Out   75

Arbor Spreader Plates

The best spring clamp to keep arbor plates out of the way while loading weight is the 1" size. The 2" spring clamp is more common – these are the ones often found in big bins in the aisles of box stores – but are really too big for the job. While a 2" clamp has to grab the arbor rod just on the tips of the jaw, the 1" clamp has a shallow enough throat and jaw opening that it can fully bite on the rod. 2" clamps get knocked off or slide down the rod if they get pushed or pulled too much. The 1" clamp is a more compact size, can still take a lanyard through the handle and does the job better.

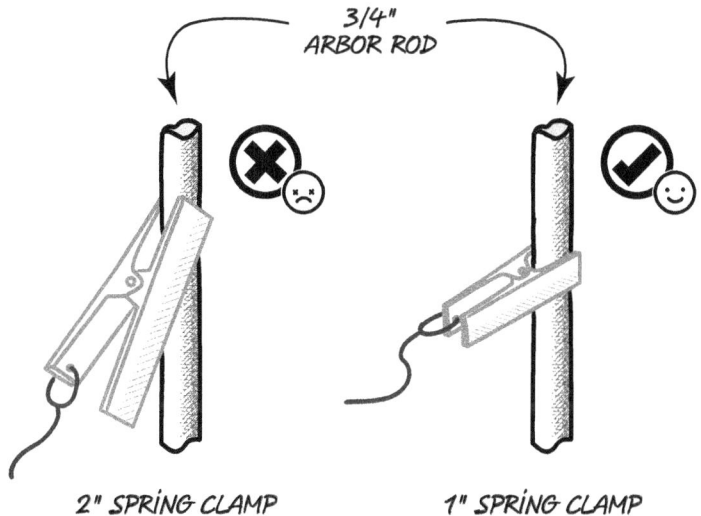

Stacking Stage Weights

Modern steel stage weights should have two opposing corners clipped off. When bricks are stacked with the clipped corners alternating left and right, pockets are formed that allow a stagehand to get a finger under the brick and lift it up more easily. Older cast iron weights often lack the corner clip but, because they are cast, they are usually designed with tapered sides. This taper is known as the "draft angle" and it used to help a part to be released from a mold during the casting process. For us, this angle can be used to create a bit of a lip between bricks *if* they are stacked consistently.

We are talking about this here, during the out, because this is when it really comes home just how important it is to load the arbors with some care. It's easy to put bricks between the rods any which way. It's getting them out again where a bit of care will pay off big.

See the *Useful Information* section in *Part 4* dedicated to arbors and stage weight for more information.

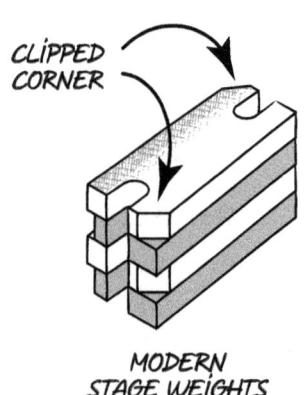

MODERN STAGE WEIGHTS

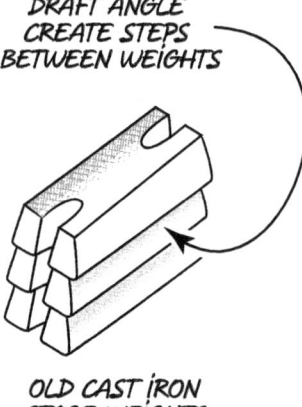

OLD CAST IRON STAGE WEIGHTS

Load Bars at the Tail

When you crack the door on a trailer you did not pack, it is always real nice to see a load bar (or two) at the tail, in the last set of E-track slots, as close to the door as possible. When you see these, you know you can finish opening the doors and no case is going to come racing out the back at you and nothing is going to come swinging down on your head. Or, if it does come racing back or swinging down, it will hit the bars and not you.

I get it when folks say, if you pack the truck right, you don't need load bars at the tail end. I get it when folks say they need every inch and there's no room for the load bars. I get it. But it sure is nice when you're opening the door and you see those bars. Right off you know someone did their due diligence, did the just-in-case thing, was looking out for you on the receiving end. And they probably don't know who I am, just that another stagehand is going to flush this trailer, and that it's real nice to see load bars set up on the tail end of the truck.

I'd like to see it be the rule on every truck, no matter what. But I get it when folks think differently.

[THIS PAGE INTENTIONALLY BLANK]

PART 2

The Shop & The Road

[THIS PAGE INTENTIONALLY BLANK]

Shop Work

A Note on Drawing Notes

The odds that a carpenter will read a note on a drawing are inversely proportional to the number of notes on the drawing.

 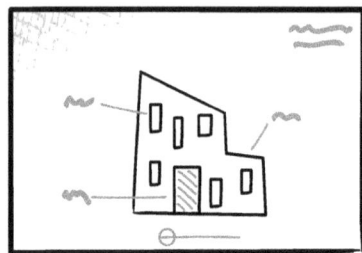

Trash Bag Drop Cloth

Quickly make an impromptu drop cloth out of a trash bag. Start by pulling a bag off the roll but leave it folded up. The end that just came off the roll should be welded together to form the bottom of the trash bag. Cut it off right along the weld. A knife will work; scissors are better. Unfold what is now a tube of plastic until you find the long weld seam. Slice down the bag using the seam as a guide. As before, a knife beats a sharp rock but scissors are best. The end result can function as a small but serviceable drop cloth or tarp. The common 42 gallon bag will yield a sheet a bit over five feet by just under four feet.

Quick Figure 8

Tracing the 8 is the intuitive way to tie a Figure 8 knot and works fine, but there's a faster method. Grab the line near the end and twist it like you're putting a cap on a bottle. One twist is 180°, a full flip of the hand, and it creates a loop. Grab that loop and twist again. Last step: feed the dead end of the line into the loop.

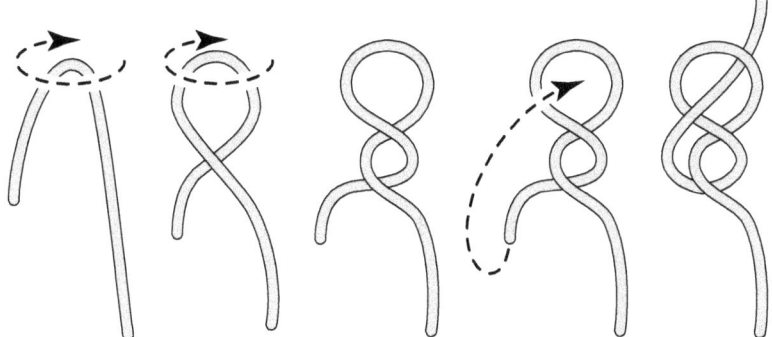

There are two ways into any loop. In this case, going in one way builds the Figure 8 and the other way builds a half-hitch. If you cap a bottle like most folk, you'll want to enter the loop on the side closer to you and exit with the line running away from you.

With a bit of practice, the quick Figure 8 method is particularly useful when tying a Figure 8 on the bight.

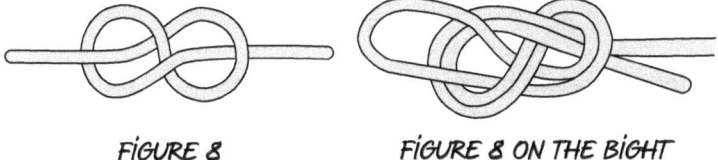

FIGURE 8   FIGURE 8 ON THE BIGHT

Bolt Length Rule

For common thru-bolted joints, such as to connect two platforms together, here is a simple formula to determine how long of a bolt is required:

$$\text{Bolt length} = \left(\begin{array}{c}\text{Total Thickness}\\ \text{of All Material}\end{array}\right) + \left(2 \times \text{Bolt Diameter}\right)$$

Always round up to the closest 1/4" increment. For example, to bolt together a couple of 2x4* platforms with 3/8" bolts:

$$\text{Bolt Length} = \left(1\frac{1}{2}" + 1\frac{1}{2}"\right) + \left(2 \times \frac{3}{8}"\right)$$

$$\text{Bolt Length} = 3" + \frac{3}{4}"$$

$$\text{Bolt Length} = 3\frac{3}{4}"$$

Let's try bolting together a couple of 1x3[†] Hollywood-style flats (also known as TV wings) with 5/16" Bolts:

$$\text{Bolt Length} = \left(\frac{3}{4}" + \frac{3}{4}"\right) + \left(2" \times \frac{5}{16}"\right)$$

$$\text{Bolt Length} = 1\frac{1}{2}" + \frac{5}{8}"$$

$$\text{Bolt Length} = 2\frac{1}{8}" \Rightarrow 2\frac{1}{4}"$$

This formula works because the length of thread on the bolt as well as the thickness of nuts and washers is determined by the diameter of the bolt. For example, regular hex nuts are always slightly shorter than the diameter of the bolt. For a 1/2" (0.5") bolt, the standard hex nut height is 0.448". This formula length is designed to accommodate a flat washer and either a lock washer and hex nut (currently an industry standard for most scenery) or a lock nut such as a nylon insert lock nut.

---

* Remember: 2x4 lumber is actually 1 1/2" × 3 1/2"
† Remember: 1x3 lumber is actually 3/4" × 2 1/2"

PART 2 - Shop Work   **85**

When calculating the total thickness of material, make sure to include *all* of the material that will end up between the flat washers. A common mistake is to neglect the crush plates, the square plates with holes that are tack welded to the steel or aluminum tube as reinforcement. They are basically big washers that travel with the tube, and they typically add up to a 1/2" of material.

The formula also provides a bit of thread beyond the nut. This extra thread aids in assembly. For example, in bolting together a flat, there may be a bit of a gap between stiles that needs to be drawn together. A slightly longer bolt is a great help. (For high precision and demanding engineering applications, extra thread is not desirable.)

One more point is worth making here. "Bolt length" is the measurement we use when buying bolts. This measurement is often – but not always – <u>different</u> from the overall length of the bolt. Here's the rule: **bolt length is the amount of the bolt that passes into or thru the material to be bolted**.

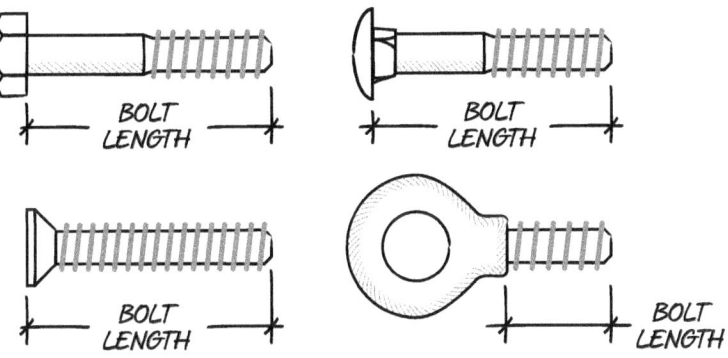

Bolt versus Screw

Ever heard of a "false dichotomy"? Bolt versus Screw is a good example. A threaded fastener might be a bolt or a screw <u>or both</u>. A bolt is a threaded fastener that is meant to be used with a nut. A screw is a threaded fastener that is meant to be used in a hole with threads. Sometimes a screw uses existing threads. Sometimes a screw creates its own threads. The locking knobs on a lighting instrument are typically screws that use existing threads. A drywall screw, on the other hand, is a screw that forms its own threads. This action is called "self-tapping". Some screws also incorporate a drill tip, such as the common Tek® screw. These screws are both self-drilling and self-tapping.

The hex head bolt typical to the theater can be used either with a nut or in a tapped hole. ("Tapped" means threads have been cut into the hole.) It is, therefore, both a bolt and a screw, and can be called either. For the stagehand sitting in tech rehearsal and looking for a rabbit hole on the subject, U.S. Customs has a publicly accessible guide called "Distinguishing Bolts from Screws". Have at it.

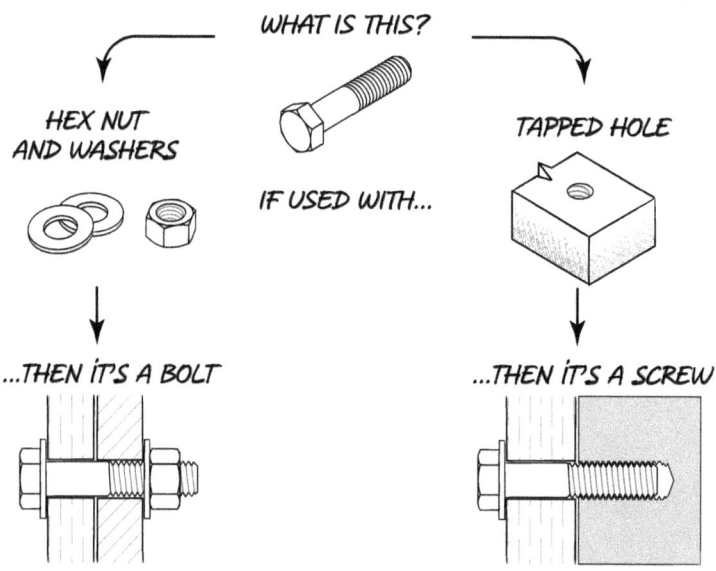

...AND IF IT'S SITTING IN A BIN AND WE DON'T KNOW HOW WE'RE USING IT YET, WE WOULDN'T BE WRONG TO CALL IT A SCREW OR A BOLT

(AND TRADITION WILL DETERMINE WHICH TERM WE USE)

Quick Tips on Buying Hardware

These are some common conventions when it comes to ordering hardware typical to the stage.

Hex Head Bolts and Nuts

- Steel with a Zinc Plated finish
- *Minimum* Grade 5 strength for both the bolt and the nut

Flat Head and Pan/Button Head Bolts

- Socket Head rather than easily-stripped Flat or Philips head
- Black Oxide finish is common but starts to rust quickly
- Zinc Plated finish is available and offers better protection

Washers

- Steel with a Zinc Plated finish
- USS size for general purposes
- SAE size for a smaller size and better clearance
- Rated washers are available to match the bolt and nut
- Lock Washers are an industry standard
- There are better options than lock washers for critical applications

Stainless Steel Hardware

- Only use when necessary, never as a stock item
- Galling is real: use anti-seize compound on the threads

Screws

- Sheet metal screws are generally useful
- Old school wood screws are obsolete
- Self-drilling screws vary widely in quality (see the "Burning in Screws" tip); buy good quality for good results

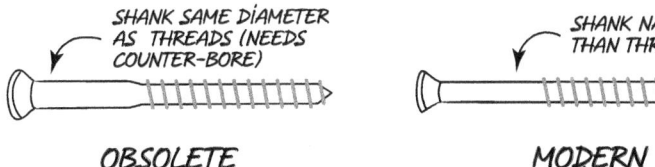

Burning in Screws

Why do self-drilling screws fail so often? One problem is that a lot of the screws on the market are for attaching drywall to metal studs. For interior work, these galvanized steel studs are often 25 gauge or 15 mil, which is about 1/64" thick. Screws that are designed for 1/64" of material are going to have a lot of trouble with the material we typically use, which is usually at least four times as thick, and often much more. Only buying the correct screw will help here. (These types of screws are rated by the thickness of material they can drill and tap into.)

The other problem happens even with good screws. Take screwing plywood to steel. The screw goes thru the plywood easily enough but as it slows down to drill into the steel, the plywood can ride up the threads of the screw, putting a side force on the screw, and snap it. To prevent this, the plywood needs a clearance hole that allows the screw to turn freely. Predrilling the plywood is ultimately the most efficient approach, but if all we have is the screw and a drill or impact driver, then we can burn in the screw. Simply put, "burning a screw in" is driving the screw thru material while running it in reverse. Instead of cutting threads into the material, the back of the threads rubs it away with friction. In screwing plywood to steel, the screw is burned in thru the plywood until the stagehand feels it get stopped by the steel, then the driver is switched to forward and the screw does its work drilling and then tapping into the steel with little interference from the plywood.*

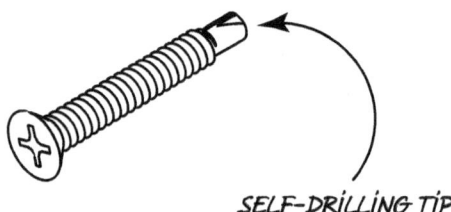

SELF-DRILLING TIP

---

* Top of the line screws can be found with wings that bore a clearance hole in plywood, then break off when they hit metal. No burning in required.

PART 2 - Shop Work 89

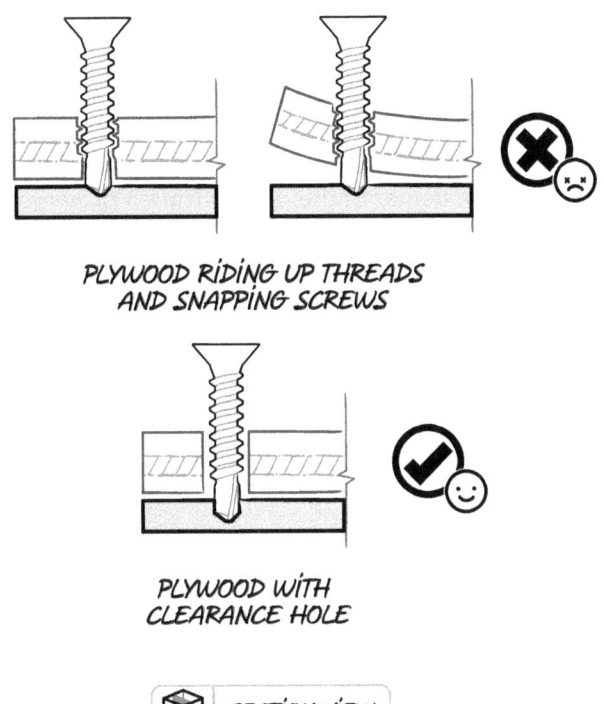

PLYWOOD RIDING UP THREADS
AND SNAPPING SCREWS

PLYWOOD WITH
CLEARANCE HOLE

SECTION VIEW

Burning in does generate a lot of friction, which creates more heat than is typical, enough to cause some smoke. Experience shows that this is not enough to ignite the plywood. There is just not enough heat and, moreover, when the screw is driven home it prevents much oxygen from getting to the plywood. But prudence dictates that we keep an eye on the plywood and never attempt this if there are flammables around. And, just as with other fasteners and other bits, the screw can get hot enough to burn skin if touched.

Grommet Punch Jig

Here is a quick and consistent way to churn out #3 grommets at one foot intervals, our industry's standard for spacing ties on soft good. Bolt the grommet press to a length of flat bar and weld a 3/8" post one foot from the center of the press. (The #3 grommet has a 7/16" hole size.) If welding is not an option, try this: drill and tap a hole, screw in a 3/8" hex head bolt and cut and file the threads flush to the plate. Then cut the head off the bolt and file smooth. An advantage of this approach is that the post can be removed if convenient for a custom project. This plate can be designed to bolt or clamp to a bench. If the press is going to be freestanding, extend the plate below the handle of the press to provide better stability.

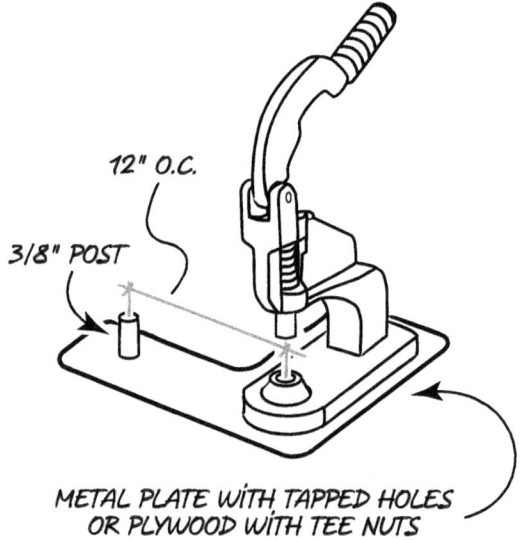

To use the jig, lay out the drapery face down (on a very clean surface) and find the center of the webbing that is to receive the grommets.* Mark center clearly and permanently with a marker. Make the first grommet at dead center. Make sure to keep the distance from the top edge of the drape to the grommet consistent. (This distance is usually set somewhere between 3/4 and 1 1/2 inches, depending on the fabric and how it is sewn to the webbing.) Now, simply drop

---

* It is also possible to lay the drapery face up and flip the entire top edge over to reveal the webbing. Laying out and punching the first grommet accurately is more difficult but hardly impossible.

PART 2 - Shop Work

the center grommet onto the post of the jig, align the top edge of the drape, then punch in the next grommet. Making a mark on the bed of the punch makes aligning the top edge easier. Keep working down the drape to the end. Add a grommet in the corner as necessary.

To do the other side, fold the goods over far enough so that the center grommet is flipped over. Now set the center grommet on the post and begin punching grommets again, working on the face of the drapery this time. If you prefer not to fold the goods, simply build the jig with two posts, one on each side of the punch.

Can we just agree?

Here's a list of things we could use, but maybe shouldn't. Let's sacrifice a little efficiency of material for big rewards in simplifying assembly and better operation.

7/16" Bolts	*Just an odd size.*
#12 Machine Screw	*Sounds like you need a 1/4" Bolt*
#3 Philips Screws	*Who has the bit set?*
Fine Thread Bolts	*Technically stronger than the same diameter bolt with coarse threads, but definitely easier to cross thread*
Ball Transfers	*Way too loud for use in a show (ok otherwise)*
1 1/8" Drywall Screws 1 1/2" Drywall Screws	*Would be useful if not for the other common sizes*
Used Drywall Screws	*Metal recycling is a better home than back on the hardware shelf*
3/64" Aircraft Cable 3/32" Aircraft Cable 5/32" Aircraft Cable 7/32" Aircraft Cable	*Too easy to confuse with other sizes*
Manila Hand Lines (also called Hemp)	*It's time to let go of organic rigging*

Got anything to add to the list?

PART 2 - Shop Work

An Inch a Yard (Fleet Angle Rule)

For every yard of distance between two sheaves, the absolute most that you can offset the sheaves is an inch. For each yard – every three feet – you gain an inch. If sheaves are 30 feet apart, you can be a maximum of 10 inches offset from each other.

If followed to the 32nd of an inch, this will keep the fleet angle at 1.59°, which is 0.09° over the recommended limit of 1.5°. So remember to use this rule as an error check for the absolute maximum. Keeping the offset down to 15/16" inch for every yard will be within spec, though it is less memorable as a phrase.

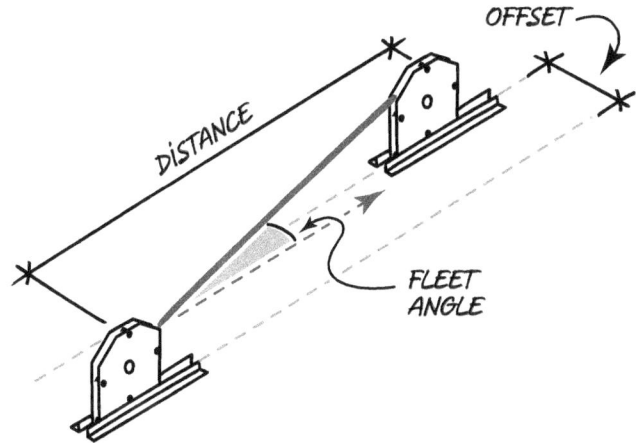

The best fleet angle between sheaves is 0°. This keeps the line from climbing up the sides of the sheave groove at all, reducing wear on the sheave and line. Whenever possible, "aim" the sheaves at each other by rotating them so that they point at each other. But this is not always possible. Some amount of fleet angle is inevitable in many situations. So, avoid it as much as you can, but know that you can get up to (but not quite) an inch for a yard when the real world interferes.

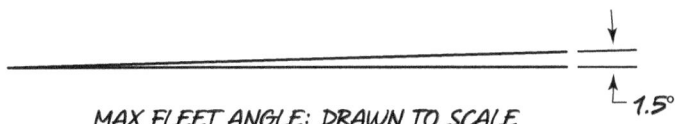

MAX FLEET ANGLE: DRAWN TO SCALE

Fleet Angle Equation

To calculate the precise number for either distance or offset with a 1.5° fleet angle, use these equations:

To Find:

Minimum distance (in feet) for a given offset (in inches):

$$\text{Min. Distance (ft)} = \text{Offset (in)} \times 3.18237$$

To Find:

Maximum offset (in inches) for a given distance (in feet):

$$\text{Max. Offset (in)} = \frac{\text{Distance Between Sheaves (ft)}}{} \div 3.18237$$

Example:

Sheaves have to be offset 5 inches to get around a sprinkler pipe in the grid.

$$\text{Min. Distance (ft)} = 5" \text{ offset} \times 3.18237$$

$$\text{Min. Distance (ft)} = 15.91185$$

Rounding up to the closest inch, sheaves should be at least 15'-11" apart from center-of-sheave to center-of-sheave. (To get from decimal feet to inches, see chart below.)

INCH TO DECIMAL FEET

1" = 0.083'	5" = 0.417'	9" = 0.750'
2" = 0.167'	6" = 0.500'	10" = 0.833'
3" = 0.250'	7" = 0.583'	11" = 0.917'
4" = 0.333'	8" = 0.667'	12" = 1.000'

Swaging Tool Identification

Copper oval swage sleeves are widely used in rigging, and for good reason. They are extremely efficient and cost-effective solutions, and have rightfully become workhorse hardware for stagehands. (For some of the finer points of swage sleeves, see the "Swages" section in *Part 4* of this book.) One major issue deserves discussion here: swages and swaging tools can be utterly confusing.

Two of the most common manufacturers in show business are Loos and Co., who make the Locoloc® series of tools, and National Telephone Supply Company, who use the tradename Nicopress®. There are others, ranging from top of the line aircraft tool manufacturers to cheap knock-offs suited at best to building a backyard fence. All of the legitimate swaging tool manufacturers have specific instructions on how to make and verify a swage. Each one does it their own way. Enter the confusion.

1/4" galvanized aircraft cable (GAC)* is probably the most common size in a theater. Most counterweight rigging systems use 1/4" GAC for the batten lift lines. A lot of stage automation defaults to 1/4" for deck tracks, counterweight assist winches, and dead haul hoists. Both Locoloc and Nicopress have single groove tools for crimping swages on 1/4" GAC. The Locoloc tool (part number 0-1/4) requires four presses. The Nicopress tool (part number 3-F6-950) requires three presses.

Adding to the confusion, for a given cable size and sleeve, a single manufacturer may require a different number of presses for different tools. For example, to crimp 1/8" GAC with a copper oval sleeve (part number 18-3-M), Nicopress makes two different multi-groove swaging tools. Both tools use the same groove: Oval M. However, the smaller tool (64-CGMP) requires three crimps. The larger tool (3V-F6:X:M) requires only two crimps. Nicopress also makes a single groove tool (3-M-850) that also uses Oval M but only requires a single crimp. Same cable size, same sleeve, same groove name – and three different numbers of crimps.

---

* Aircraft cable is a specific type of wire rope. It is also called "Specialty Cord". Smaller sizes tend to be 7x7 construction and larger sizes (including 1/4") tend to be 7x19 construction. It is available in both galvanized steel and corrosion resistant materials. Galvanized steel is more common and stronger.

Best practice is to make sure that the information the user needs travels with the tool. One approach is to engrave the number of swages required right next to the groove on the tool. Another approach is to attach a chart with sleeve part number and presses required to the handle of the tool. To protect the chart, packing tape is ok but clear heat shrink is ideal. Swaging is a great way to rig, but it's important to remember that the part numbers can be complicated and users need the right information – as well as the right tool, right swage, right cable and right go gauge* – to be successful.

---

* Yes, "go gauge" is the right name for the most commonly used gauges. *Nicopress Technical Bulletin TB-2* answers this question directly. There is an explicit difference between a Go and a No-Go gauge. (A Go-No-Go combines both gauges into one tool.) There are all sorts of these gauges used for industrial quality control, such as plug gauges to check hole sizes. For swaging tools, the sheet metal gauge is a "go gauge" because, as described in *TB-2*:

"if it goes, it passes - if it doesn't go, it fails".

A No-Go gauge would check for over-crimping. We do not need this gauge with common swaging tools and sleeves because the jaws act as their own limit. (But maybe there is a tool that I've never heard of that does need a Go-No-Go gauge; always confirm how a tool works with the manufacturer.)

Paint Pen Inlay

Having trouble reading the stamped sizes on the drill gauge in the dark? Trying to use a swaging tool and go gauge on a loading bridge with inadequate work light? Any text that has been stamped into a tool or gauge can be made more legible by using a paint pen. Scribble the paint on the stamping until it fills the text, then wipe the remaining paint off. Try to keep the rag from pressing in and pulling the paint out, we only want to wipe the surface. Done right, all of the text should now pop and be easily read.

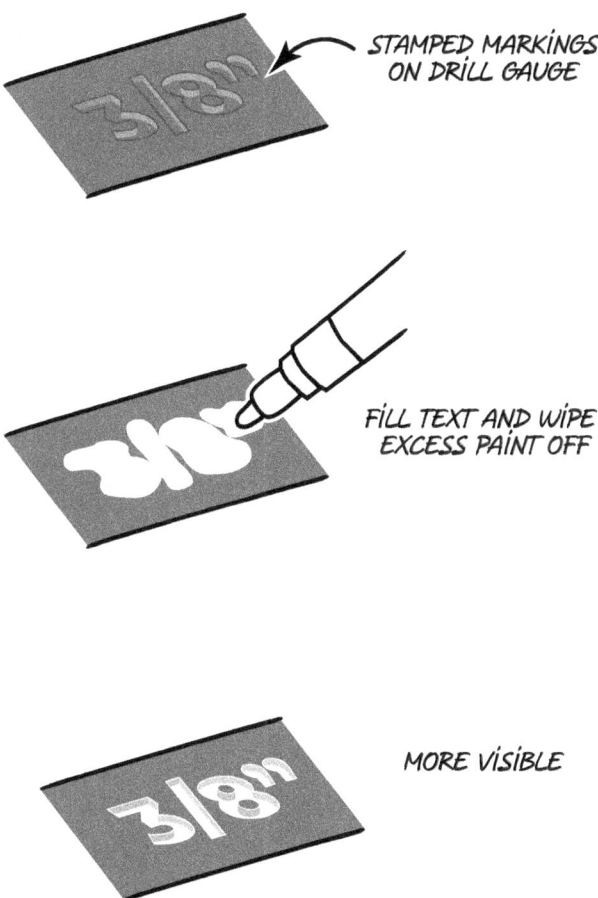

Impact Tapping

Leave the tap wrench and can of oil in the tool room. Tapping can be made more productive with an impact driver using impact tapping bits. Use rub-on stick lubricants for less mess and less waste. For smaller thread sizes (#10 and under) combination drill-tap bits designed for use in impact drivers are very efficient. There are combo bits for larger sizes, but using a separate drill along with an impact driver and tap offers more control over drilling speed and less cost per bit. Adapters are available for mounting conventional taps to impact drivers, just make sure the bits can take an impact load. This approach works best for thru holes in bar and plate; always check the manufacturer's specs on thickness and other requirements. Caster plates have never been this easy.

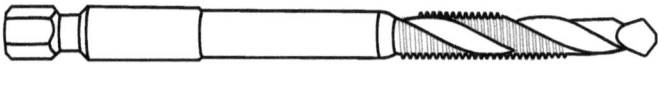

COMBINATION DRILL-TAP BIT

Stagger Casters

When a wagon rolls over a seam or gap in the stage deck, if all of the casters hit the obstruction at the same time, the wagon shudders quite visibly. If the casters are staggered so that each one hits individually, the wagon will look like its gliding across the stage. For relatively large gaps like deck track grooves or the clearance space around a lift, try grouping the casters in staggered pairs. As one caster floats over the gap, the other takes the load.

Grounding versus Grounded

Black, white and green: pull open a stage pin connector and these are the typical wire colors. Black is hot, white is neutral and green is ground. The National Electric Code, however, uses "grounding" and "grounded" for the neutral and ground. Which is which? Ignore the colors for a moment and remember that the groundin**g** conductor has an extra G and is for **g**round. The n**e**utral has an E and is the ground**e**d conductor.

Rot**a** Lock or Rot**o** Lock?

What are the odds two completely different types of hardware, both widely used on stage, would have such similar names? Here's a way to remember which is which: the saddle of a Rota Lock sort of forms an A when you look at it.

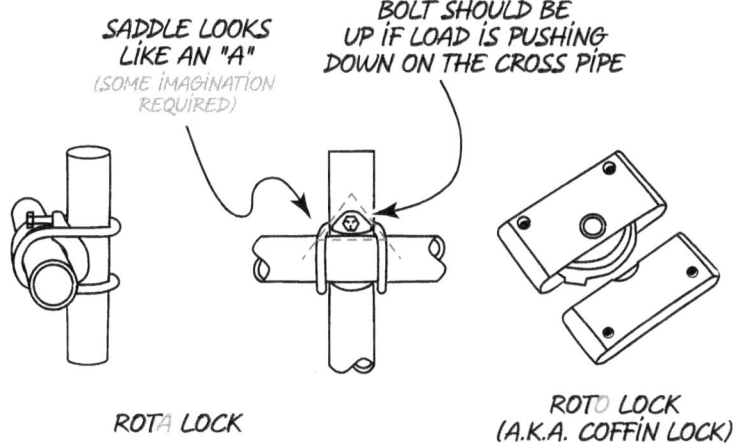

If you're looking for a Rota Lock that can go between different sizes of pipe, try a search for "Pipe Sway Brace Clamp". Sway Braces are used to stabilize plumbing systems and the pipe fitters often use pipes as the bracing member.

Fail Safe

Fail safe is an important term in engineering. It has also grown a popular definition. The popular definition is understandable in that if we had no experience with the term but were asked to define it, we might guess that fail safe must be something that is safe from failure. This is wrong. Fail safe, as used today by practicing engineers and designers, means **something that fails in a safe manner**. The popular definition assumes something can be made that will never fail. Impossible. The engineers and designers know that anything can fail. But we can plan for how it fails. (For more on these concepts, see the works cited in the *References*.)

Here's an example from everyday life: the doors on a passenger elevator. We know that the doors typically have a bump switch or a photo eye sensor. When the doors of the elevator are closing, if we wave our hand in front of the sensor or push the bumper, the doors stop closing. This prevents anyone or anything from getting caught in the door. What happens if the bump switch or photo eye sensor gets disconnected? Will the door be able to crush our hand? Not in a fail safe system. The door mechanism is wired so that all of the switches and sensors have to be connected before it can work. If anything is missing, a circuit is left open and the doors can't close. The system has failed – the elevator can't function if the doors can't close – but it has failed in a safe manner.

Chasing Air Leaks

Pneumatic systems are useful. Simple, affordable systems can still deliver high power density (lots of force in a small package) with good energy storage options that *can* be operated relatively quietly. Pretty much every shop uses air tools such as nail guns. On stage, pneumatics run wagon brakes and other effects. There are disadvantages, however, and one of the big ones is air leaks.

The tried and true way to find an air leak is to apply soapy water to the parts of the pneumatic system. If there is a leak, it will cause the soapy water to bubble aggressively. (The soap captures the air in bubbles; this is the same thing that happens with toy bubble blowers.) A small brush and cup offer the least messy delivery. For speed, a spray bottle covers a lot of area quickly. Leaks are most common at the threads of fittings, but can come from any part. For a system that is definitely leaking but the leak cannot be found, check the exhaust line on the valve. If the exhaust line has a muffler the leaking air can diffuse enough to not cause the soapy water to bubble. Remove the muffler, add soapy water, and check each valve position. With wagon brakes, for example, check both with the brakes up and with them down.

While most any common soap can be used with compressed air systems, be careful applying this to other gases. **Never use soapy water on oxygen tanks.** As soap dries, it leaves behind residues that can cause an explosion when mixed with oxygen.

In factories and pipeline systems, gas leaks of all sorts are found with ultrasonic detectors. (Imagine trying to find a leak in a fifteen-hundred acre refinery with a spray bottle.) While definitely a tool that an organization and not an individual stagehand should buy, there are affordable options.

Fixing air leaks, especially with shop tools, is a great way to make our work more sustainable. Compressors consume a *lot* of power, and leaks make them use more than is necessary. It is an easy step towards a more environmentally and fiscally responsible shop and stage.

Pneumatic Muffler

Need a muffler for the exhaust line on a pneumatic valve? Many of the common industrial options can be inadequate for use on stage. While they do protect the exhaust line from contamination, they simply do not reduce the noise enough. There are high-end options and shop-built solutions that are successful alternatives. But, in a pinch, stuff a rag in a soda bottle then run a hose from the exhaust port of the valve deep into the bottle. Make sure the bottle and the hose are adequately secured, such as by cable-tying both to framing. The larger the bottle and the more rag that is stuffed in, the better the noise reduction.

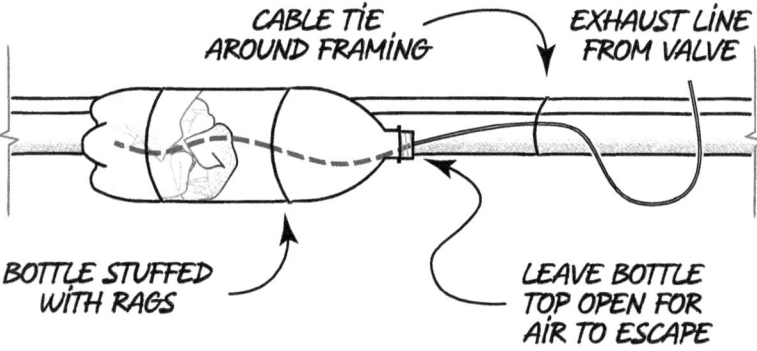

Right to Work ≠ At-Will Employment

A lot of folks are not very clear on what these terms mean. Worse, all too often folks confuse one for the other. In an at-will employment situation, the employer can fire the stagehand for any reason as long as that reason does not violate certain specific laws. These laws, both state and federal, set up protected categories. For example, a stagehand cannot be fired because of their race or sex anywhere in the United States. Some state legislatures and local governments have extended that protection to additional categories. But if the stagehands are working at-will and a producer walks in the door and decides to cancel the show, that's it. From that moment on: no more gig, no more pay (beyond what is owed for work already done) and no recourse. On the flip side, a stagehand can also quit the job whenever they want without legal repercussion.

The opposite of at-will is work under a union contract. Unions negotiate contracts with employers. That's why they exist; if employment contracts aren't getting negotiated, it isn't a union. These contracts usually create employment situations that are no longer at-will. Conditions vary from contract to contract, but provisions such as minimum length of work call and "discipline or discharge only for just cause" are typical. In this case, when the producer decides not to do the show, the stagehands will get paid the minimum call, which might be equivalent to four hours pay, or the full day, or even the full week, depending on the agreement.

Right to Work doesn't actually have anything to do with the relationship between the employer and the employee. It deals with the relationship between the employee and the union. In a Right to Work state, even if a union exists at a place of business, employees of that business do not have to join the union. They also do not have to pay dues to the union. Union supporters generally do not like Right to Work laws.

The states in the South and the Midwest are more likely to be Right to Work states than the Northeast or the West Coast. In the Northeast and the West Coast, when unions have a contract with an employer, all employees that benefit from the union's contract have to pay dues to the union. That is to say, anyone whose pay rate is advocated for by the union, pays the union.

RIGHT TO WORK STATES
(AS OF 2019)

KEY: RIGHT TO WORK (22)

Even if the employee chooses not to join the union, a percentage of their paycheck is owed to the union. It is very common for the employer to send this portion of the employee's wages directly to the union.

Unions face a problem. Employers at non-union shops can match the rates and benefits of union shops in the same area in order to attract workers. The workers, in the short term, see that they get the same compensation at either shop, but at the union shop they also have to pay dues. Unions, to succeed, also make demands on the time and energy of their members. People have to show up to meetings, vote in elections, walk a picket line if necessary. The problem is that workers might be shortsighted and work at the non-union shop. This denies the union shop of the labor all businesses need to succeed and drives the union shop out of business. Once the unions are gone, the employers no longer have strong competition in terms of rates and benefits. They can cut both wages and benefits without fear of losing workers. Probably more common than cutting wages is a failure to raise them to keep up with the cost of living. As things become more expensive thru inflation, the wages remain the same or increase at a much slower rate, which means the workers are able to buy less and less of what they once could.

Here is an example of wages failing to keep up with inflation. In March 1956, three years into Eisenhower's Presidency, the Federal Minimum Wage became $1 an hour. In September 2020, the Federal Minimum Wage was $7.25 an hour. That seems like a big difference but, in fact, if the Federal Minimum Wage had kept up with inflation, it would have been about 34% more ($9.71 an hour). Minimum wage workers in 2020 can afford less than minimum wage workers in 1956.[*]

It is a common mistake to believe that if a state allows at-will employment, it must be a Right to Work state. In fact, while the country is roughly split on Right to Work, at-will employment exists in all of the states as of September 2020. There are other caveats and exceptions that vary state-by-state. Montana has a significant exception.[†] But you can be an at-will employee in any state.

This might be the most controversial topic we touch on in this book. How ever any of us feel about Right to Work and at-will employment, it is important for us to use the terms correctly. See the *References* for more information from both sides of the debate.

---

[*] These numbers all come from the Federal Government. The Department of Labor has a history of minimum wage and the Bureau of Labor Statistics maintains an inflation calculator. See the *References*.

[†] In general terms, Montana law establishes a probationary period during which an employee works at-will. After this period, an employee can only be fired for "Good Cause". See the *References*.

[THIS PAGE INTENTIONALLY BLANK]

PART 2 - Travel

Travel

Here are a few tips and tricks on traveling for work. Admittedly, this barely scratches the surface of everything people learn touring shows, transferring productions, and attending conferences. (Anyone interested in contributing to the next edition, here's a great place to start...)

Luggage Carousel Tool Sale

Many of the cases popular with stagehands for personal gear use two-stage latches. At root, these latches have small pry bars built into the latch, which allow the case to be locked shut more tightly with less force from the user's fingers. (Single-stage latches on less expensive cases can be a real pain to open.) One issue with two-stage latches is that some users will close the latch only as far as the first stage. All too often, airport security officers fall into this category. When they fail to fully latch the case after searching it, all too often the lid springs open and the contents dump out as the case hits the conveyor belt leading to the luggage carousel. The stagehand waiting for their case will be greeted with a parade of their personal tools laid out as if for a tag sale.

A lot of cases have provisions for two padlocks and using both of them will help prevent this problem. With the locks on and the latches open, the lid can still open a bit, but as long as any small items are packed in organizer bags, the contents will remain with the case. An alternative approach is to use cable ties to secure the lid. Be sure to include replacement ties in the case for when the original ones are cut off by airport security to search the case. Why airport security will work either locks or cable ties correctly – but not the latches – is a question for a different book.

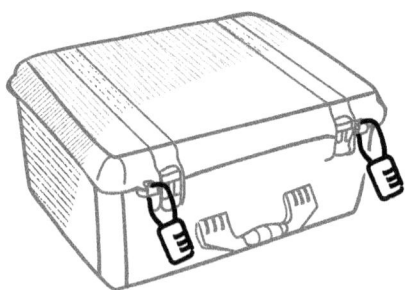

PART 2 - Travel

Trade Show Name Tag

Tired of your name-tag-on-a-lanyard bouncing around on your midriff? Would it be nicer to get it up a little higher, maybe at the height where you would clip or stick any other name tag? Simply tie a knot in the lanyard to take out some of the slack. A figure 8 will do, but not a bad time to get creative if you're into macramé.

Hotel Advice

Here is one simple but important tidbit: get the room numbers of whoever you're on the road with. Phone service can fail, especially abroad, and some front desks won't give out the information. For problems ranging from proving residence in the hotel to receive lost luggage to someone sleeping in, get the room number.

[THIS PAGE INTENTIONALLY BLANK]

PART 3

Fundamentals & Trivia

[THIS PAGE INTENTIONALLY BLANK]

Fundamentals

We tend to forget how confusing our jobs were when we first learned them. Many people lucky enough to know how to swim utterly fail to imagine what being in the water is like for people who cannot swim. Same thing happens with hard-won work skills. Here are some fundamentally important concepts that experienced stagehands ought to know *and* ought to realize that novice stagehands will be completely ignorant about. This isn't a list of everything fundamental, but it does hit some of the critical ones.

Bring tools.

Tools vary by position. Not infrequently, this means a pair of gloves and a c-wrench. Not infrequently, it means a thirty-five pound bag of carpentry. Sometimes, the primary tools are a pair of headphones and the knowledge of how to run a sound console. The idea is the same: be ready to work when you show up.

Being early is on time. On time is late.

At the root of punctuality in show business is respect for the audience. There is a start time written on the tickets and we ought to be ready to go at that time. The audience might not be ready at that time, and the curtain might be held on their account, but we should be ready. (And, of course, performers can vary in this area, but that is a subject for a different book.) In order to be ready at the advertised time, many different departments have to accomplish many different tasks, from checking for burned-out lamps to making sure the stage is clean. Every step in a pre-show routine matters, and many steps rely on another step happening first. The logic is that of the "For Want of a Nail" proverb. And it all starts with everyone being in the venue at the agreed upon time, ready to work.

A lot of work happens in the shop and before or after a show. There's no audience involved, but we still insist on punctuality. Instilling a culture of punctuality might be justification enough but, in fact, **it ought to be out of respect for each other that we show up just a bit early for work**. If we were planning on picking up something big with four people, what happens when only three show up? Do the three now each have to do that much more work? Does the job have to be put on hold and, when the fourth arrives, does it suddenly become a rush, adding stress and risk to the work?

The best sort of work happens with a great deal of mutual respect. This is visible not only in how people talk to each other, but in how the work is done. A stagehand shows up early for a call and there is a place they can go to hang up their jacket, change into work boots, finish a cup of coffee. If it's a theater, maybe they are just sitting in the house; if it's a shop, maybe they have their own work box or a locker in a break room. They can chat with the rest of the crew. If the manager of the call is there, they can be part of the conversation too, but no one starts talking about the tasks for the day until the work day starts. This is the sort of environment where there are carts and sawhorses available so no one has to wreck their body. Where the stagehands know how the equipment works and treat it with care; gear doesn't get sent back to the rental house for simple problems that could have been solved on the spot. This is not simply aspirational – theaters and shops like this do exist – and on a daily basis, it really does all start, quite literally, with folks being punctual.

How early is early enough? A good approach is to think about what can go wrong on the way to the call. If you miss a train, how long until the next one? If there's a fender bender on the highway, how much time does that usually add to a drive? Some folks live in places where they have to consider freight trains, which can block a road for minutes on end. Other folks have draw bridges to consider. However long the typical delay is, aim to show up at the job at least that much earlier. Most of the time, you'll have a nice buffer. Occasionally, it will be tighter, but you'll still be ready to work when the call starts. You might even find that the work itself becomes less stressful than the commute in.

And if you are going to be late, let whoever is managing the call know as soon as you know. Don't hope for a miracle, just give people as much of a heads up as you can.

Stage Directions

Stage directions for stagehands are a bit like math for an accountant or a foreign language for a diplomat. Fluency is both essential to success and requires practice to master. The good news is that fluency becomes effortless over time. There are many different conventions, but the essential compass of the theater is built from two simple principles.

Principle #1   All directions on *stage* are from the perspective of the *performer*

Principle #2   All directions in the *house* are from the perspective of the *audience*

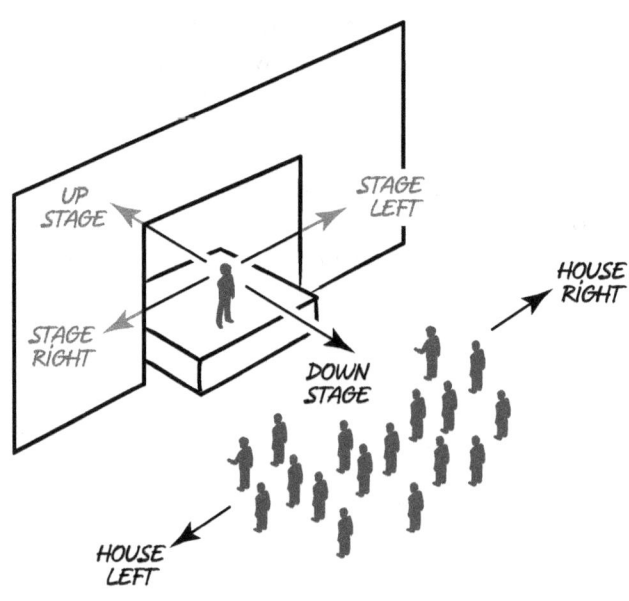

PART 3 - Fundamentals

The use of left and right is pretty sensible. We only need to remember if we're on the stage or in the seating to remember which perspective to use. What about the use of up and down, as in "up stage" and "down stage"? (Check out the previous drawing to see the primary directions.)

If we were designing a new language, we might pick different words, but we're stuck with the language we have. One way to remember which way is up and which way is down is to remember that stages are often tilted at an angle. If there is a group of performers on stage, the folks closer to the audience need to be lower than those behind them in order for everyone to be seen. We do this all the time with risers for a chorus, for example. In fact, many stages used to be built with a permanent angle, called a rake. Going up the rake (up stage) moves you away from the audience towards the rear of the stage. Going down the rake (down stage) puts you right in front of the audience.

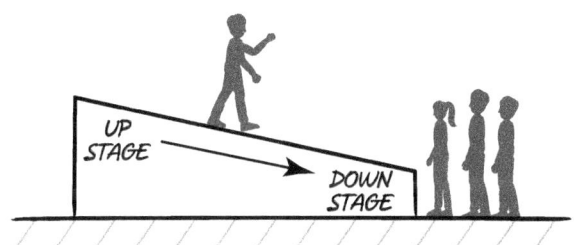

Let's add in a little more complexity. We know that there are four primary directions. But sometimes things need to move diagonally. So, we have four ways to combine the primary directions. They represent the corners of the stage, more or less. Out in the house, where the audience sits and where cameras are sometime set up, directions are usually limited to left and right. When there is a camera, it is treated as the audience, with "camera left" and "camera right" the same as "house left" and "house right".

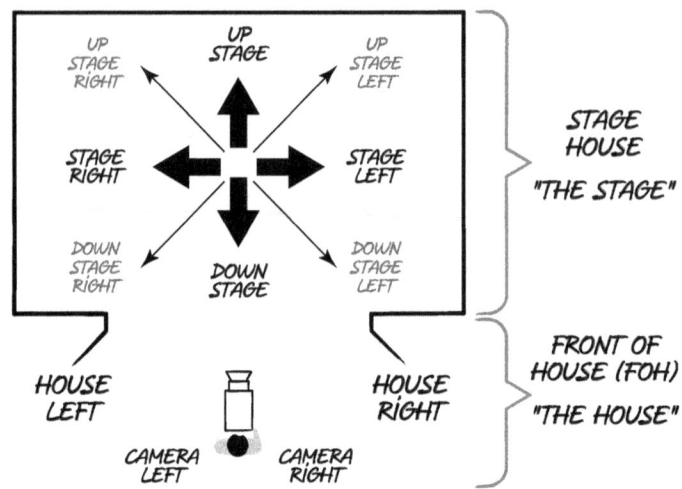

Finally, there is another system of stage directions common enough to be considered fundamental: the concept of "on stage" and "off stage". This is a slightly more formal version of saying "move that way" and pointing. Getting things on and off of the stage is the goal, and we have developed a simple language to achieve it: "on stage" means get it more towards the audience's view and "off stage" means get it out of sight.

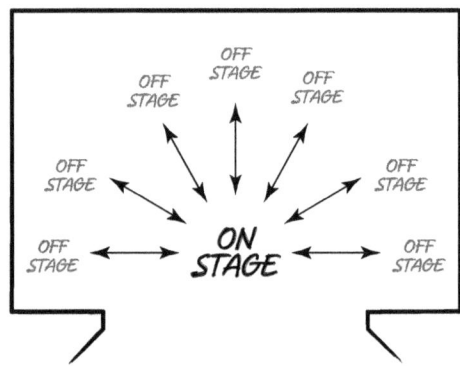

A Proposal* on Stage Directions

Looking back on the stage direction diagrams in the previous section, we notice that there are many more directions for people on stage than there are for people in the house. From a historical perspective, this makes sense because stagehands once did all of their work on stage and almost none in the house.

Times have changed.

Every year seems to add more and more equipment to the Front of House area. (Front of House is another name for the seating area of a proscenium theater.) The only directions we have to manage all of this equipment is "House Left" and "House Right". At the risk of confusing the issue by introducing something new, it seems entirely appropriate to propose that "**Down House**" (moving towards the stage) and "**Up House**" (moving away from the stage) should be added to the vocabulary. Just as the stage can be raked towards the audience, the audience is very commonly raked towards the stage. This means the same up/down logic can be applied. Moving "up house" is moving up the rake of the audience, away from the stage.

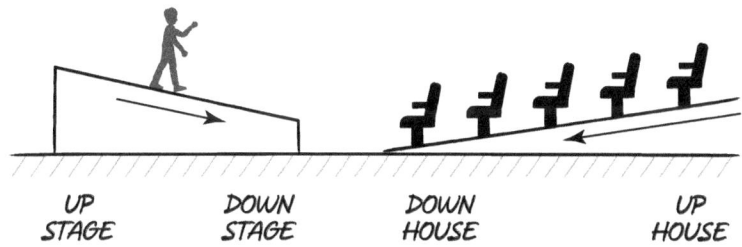

| UP STAGE | DOWN STAGE | DOWN HOUSE | UP HOUSE |

Trying to use "up stage" and "down stage" in the house can be very confusing, because the rake is now in the opposite direction and "house left" and "house right" are reversed relative to "stage left" and "stage right". So here we propose that only "house" terms are used in the house and "stage" terms are used on the stage.

---

*We are calling this a proposal because "up house" and "down house" are not commonly used. However, this is such a straightforward extension of the stage direction logic, that somebody somewhere has to have come up with this already. I suspect there are venues that already use these terms all the time.

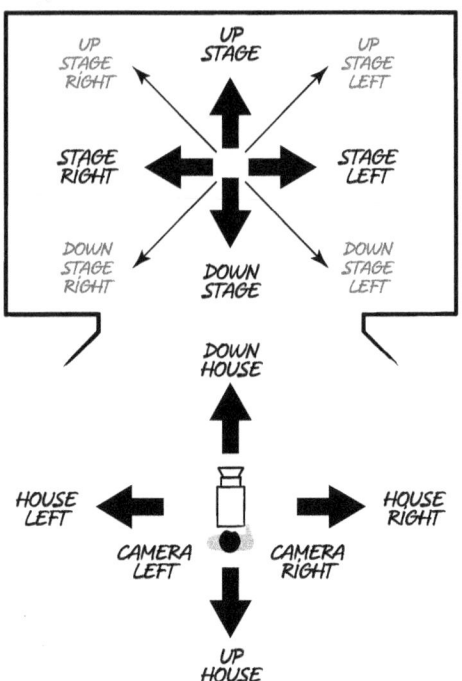

PROPOSED STAGE DIRECTIONS

PART 3 - Fundamentals

Electrical Overcurrent Protection

In entertainment power distribution for a given system, we can often (but not always) hold **voltage constant**. Any changes in voltage happen with the electrical company long before we get our hands on it or, at the other end of the system, inside the devices. For the stagehand running cables from source to device, the voltage is typically constant. In these systems, it is the **amperage that varies**. (The amperage is the amount of current that the device draws, measured in "amperes" which we usually call "amps".) It is for the amperage that everything will need to be sized. Just as the shackle and wire rope need to be sized for the weight of an object, a circuit breaker and electrical cable need to be sized for the draw of an electrical device.

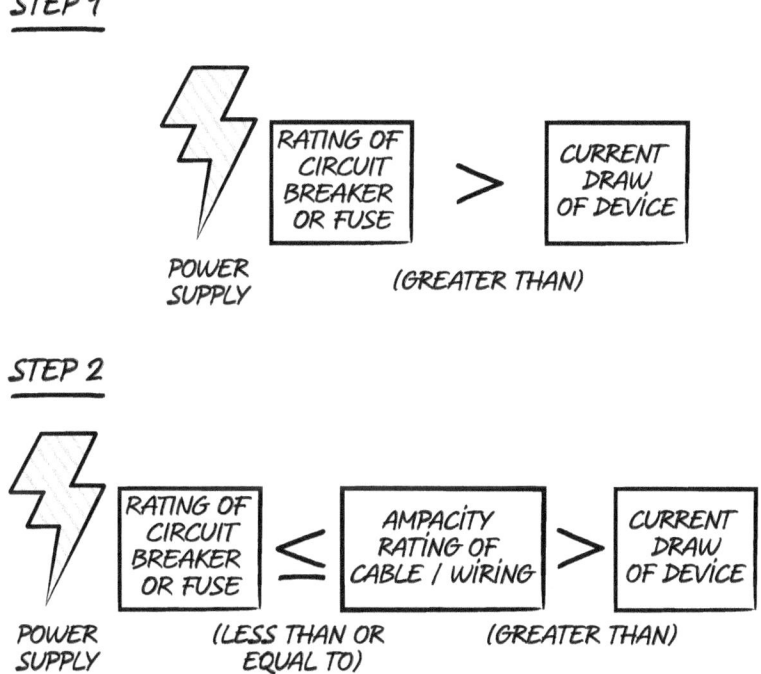

Here's an example: we have a light that draws 28 amps. The circuit breaker in the distro needs to be rated for more than the draw. Let's say it is rated for 30 amps. Next, we have to size the cable that runs from the distro to the light. **This cable has to be rated for the size of the circuit breaker.** It needs to be rated for at least 30 amps.* We call this rating the "ampacity" of the cable.†

What happens if we replace the light with a newfangled LED that draws only 12 amps? Can we downsize the cable to a lighter and cheaper 15 amp cable? We can if we <u>also</u> downsize the breaker. If we leave the 30 amp breaker in the distro, the cable has to stay the same. Why? Consider what happens if the old light gets put back into service. On one end we have a light drawing 28 amps. On the other end we have a circuit breaker able to supply 30 amps. In the middle we have a cable that can only carry 15 amps before it begins to overheat. Overheating cables and wires are a common way for a building to catch on fire.

In discussing electrical safety, we often focus on the risk from shock and arc flash. These are very dangerous hazards that need to be protected against. But it is also important to understand the more general fire risks of electricity, such as overheating cables run in places we can't see them. Between the years 2012 and 2016, an average of 148 workers died each year from electrocution. For those same years, an average of 440 people died each year from electrical fires in the home.

There is a reason that the National Electrical Code (NEC) is published by the National <u>Fire</u> <u>Protection</u> Association.

---

* The rating will include several factors. These include voltage and type of cable. In general, only "hard service" type cables are allowed on stage. The length of the cable will also be important. See the *References* for detailed resources. Right now, we are focusing on the concept.

† "Ampacity" is a portmanteau of "amp" and "capacity". This is worth pointing out because portmanteau is a fun word to use. See the *References* for more on the language of electricity.

PART 3 - Fundamentals

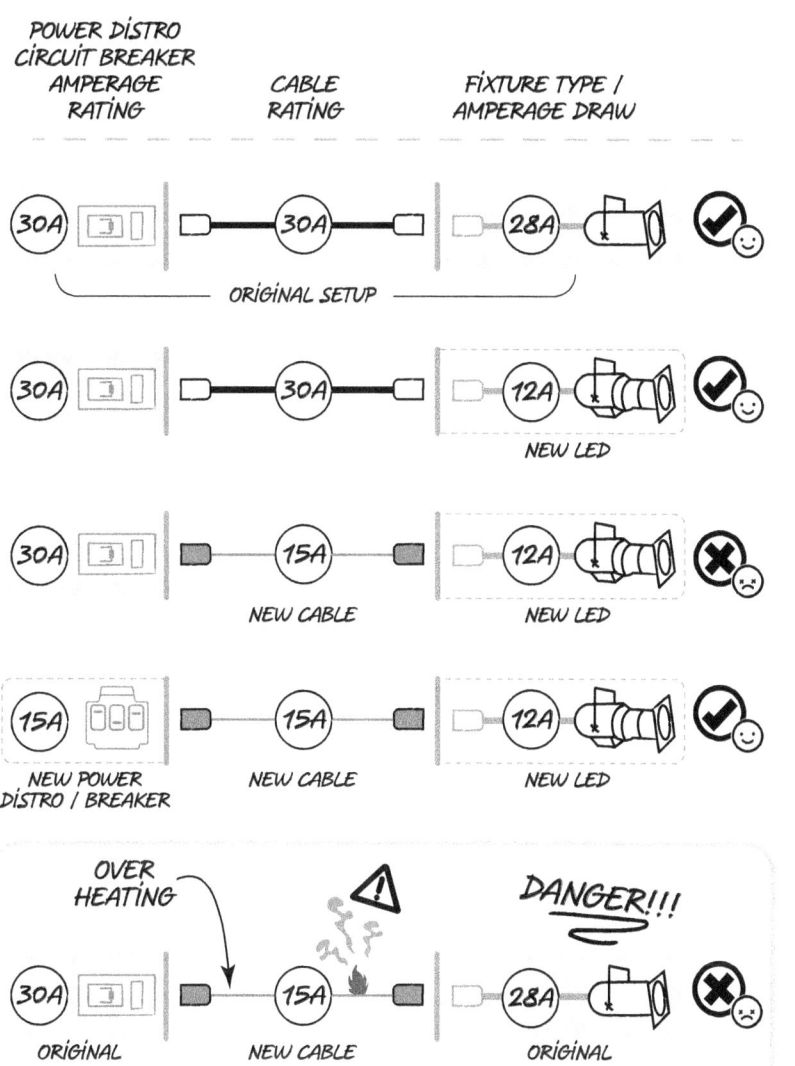

Note:
This example is meant to demonstrate a concept. Do not use the numbers in a sketch to make real world design decisions.

Going back to our example, let's say we downgraded both the breaker and the cable to 15 amps. What would happen if the old light was plugged into the new cable? It would draw 28 amps, which is more than the 15 amp rating of the breaker and so the breaker trips. This would be a non-functioning system, but it will have failed in a safe state.

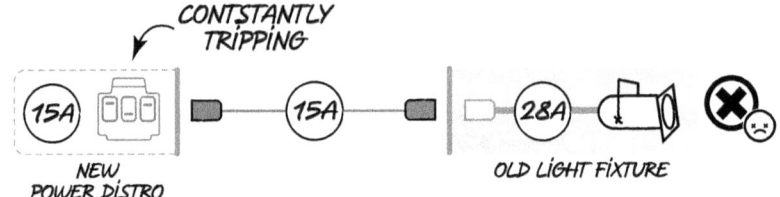

Proper sizing of conductors (cables) and overcurrent protection devices (circuit breakers and fuses) is but one of several essentials in the safe use of electrical power. It is also less obvious than some of the other essentials. Stagehands who would never cut the ground pin off a plug or drive a forklift over feeder cables may build a cable from 18/2 zip cord and plug a string of lights that draws 19 amps into a dimmer with a breaker rated for 20 amps. (The zip cord is rated for much less, and is also expressly prohibited for use on stage by the National Electrical Code.) Zip cord used this way has burned down more than one theater. For more information on electricity, check out the works cited in the *References*.

> A word from the NEC:
>
> The official language in the code for the concept we have been explaining can be found in Article 520. (Article 520 is dedicated to the theater and "similar locations".) Section 520.9 states: "Receptacle ampere ratings and branch-circuit conductor ampacity shall not be less than the branch-circuit overcurrent device ampere rating."
>
> A lot of factors go into establishing the "rating" of these parts. For example, is the load continuous or intermittent? These factors are all available in the NEC, but you really have to understand the jargon. The electrical resources listed in the *References* can help.

Bridle Tension

The forces on a rigging system are more than just the weight of the object being picked up. Any object can generate forces much higher than its self-weight. The simplest example of this is among the most dangerous: shock loads. Allowing an object to free fall and then be "caught" by a rigging system can generate enormous forces. The farther the fall and the stiffer the rigging, the greater the forces. (Stiffer means hanging things with materials that don't stretch much, like steel and polyester.) But shock loads are usually an accident. Outside of stunt work, no one designs a shock load into the system. Bridles, on the other hand, *are* done intentionally. And bridles can generate forces many times higher than the weight of the object being picked up.

For a gut sense of bridle tension, imagine two stagehands picking up a bucket. The higher they lift the bucket, the more effort is required, even though the weight of the bucket itself never changes. To increase the height of the bucket, the stagehands have to pull more against each other.

The flatter a bridle becomes, the more force it generates in the legs of the bridle. How does this happen? The object's weight is the object's weight, so the total vertical force remains the same. But all bridles also generate a horizontal force. The stagehands with the bucket both feel their hands being pulled down and their shoulders being pulled towards each other. The flatter the bridle, the more the anchors (or, in this case, the stagehands' shoulders) are pulled in toward each other. Depending on the situation, either the rigging or the anchor can fail with this additional force.

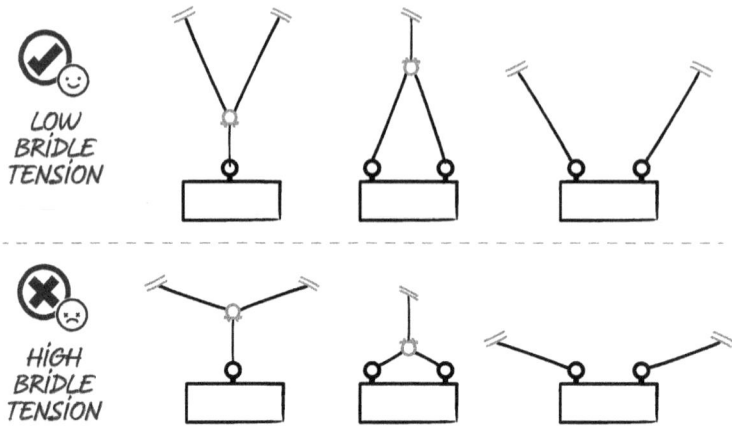

When discussing bridles, many folks in show business immediately think about big concerts that rig from the steel beams of an arena's roof. But bridles happen in all sorts of rigging. They can happen at either end of the load path. A sling basketed around a truss, for example, acts as a bridle. A ratchet strap holding a case to the wall of a trailer also acts as a bridle. In this case, we can only apply so much tension to the ratchet strap. What varies, depending on how steep or flat the strap is relative to the case, is how much of the strap's tension goes into pushing the case into the wall versus pulling the anchor points towards each other.

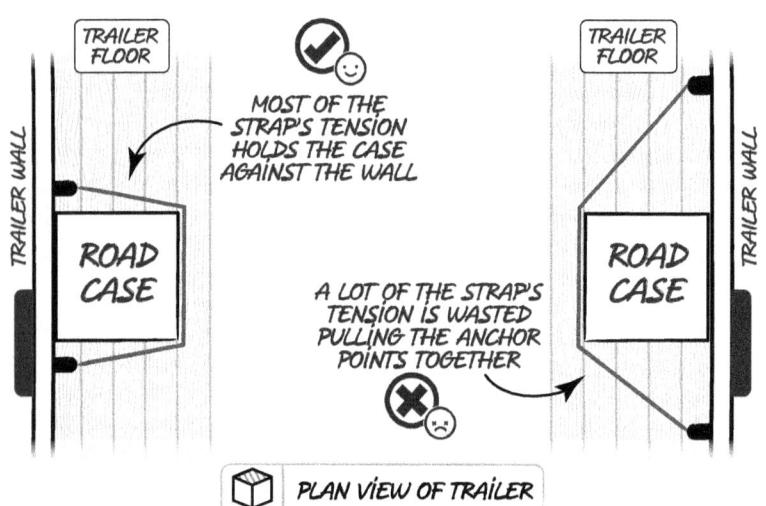

Where is the line between an acceptable bridle angle and too flat of a bridle angle? It depends on what is being used to build the bridle and where the bridle is being used. An engineer can design a wire rope system that is functionally a very flat bridle. Horizontal lifelines for fall arrest systems are exactly that, and typically use some very beefy components and shock absorbers. Conversely, when a rigger is wrapping a truss with a round sling, a common rule of thumb is to keep the bridle angle of the sling at 90° or less. Applications will vary; the critical takeaway is that bridle angle can quickly generate forces greatly in excess of the weight of a load. The closer the bridle gets to flat, the exponentially higher the forces become.

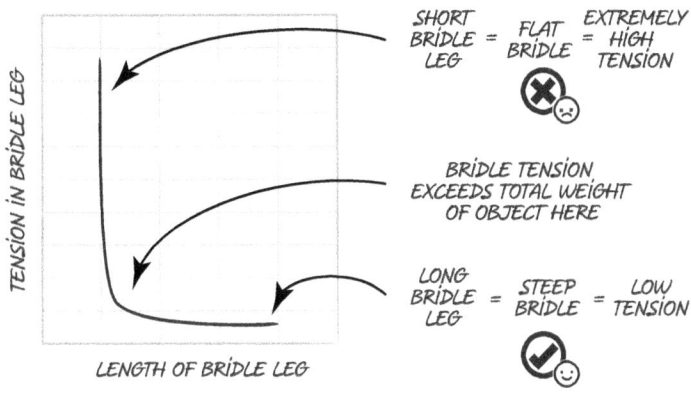

EXAMPLE BRIDLE TENSION CHART

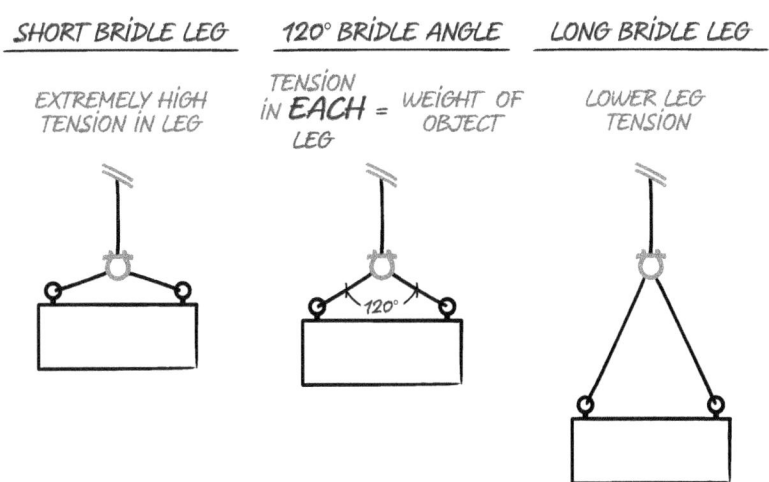

Power Transmission by Rotation

For a given source of power, the output speed and the output force are inversely proportionate to each other. The motor in a winch can be made to spin the drum faster, but the drum will have less torque.* Less torque means that it will pull the line coming off of the drum with less force. This is the same concept as riding a geared bicycle. One set of gears will turn the wheels slower but climb hills better. Another set will be faster, but only work on flatter terrain. (This assumes the bike rider is always applying the same amount of pedaling power; in the real world, we tend to apply more power as we deal with inclines.)

Power transmission by rotation is one of the most common concepts in machinery. Many industrial sewing machines found in the costume shop and drill presses found in the scene shop use belts and pulleys to set the speed. (Both machines can of course also be found in the prop shop.) Typically, on either type of machine, the speed can be modified by changing the size of the pulley. If the machine has a stepped, multi-groove pulley, the speed can be modified by changing which groove the belt sits on. Similarly, deck winches are often designed such that the speed and force can be adjusted by changing sprocket sizes. This form of power transmission is also essential to the operation of many moving lights. Even in cases were the system should not be modified by the user, as with moving lights, understanding how the power transmission works is foundational to understanding the system as a whole. **If power is constant, to increase force, speed must go down. And vice versa.**

$$Power = Force \times Speed$$

---

* Torque is twisting force. We tighten a nut, for example, by applying torque with a wrench.

PART 3 - Fundamentals

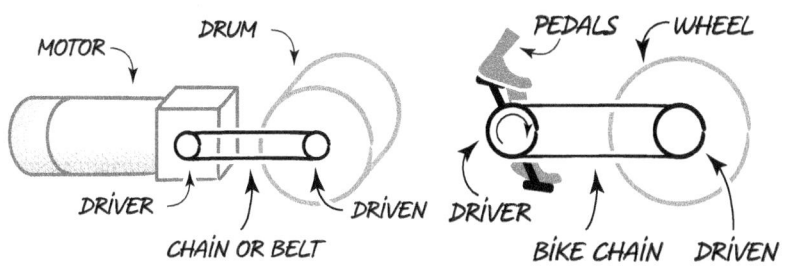

DRIVER = DRIVEN → SAME SPEED, SAME FORCE

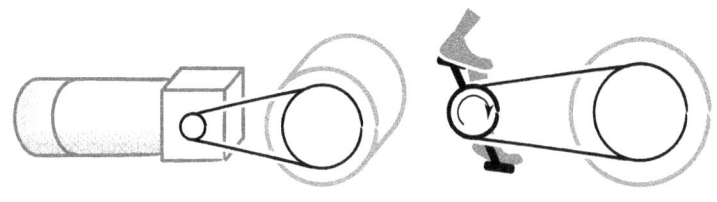

DRIVER < DRIVEN → SLOWER SPEED, MORE FORCE

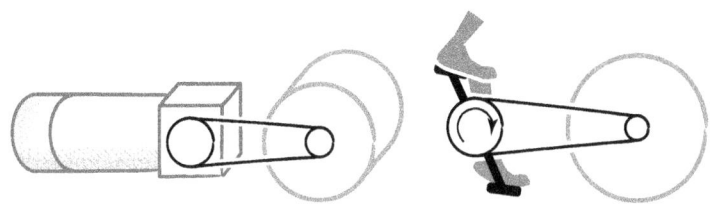

DRIVER > DRIVEN → FASTER SPEED, LESS FORCE

Power Transmission by Purchase

Purchase, in a rigging system, simply means a line that leads to an object. The hand line of a counterweight line set, for example, is also called the purchase line. Manipulating the transmission of power by changing the number of purchase lines is a very common technique. Many stagehands are familiar with converting a 1-ton chain motor to a 2-ton chain motor by adding a hook block. Other systems, especially when using pneumatic and hydraulic cylinders, are also common to stage machinery and props.

As with the previous *Fundamental*, "Power Transmission by Rotation", another name for these systems is "Mechanical Advantage/Disadvantage". We are using the term "Power Transmission" because it better captures the essential concept that — whether it is a stagehand or a motor — **for a given power source any gains made in speed must include a loss of force. And vice versa.**

Increasing the force while decreasing the speed is common for rope and pulley systems, such as with block-and-tackles.* The reverse — decreasing force and increasing speed — is much less common with rope systems and much more common with pneumatic and hydraulic cylinders. What works best depends on the nature of the power source. Stagehands can pull lots of rope reasonably quickly but can only lift so much, so pulling more rope to lift a heavier load is a good trade off. Cylinders, on the other hand, can only be so long, which means their rods can only pull so far. But cylinders can generate high forces. So pulling less rope with more force works well for cylinders.

The number of lines going to the load and the number of lines going to the power source are written as a simple ratio. By convention, it is written as a ratio of the purchases on the load relative to the purchases on the power source.

Load : Power

---

* Block-and-tackles are also called block-and-falls: "tackle" and "fall" are both alternative names for rope.

PART 3 - Fundamentals

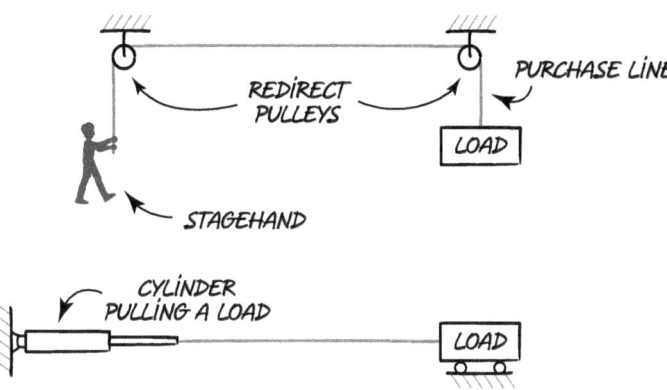

| 1:1 PURCHASE | → | SAME LOAD AND DISTANCE |

Example:

| 80 lb Pull of 3 feet | → | 80 lb Load moves 3 feet |

It is important to note that in the case of the cylinder moving an object horizontally, when we say "load" we mean the force required to move the object. When pushing and pulling, this is most likely going to be very different than the object's weight. Just as a stagehand can roll around a 730 pound Genie® lift without too much effort but would have a lot of trouble picking it up, the forces required for pushing and pulling are typically very different from lifting and lowering. But purchase systems are just as effective at pushing and pulling as they are at lifting and lowering, so it's worth showing it being done both ways.

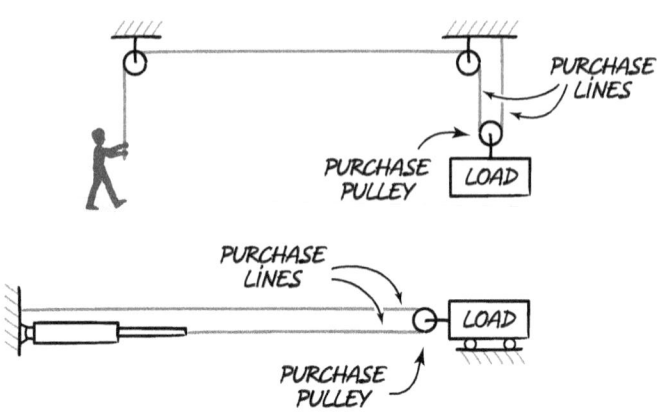

2:1 PURCHASE	→	TWICE THE LOAD, HALF THE DISTANCE
80 lb Pull of 3 feet	→	160 lb Load moves 1.5 feet

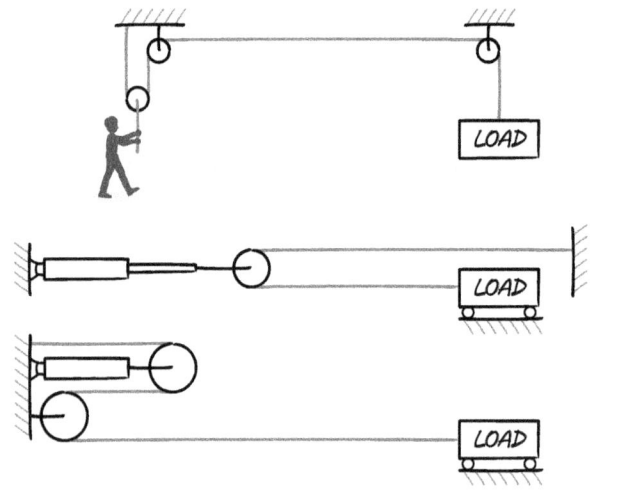

1:2 PURCHASE	→	HALF THE LOAD, TWICE THE DISTANCE
80 lb Pull (or Push) of 3 feet	→	40 lb Load moves 6 feet

PART 3 - Fundamentals

Purchase systems can be expanded to lift heavier loads more slowly or lighter loads more quickly. Block-and-tackles are designed to lift or pull heavier loads, and usually use at least three purchase lines.

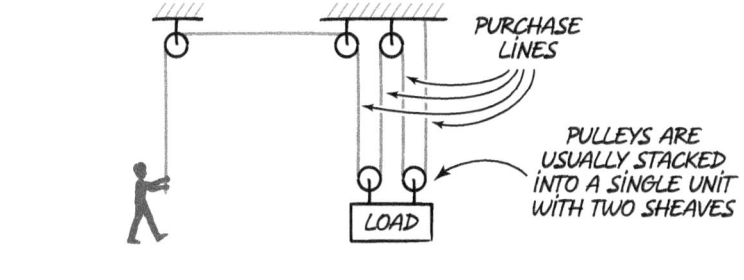

4:1 PURCHASE	→	4 TIMES THE LOAD, 1/4 OF THE DISTANCE
80 lb Pull of 3 feet	→	*320 lb Load moves 0.75 feet*

Purchase systems can also be combined. Combined systems are much less common, though a 3:2 purchase can be useful in situations where the power source needs just a bit of an assist. This can come up, for example, in performer flying systems. Combinations other than 3:2 and 2:3 are pretty rare.

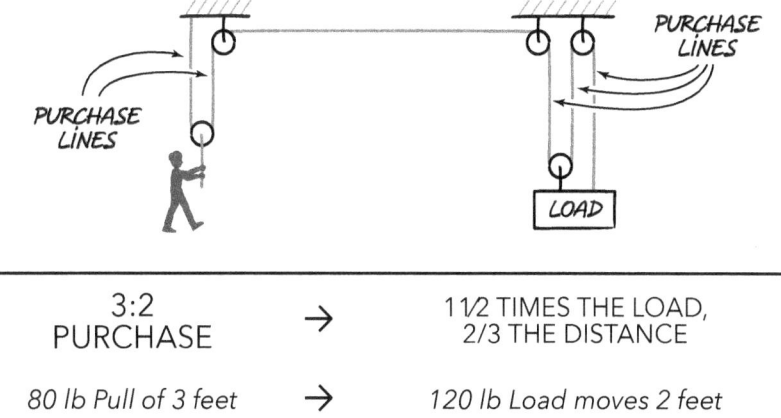

3:2 PURCHASE	→	1 1/2 TIMES THE LOAD, 2/3 THE DISTANCE
80 lb Pull of 3 feet	→	*120 lb Load moves 2 feet*

We have made some simplifying assumptions here, such as neglecting the forces required to overcome friction and to accelerate an object. In the real world, some amount of force will be lost to friction. Some amount of force will also be needed to accelerate and decelerate a load, which is the force to overcome inertia. (The more time we take to slow down or speed up, the less force is required to overcome inertia.)

Even in more precise real world calculations, where the forces involving friction and inertia are taken into account, the designers and engineers start from the ideal, which we have presented here. That is to say, none of this is a simplified version of the physics but the essential first step in understanding the physics.

More steps can be taken to refine the results and be more precise. How many steps that need to be taken will depend on the circumstances. The design of an elevator or an airplane will need more refinement than the question of whether the stagehand needs a 3:1 or 6:1 block-and-tackle to lift a speaker. For a more thorough treatment, check out the physics section in the *References*.

Orthographic Projection

When a stagehand gets a stack of drawings for a show, they will have to make sense of a lot of visual information. This information will typically follow **drafting conventions** drawn from the worlds of architecture and engineering, as well as other fields such as fashion and computer science. We have, over time, picked the tools from these other fields that most suit our work. While this makes our drawings rather idiosyncratic, there is a common core of conventions. Foremost among these is the use of orthographic projection: the technique of translating an object drawn on a page in two dimensions into a physical reality of three dimensions. To understand this process, we need to first think about how our vision works.

We see the world in perspective. If we stand on some train tracks and look at them as they run off into the distance, the rails of the tracks appear to converge and the cross ties get smaller and smaller. We know the rails don't actually converge – the train would derail if they did – but the trick of the eye helps us to judge the distance of objects. The farther something is, the smaller it looks. This is useful for navigating the real, three-dimensional world.

Perspective is a type of projection. Projection simply means how we take an object and represent it on a two-dimensional surface. Going back to how we see the railroad tracks, there is actually a perspective projection happening inside your eyeball: light passes thru the lens of the pupil and literally projects itself on the back wall of your eye, which is made out of receptors. A camera does the same sort of projection, using a lens similar to the pupil and a back wall of either film or electronic receptors. An artist can simulate this projection on a piece of paper by picking a vanishing point, then drawing objects converging towards that point.

Not all projections use the same technique. Some projections ignore the fact that we see in perspective. Take, for instance, a map of the world. In this case the big problem to be solved is that a sphere – the earth – has to be projected onto a piece of paper. There are several different techniques, each of which distorts the world's proportions to some degree. Greenland, for example, often looks significantly larger on a paper map than it does on a desktop globe.

(The globe is more accurate than the map: Greenland is much smaller than South America.)

An orthographic projection is a graphic technique that attempts to represent an object with dimensional accuracy. Most noticeably, parallel lines stay parallel. The rails of a train track never converge in an orthographic projection. This is an artificial projection in that it represents the world differently than our eyes see it. In truth, all projections – including the one inside a human head – are artificial.* Each of them is an interpretation that only captures a part of the world. So how does the orthographic projection work?

A generally useful metaphor used for orthographic drawings is the **Glass Box**. Most textbooks on drafting in any discipline use this metaphor. For a particularly elegant and theater-specific text, see W. Oren Parker's excellent *Sceno-Graphic Techniques*. We will follow Parker's approach to the common metaphor of the glass box. The metaphor goes like this: start with an object you are interested in. This could be a moving light or a speaker. Frequently, it is the entire theater. Imagine placing this object inside a glass box, something like a big square fish tank. Now imagine filling the box with a clear epoxy such that the object is fixed right in the center of the box.

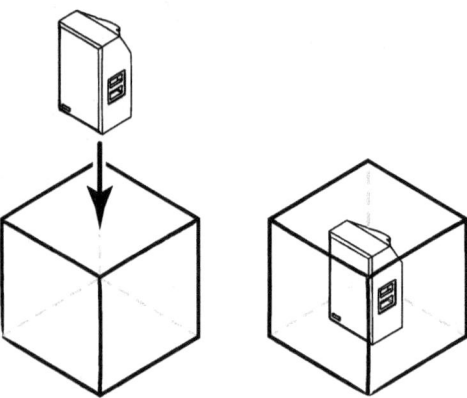

---

* One of the best proofs that our vision is a fallible construction are optical illusions and visual paradoxes. M.C. Escher made his living off the fact that what we see can differ from physical reality.

PART 3 - Fundamentals

Imagine some stagehands standing around this box. If each one looked as squarely as possible at the box and traced what they saw on the box with a marker, they would be creating an orthographic projection. By looking squarely at the object, we are minimizing our tendency to see in perspective.

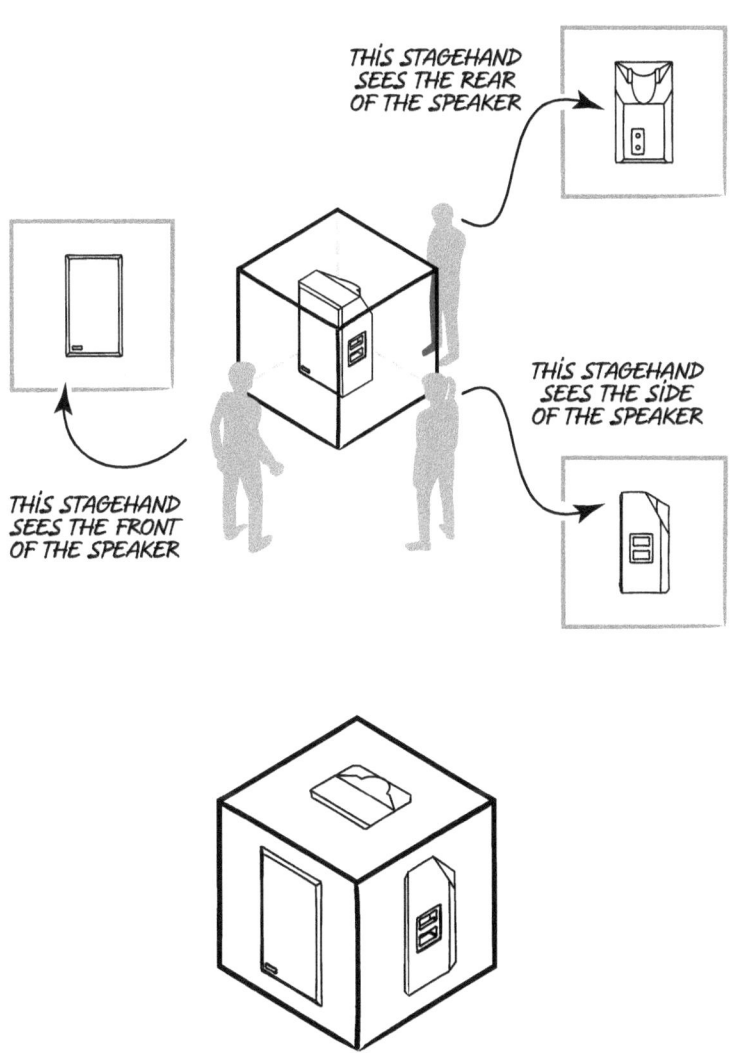

Once we have drawn on all of the sides of the box, we take the object out (complete with epoxy which fortunately does not stick to the box), then unfold the box. This unfolded box now has six different views of a three dimensional object laying flat.

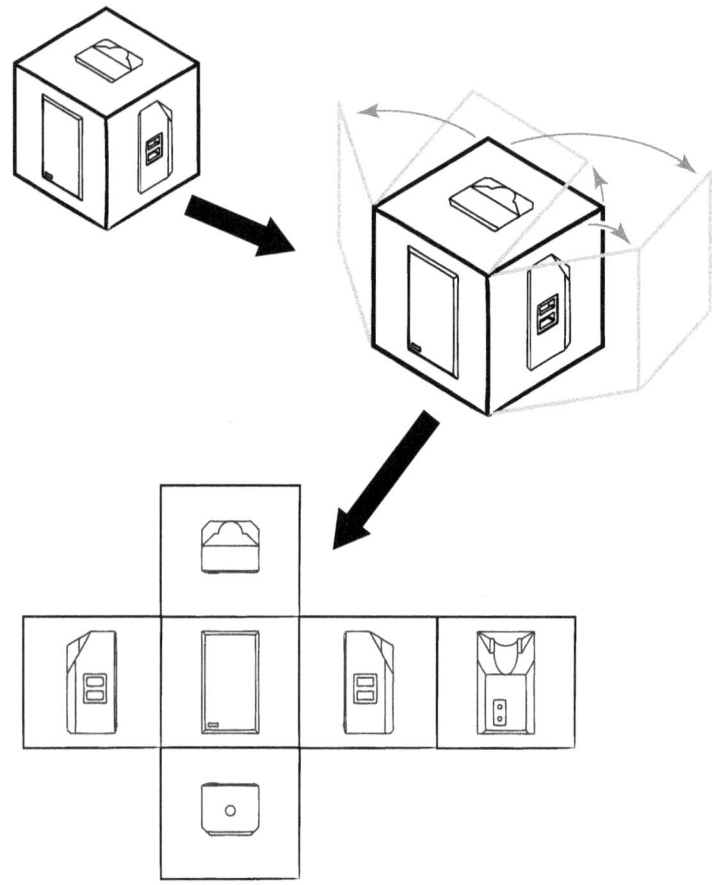

Why are orthographic projections important? Because they are essential in communicating accurate information about an object. Orthographic projections allow a drawing to be dimensioned accurately and precisely. They allow different carpenters to build different parts of a show and have it all come together correctly at load-in. (This would not happen if each was just making a best guess off of a perspective sketch.)

PART 3 - Fundamentals

Why can orthographic projections be difficult? Because we see in perspective. When given orthographic drawings, our brains have to reassemble the images into a three-dimensional model in our mind. With practice, this becomes second nature. Early on, it takes a concerted effort.

Consider the following orthographic image that Parker presents in *Sceno-Graphic Techniques*. These are three of the six sides of an object. Imagine it is a build drawing handed to a carpenter. Can you see what Parker wants you to build? Try imagining what it is before moving on.

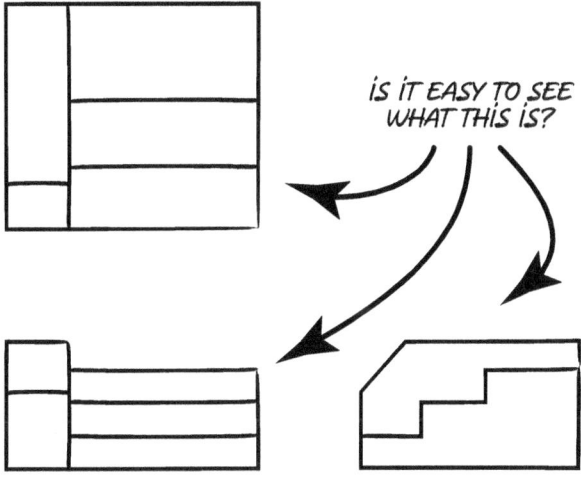

The following is Parker's pictorial drawing of the same object. It is much easier to understand conceptually. On the flip side, the exact proportions are harder to judge.

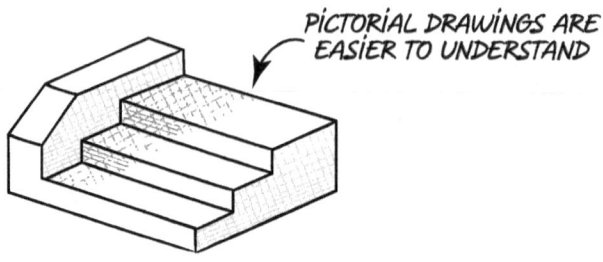

What exactly is harder to judge? Here's an example: looking just at Parker's pictorial drawing, can you tell where exactly the beveled portion of the stairs end? Is it before the start of the second step, in line with the leading edge of the second step, or does the bevel actually end after the second step begins?

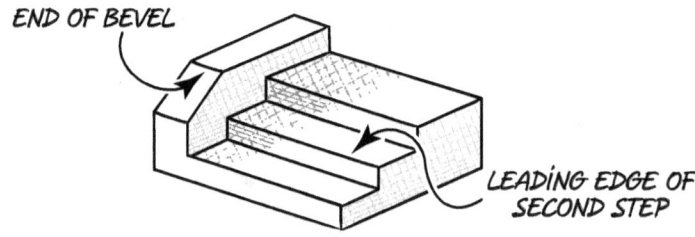

Flipping back to the orthographic drawings, it is easier to answer this sort of question with the orthographic projection. Moreover, **a stagehand can find all the dimensions they need from an orthographic drawing by measuring the drawing itself, if they know the scale that was used**. A pictorial drawing cannot be measured in this way. For pictorial drawings that mimic how we see in perspective, the scale for each line varies based on its orientation.

Screwing up orthographic projections happens all the time. Folks drafting the working drawings put top views on the bottom and left views on the right. Designers are notorious for putting section views in the wrong place. (A section is a type of orthographic view that shows a slice of an object.) Carpenters on the floor also make mistakes and set pieces get built backwards. It doesn't help that

PART 3 - Fundamentals **141**

there are actually two ways of doing orthographic projections. The method we've been describing, which is called third angle projection, is the most common in the USA. The other technique, first angle projection, is more often found outside of the USA. It is good practice to indicate which type of projection is being used in a drawing. A common graphic symbol for doing that is shown below. For more information on first angle projection, see the resources listed in the *References*. For now, just be aware that there is a trap here.

THIS SYMBOL INDICATES THAT THIRD ANGLE PROJECTON IS BEING USED IN THE DRAWING

(TYPICAL IN THE U.S.A.)

THIS SYMBOL INDICATES FIRST ANGLE PROJECTION

We've gone from the actual object to a paper representation of it. We put a speaker in a glass box, then turned it into a drawing. More often than not, however, a carpenter on the floor of a scene shop is expected to go the other way: from the paper representation to an actual object. Consider the construction drawing of a funky step unit that a carpenter just got handed. There are three orthographic views of the step unit.

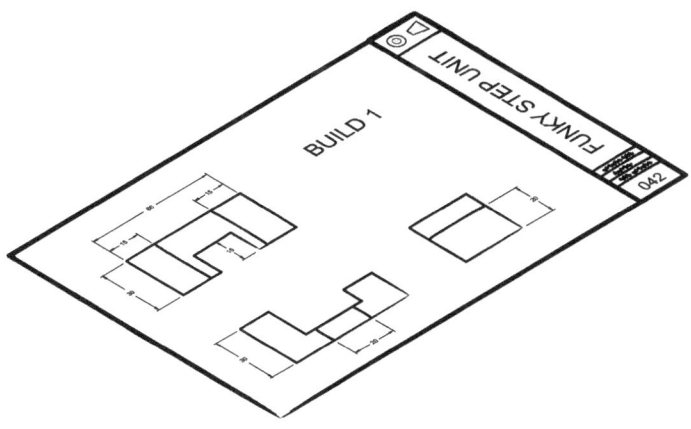

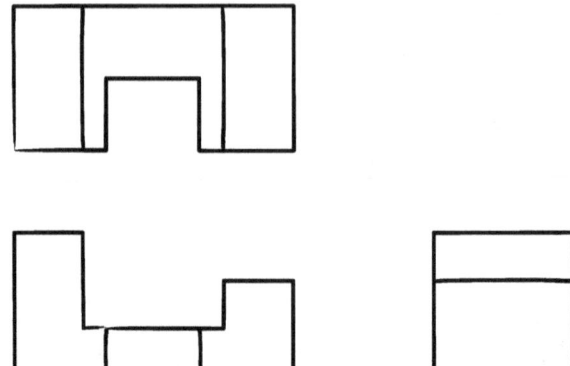

Here are the orthographic views without the dimensions. The carpenter, a visual thinker, sketches two pictorial representations of the object. Which one of them is correct?

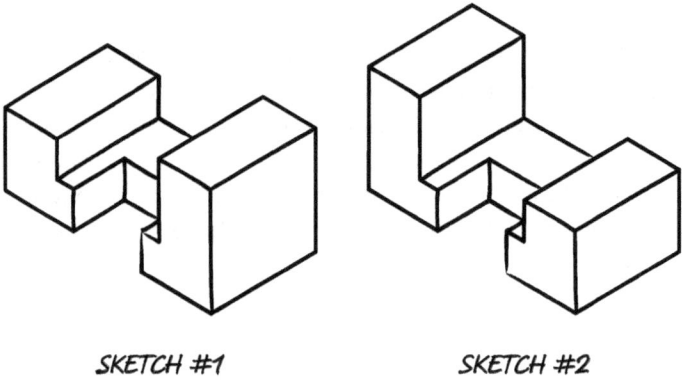

SKETCH #1   SKETCH #2

When working from the orthographic to the real image, one trick is to work back to the glass box. With the orthographic views all of the same scale and properly placed, the carpenter can literally cut them out of the paper and fold them into a box. Being able to spin the views around in the hand can help really make the relationships between views clear.

PART 3 - Fundamentals **143**

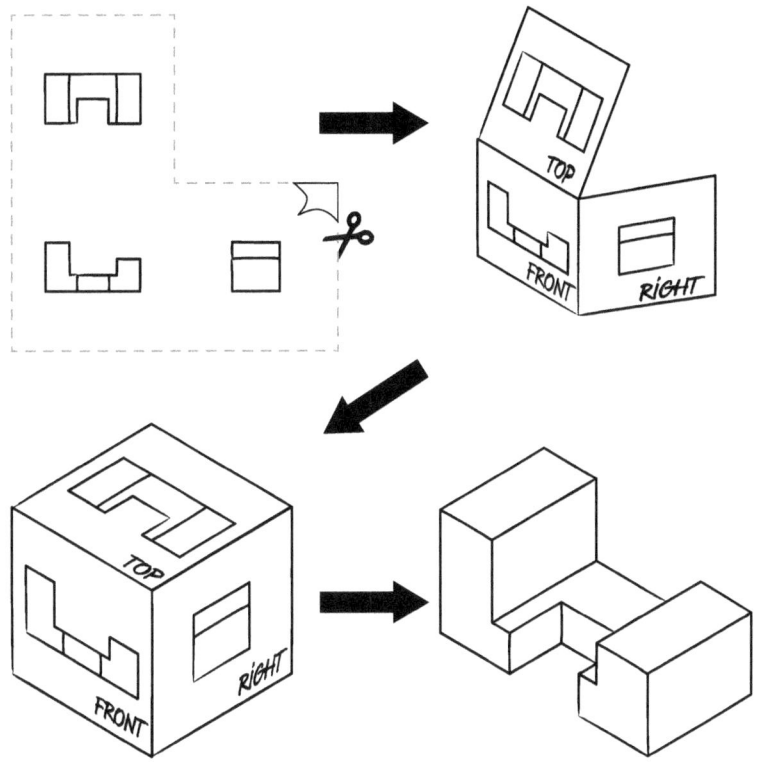

As we can see from the folded paper box, the Sketch #2 was correct. The other sketch reverses the taller and lower sections, relative to the U-shaped cut out. Now the carpenter is ready to build this funky thing... just as soon as they go and get a fresh copy of the drawing from the drafting department.

A larger scale version of the orthographic step unit is included on the next page, if you want to try cutting out and reforming it into a box yourself.

[THIS PAGE INTENTIONALLY BLANK]

PART 3 - Fundamentals

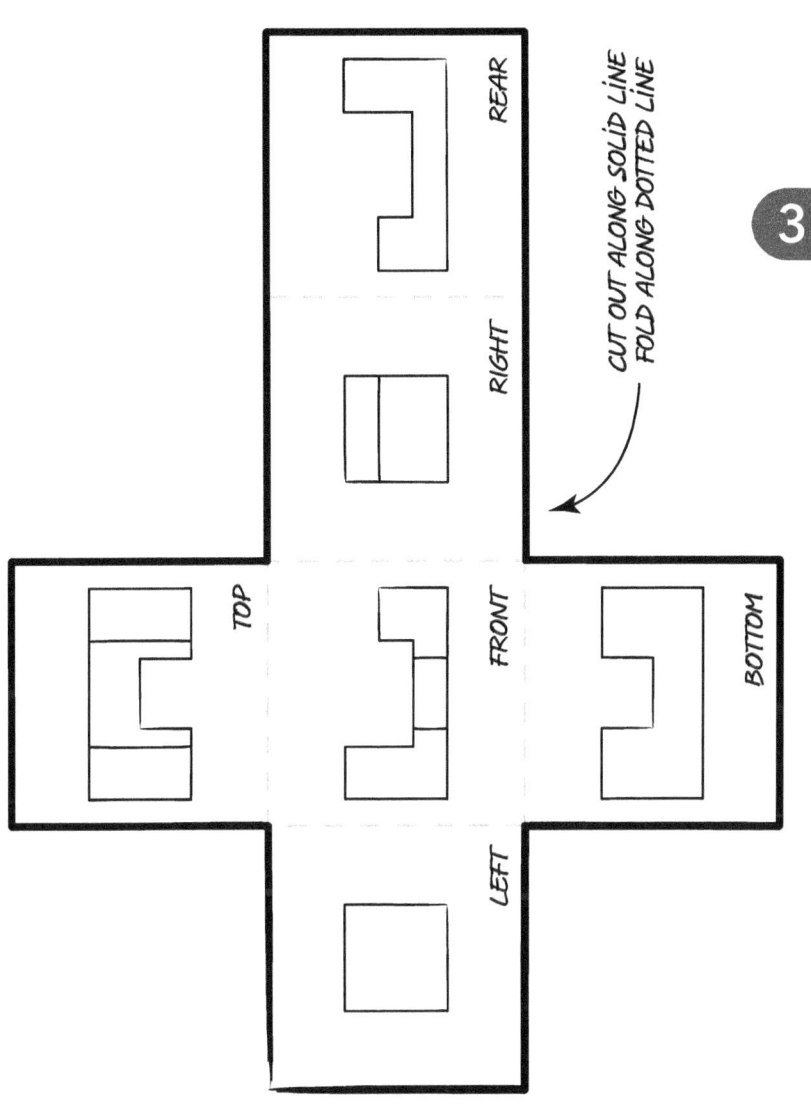

BE ADVISED: IT IS NOT RECOMMENDED TO CUT OUT DRAWING IF USING AN E-READER

[THIS PAGE INTENTIONALLY BLANK]

PART 3 - Fundamentals   **147**

Don't Run in the House

Places of public assembly have some inherent dangers. When people gather in large groups, it is easy for lots of them to get hurt quickly. Sometimes, outside forces can hurt these people, such as a fire filling the room with smoke. Sometimes, these people can hurt themselves, such as all running for the exits and trampling each other. These dangers are very real and unfortunately need to always be at the forefront of our thinking.

Imagine a stagehand on a show call. They are wearing all black, have a comm headset, probably an array of tools on their belt or in an apron. All very official looking. When the audience sees this stagehand go running down the aisles of a theater, they will immediately assume that the building is about to blow up. Or that the star of the show has just died. Or something equally horrible. At a minimum it will be a disruption. At worse, it can start a panic.

When should a stagehand run? To prevent someone from getting injured or killed. What if they need to run to make a scene shift or a quick change? In cases like this, frankly, it sounds like the show needs to hire another stagehand.

[THIS PAGE INTENTIONALLY BLANK]

PART 3 - Trivia **149**

Trivia

Just for fun.

Did you know...

(To learn more, follow the end note number to the next section.)

Louis Daguerre, who invented photography with Nicéphore Niépce, got his start in the theater. He was a scenic designer, a scenic painter, a stage machinist, and an entrepreneur that built custom theaters for scenic spectacles. He arranged for the French government to pay him a lifelong pension and make the secrets of photography free to the world (except England, where Daguerre had a patent).[1]

George Washington's favorite play was *Cato* by Joseph Addison. He reportedly made his officers watch it to inspire their virtue.[2]

Bram Stoker, author of *Dracula*, was a theater manager. Among his other literary activities, he wrote a brief history of stage lighting.[3]

Gel, the sheets of plastic we cut up and use to change the color of light, used be an actual gel. Gel is short for gelatin. Early theater electricians would pour hot liquid gelatin out onto pans and let it cure to make sheets of gel. Now we use plastic, but still call it gel. (Soon, thanks to LEDs, the fact that we used gel at all is going to be trivia.)[4]

Gaff Tape was invented by Ross Lowell, a cinematographer and general camera/lighting wonk, in 1959.[5]

The first Broadway show to use an electronic light board was *A Chorus Line* in 1975. Electronic boards were used in the original production at The Public. When the show moved to Broadway, if a new board had not been purchased, half the cues would have to have been cut from the show. Tharon Musser won the Tony for her Lighting Design and the show is often cited as foundational to modern Broadway lighting.[6]

The first year of the Tony awards – 1947 – a special Tony was given to P.A. MacDonald, "for intricate construction for the production of *If the Shoe Fits*". The set was a giant story book where, as the pages turned, a new scene would pop up mechanically from the pages. Designed by Edward Gilbert and built by MacDonald, the set was praised but the rest of the show was panned.[7]

The only Tony award ever given to audience members was in 1947, to Ira and Rita Katzenberg, "for enthusiasm as inveterate first-nighters".[8]

It was illegal to move shows between cities by truck until 1948. The Interstate Commerce Commission finally granted the right to do so to the company Highway Express, which became Clark Transfer. Up until this point, all touring was done by railroad.[9]

The first recorded "hot mic" incident was Anna Maria Alberghetti, the star of *Carnival!* on Broadway in 1961. Wireless mics were a new phenomenon and performers had to switch them off themselves between scenes. One day during tech, Alberghetti forgot and her trip to the bathroom was broadcast over the house PA.[10]

The first person to "drop the mic" was either Eddie Murphy in 1983 during his *Delirious* stand-up routine or Judy Garland after singing *By Myself* on the Ed Sullivan show in 1965. Eddie Murphy probably deserves the credit, given how he perfected the move in 1988 playing (among other roles) the singer Randy Watson in *Coming to America*.[11]

There is an old chestnut out there that whistling on stage is bad luck. The explanation goes that the stagehands in the flies used whistles to communicate and whistling might inadvertently bring some scenery down on the whistler's head. It never made much sense that stagehands would be whistling during shows to fly scenery, but apparently the folks at the old Metropolitan Opera House did in fact communicate by whistle during changeovers, once upon a time. So if you find yourself standing on the Met stage in the late 19th century during a changeover, avoid whistling.[12]

The term "robot" was coined in 1920 by playwright Karel Capek in his play *R.U.R.* It is derived from a Slavic word meaning servitude, forced labor, and drudgery. Wonder how someone who worked in the theater came up with such an idea.[13]

Karl Peterson is very well represented in the stagehand's tool bag. He patented the modern form of c-wrench in 1915 (there have been a lot of adjustable wrenches over the years; his is what we use), and he also patented a pair of pliers/cutters and a pipe wrench. His company's name was Crescent Tool Company.[14]

The most famous c-wrench in the world is on display at the Smithsonian National Air & Space Museum. It belonged to Charles Lindbergh. Legend goes that the only tools he carried crossing the Atlantic were a pair of pliers and that wrench.[15]

Time will tell, but perhaps the most famous wrench of any type is the very originally named "wrench" that was designed on earth and emailed to the International Space Station, where astronauts made it real with a 3D printer in 2015.[16]

Rota locks were originally developed for building cattle pens. They were a means of joining pipes such that the cows would not hurt themselves on any exposed fasteners.[17]

The British alternative to the A-frame trestle ladder and the Genie®-style MEWP lift is the Tallescope, a sort of cross between a scaffold, a ladder, and a lift.[18]

In 1930, George Bernard Shaw joined a long tradition of pessimists by predicting the death of the theater. As the writer of such plays as *Pygmalion*, he was more than passingly familiar with the art form. Like a lot of folks at the time, he thought movies would destroy it. He predicted, "The poor old theater is done for!...There will be nothing but 'talkies' soon".[19]

Twenty-six years after G.B. Shaw predicted the death of the theater (see previous), *My Fair Lady* opened on Broadway, ran for over 2,700 performances and set a new record for Broadway grosses. It was an adaptation of Shaw's play *Pygmalion*.[20]

John Steinbeck, working as a reporter during World War II, stayed optimistic about the practice of theater even as the physical venues were being bombed into rubble all over the world: **"The theater is the only institution in the world which has been dying for four thousand years and has never succumbed. It requires tough and devoted people to keep it alive"**.[21]

The Steinbeck quote about the theater (see previous) is the most commonly tattooed phrase on a stagehand. It is usually found between the bowline tattoo and the c-wrench tattoo. (Yes, this is a joke, but it *could* be true...)[22]

The theater may survive over the long term but, about 26 years after Shakespeare died, it was completely outlawed in London for two decades.[23]

One of the first acts of the American government was to ban theater. Specifically, the First Continental Congress, having been formed in September 1774, issued the ban in October. Apparently this was more important than declaring independence, which didn't happen until July 1776.[24]

Do you spell it theater or theatre? Some say the art is spelled "theatre" and the building is spelled "theater". In truth, the "re" spelling is simply the older, British spelling and "er" is the newer, American spelling. The same difference exists with centre/center and fibre/fiber. Most folks probably just use whichever version they first learned, but there are certainly some folks who want to feel fancy and use the "re" version because it sounds more European. In 2015, there were around 500 performing art organizations that were members of the Theatre Communication Group. Over 300 used a variant of theater/theatre in their institutional name. Of these, only a quarter of them spelled it the American way. For what it's worth, *The New York Times* agrees with the minority here. The newspaper changed its preferred style from the "re" to the "er" spelling in the 1960's.[25]

If you want to learn more...

1. Encyclopedias including Wikipedia and Britannica cover the broad strokes. For an in depth treatment, see Daguerre's book *History and Practice of Photogenic Drawing*, as translated into English by J.S. Memes and digitized by Google (London: Smith, Elder and Co, 1839).

2. For a three-page summary, see Henry C. Montgomery's "Addison's Cato and George Washington" in *The Classical Journal*, volume 55, number 5 from February 1960, pages 210-212.
www.jstor.org/stable/3294386

3. Bram Stoker, "Irving and Stage Lighting", *The Nineteenth Century and After: A Monthly Review*, May 1911, pages 903-912. Also available here:
www.bramstoker.org/pdf/nonfic/lighting.pdf

   For more of his writings about theater, see:
www.bramstoker.org/nonfic.html

4. Sheet gel quickly became available commercially, though home brew gel was still made, probably by cash-strapped theaters. Rosco Laboratory has a blog and YouTube series that discusses the origin of Rosco's gels. For an in depth treatment, see: chapter 9 of Theodore Fuchs' *Stage Lighting* (Boston: Little, Brown, 1929). Other significant sources on this period include Stanley McCandless' *A Method of Lighting the Stage* (New York: Theatre Art Books, 1932) and Louis Hartmann, *Theatre Lighting* (New York: D. Appleton and Co., 1930).

   According to Hartmann's preface, he was tricked into writing his book by McCandless. You can read it here:
userpages.umbc.edu/~cobb/335/hartman/slight.htm

5. See the glossary of Ross Lowell's book *Matters of Light & Depth* (Philadelphia: Broad Street books, 1992), page 198.

6. "For 'Chorus Line,' a 'Moon Shot' of Broadway Lighting", *The New York Times*, 17 September 1975, page 40.

7. For first notice of the show, see "'If the Shoe Fits' Arrives Tonight", *The New York Times*, 5 December 1946, page 52.

    See also Dan Dietz, *The Complete Book of 1940s Broadway Musicals* (New York: Roman & Littlefield, 2015). For the award, see the archive on the Tony Awards website for 1947: www.tonyawards.com/winners/year/any/category/special-tony-award/show/any/

8. For the award, see the archive on the Tony Awards website for 1947: www.tonyawards.com/winners/year/any/category/special-tony-award/show/any/

9. For a portrait of Clark Transfer and longtime president Norma Deull, see the fourth chapter of Robert Simonson's engaging book *On Broadway Men Still Wear Hats* (Hanover, NH: Smith and Kraus, 2004). For a good history of ICC regulation after World War II, see Fritz R. Kahn's "Motor Carrier Regulatory Reform – *Fait Accompli*" from the 1979 Winter issue of *Transportation Journal*, volume 19, number 2, pages 5-11. www.jstor.org/stable/20712554

    A brief history is also available on Clark Transfer's website. clarktransfer.com/like-to-know-how-we-got-here-new/

10. For a telling of the story from someone who was there, see Lloyd Burlingame's interesting memoir, *Sets, Lights, & Lunacy*, (New York: Design Adventures, 2013), page 33.

11. The Wikipedia article "Mic Drop" names these moments and clips on YouTube confirm the action. See also Slate's Brow Beat culture blog post, "When Did People Start Walking Off the Stage Like This? *Drops Mic*" by Forrest Wickman from January 25, 2013.
    www.slate.com/culture/brow-beat

12. For an excellent description of the old Met before it moved to Lincoln Center see: Albert Hopkins, "Book III: Science in the Theatre," *Magic: Stage Illusions and Scientific Diversions, Including Trick Photography* (New York: Scientific American, 1898). Whistling is referenced on page 265.

13 For a brief etymology, see Science Friday's Science Diction podcast, episode "The Origin of the Word 'Robot'", April 22, 2011.
www.sciencefriday.com/segments/the-origin-of-the-word-robot/

See also:
John Jordan, *Robots* (Cambridge, MA: MIT Press, 2016).

14 For the classic c-wrench, see patent: US1133236A
For the pliers and pipe wrench, see patents: US794249A, USD47389S, and US735289A.

For more about Crescent Tool Company, see the chapter dedicated to it in David N. Keller, *Cooper Industries*, 1833-1983 (Athens, Ohio: Ohio University Press, 1983).

See also this story in the Jamestown Gazette:
jamestowngazette.com/crescent-tool-company/

15 Smithsonian Inventory Number A19330037001
airandspace.si.edu/collection-objects/wrench-adjustable-charles-a-lindbergh/nasm_A19330037001

16 The story of the wrench can be found on NASA's website, as well as the .stl file, which you can download and use to print one for yourself.
nasa3d.arc.nasa.gov/detail/wrench-mis

17 Primary source here is from the UK. The catalog for Flint's Theatrical Chandler, the UK's foremost theatrical supply house, includes this tidbit. The 2013 catalog has it in section 2, page 83.

The original patent for the rota lock (US3107932A) does not mention this use specifically. But the patent may have been written to be as general as possible. In any event, this trivia is a good reminder of one of the rota lock's advantages: no sharp edges or exposed hardware.

18 tallescope.co.uk

19 A quote of Shaw's from the New York Herald Tribune from August 7, 1930, as quoted in Christopher Cerf and Victor Navasky, *The Experts Speak*, 2nd ed. (New York: Villard, 1998), page 189.

20 For an amusing anecdote on the failure to predict My Fair Lady's success, see Christopher Cerf and Victor Navasky, *The Experts Speak,* 2nd ed. (New York: Villard, 1998), page 186.

For an example of coverage of My Fair Lady's success, see "'Fair Lady' Radiant $10,000,000", *Variety*, 3 December 1958, page 1.

21 Drawn from a 1958 collection of reporting originally filed during the war. The collection has been reprinted several times, for example: John Steinbeck, *Once There Was a War* (New York: Penguin, 2007), page 17.

22 Ok, so there's no source on this one, and maybe it isn't true, but wouldn't it be nice if it was?

23 Jane Milling and Peter Thomson, ed., *The Cambridge History of British Theatre*, volume 1 (Cambridge: Cambridge University Press, 2004), page 439.

24 Heather S. Nathans, *Early American Theatre from the Revolution to Thomas Jefferson* (Cambridge: Cambridge University Press, 2003), page 37.

25 For perhaps the best review of this subject, including an analysis of the *Times'* usage, see the July 20, 2015 blog post from TCG by Rob Weinert-Kendt, "Re: the 'Re' in Theatre".

Noah Webster, from whom the iconic American dictionary Merriam-Webster draws half its name, was long a proponent of rationalizing English spellings into American spellings, such as moving from "re" to "er". A 2019 article in *The Atlantic* nicely sums up Webster's motivation: "**There is to be no elite in America, no linguistic differentiation between classes and regions**."

The Atlantic article is from May 28 and was written by Peter Martin, who expands on the subject in his book *The Dictionary Wars* (Princeton, NJ: Princeton University Press, 2019).

In an effort to follow in Webster's esteemed footsteps, this book has adopted some non-traditional but frankly more rational approaches to spelling and punctuation. This is done at the risk of being censured by pedants. Attention to current norms of spelling, grammar, and punctuation does matter to clear communication. But so does logic.

[THIS PAGE INTENTIONALLY BLANK]

Part 4

A Collection of Occasionally Useful Information

[THIS PAGE INTENTIONALLY BLANK]

Wrench Charts

STANDARDS FOR THREADED HARDWARE

Hex Head Bolt	SAE J429
Hex Nut (under 1/4")	ASME B18.6.3
Hex Nut (1/4" and above)	ASME B18.2.2
Heavy Hex Head Bolt	ASTM A325
Heavy Hex Head Nut	ASTM A563
Flange Hex Head Bolt	SAE J429
Socket Head Cap Screw	ASTM A574
Flat Head Socket Cap Screw	ASTM F835
Button Head Socket Cap Screw	ASTM F835
Socket Set Screw	ASTM F912
Square Head Set Screw	ASME B18.6.2
Socket Head Shoulder Screw	ASTM A574

STANDARDS FOR THEATRICAL AND RIGGING HARDWARE

Shackles	ASME B30.26
Wire Rope Clips	ASME B30.26
Steel Cheeseborough (Scaffolding Clamps)	EN 74 / BS 1139

Note: a single fastener can meet multiple standards. The standards listed above are typical, but it is not an exclusive or exhaustive list. Also, fastener sizes that are very large, very small or otherwise uncommon may fall under different standards

STANDARD HEX HEAD BOLT

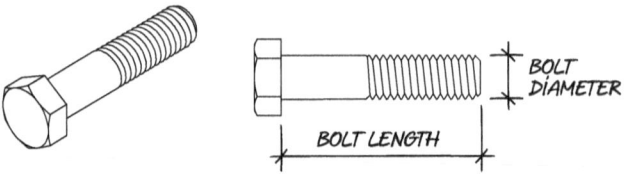

FLANGE HEX HEAD BOLT

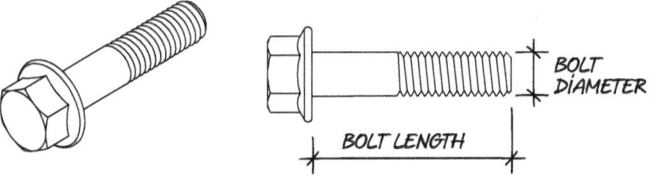

BOLT HEAD MARKINGS
(should also have manufacturer's mark, shown here as "MFG")

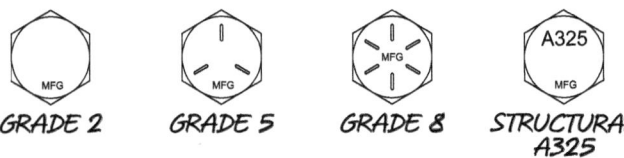

HEX NUTS

NUT MARKING
(there is more variation with nuts than with bolts; these are common but not the only form of markings; see the References)

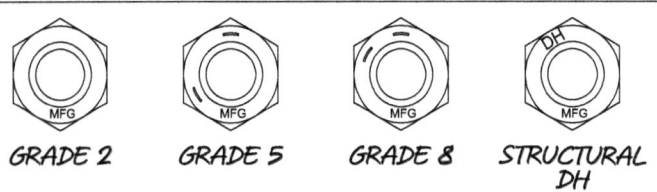

Hex Head Bolts: Wrench or Socket Size
Limited to Typically Used or Commonly Available Sizes

Bolt Diameter	Hex Head Bolt	Hex Nut	Flange Hex Head Bolt / Nut	Heavy* Hex Head Bolt / Nut
#4		1/4"		
#6		5/16"		
#8		11/32"		
#10		3/8"		
1/4"	7/16"	7/16"	3/8" | 7/16"	
5/16"	1/2"	1/2"	1/2"	
3/8"	9/16"	9/16"	9/16"	
7/16"**	5/8"	11/16"		
1/2"	3/4"	3/4"	3/4"	7/8"
5/8"	15/16"	15/16"		1 1/16"
3/4"	1 1/8"	1 1/8"		1 1/4"

Bolt over 3/4" diameter are typically available in a limited range of lengths

7/8"	1 5/16"	1 5/16"		1 7/16"
1"	1 1/2"	1 1/2"		1 5/8"
1 1/8"	1 11/16"	1 11/16"		
1 1/4"	1 7/8"	1 7/8"		2"
1 1/2"	2 1/4"	2 1/4"		
1 3/4"	2 5/8"	2 5/8"		
2"	3"	3"		

* "Heavy" is a generic term for structural bolts used in heavy construction A325 bolts and DH nuts are a common grade of structural hardware

** 7/16" hardware not recommended due to risk of confusion with other sizes and due to the bizarre difference between bolt and nut size

CAP SCREW

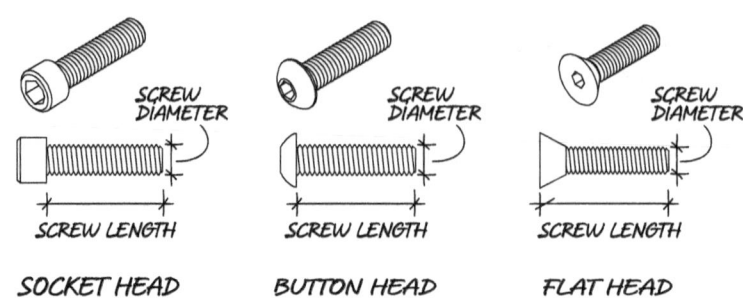

SET SCREW

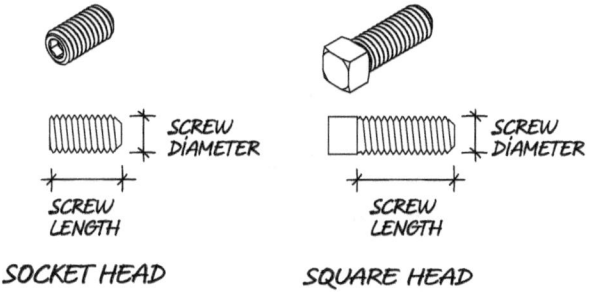

SHOULDER SCREW

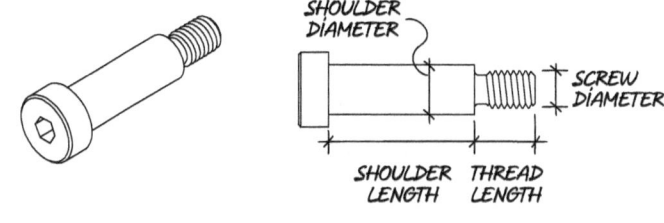

Socket Head Screws: Allen/Hex Wrench Size
Typically Used or Commonly Available Sizes

Screw Diameter	Socket Head Cap Screw	Flat Head Socket Head Cap Screw	Button Head Socket Cap Screw	Socket Set Screw	Square Head Set Screw*	Socket Head Shoulder Screw (ø = Shoulder Diameter)	
#4	3/32"	1/16"	1/16"	0.05"		ø 1/8"	5/64"
#6	7/64"	5/64"	5/64"	1/16"		ø 5/32"	3/32"
#8	9/64"	3/32"	3/32"	5/64"		ø 3/16"	3/32"
#10	5/32"	1/8"	1/8"	3/32"		ø 1/4"	1/8"
1/4"	3/16"	5/32"	5/32"	1/8"	1/4"	ø 5/16"	5/32"
5/16"	1/4"	3/16"	3/16"	5/32"	5/16"	ø 3/8"	3/16"
3/8"	5/16"	7/32"	7/32"	3/16"	3/8"	ø 1/2"	1/4"
1/2"	3/8"	5/16"	5/16"	1/4"	1/2"	ø 5/8"	5/16"
5/8"	1/2"	3/8"	3/8"	5/16"	5/8"	ø 3/4"	3/8"
3/4"	5/8"	1/2"		3/8"	3/4"	ø 1"	1/2"
7/8"	3/4"	9/16"		1/2"	7/8"	ø 1 1/4"	5/8"
1"	3/4"	5/8"		9/16"	1"		
1 1/8"	7/8"					ø 1 1/2"	7/8"
1 1/4"	7/8"					ø 1 3/4"	1"
1 1/2"						ø 2"	1 1/4"

* Square Head Set Screw use open end wrench, not hex/allen key

Rigging & Theatrical Hardware

WIRE ROPE CLIPS

Wire Rope Size	Wrench / Socket Size	Minimum Number of Clips	Turnback*	Torque (ft lb)
1/8"	3/8"	2	3 1/4"	4.5
3/16"	7/16" [1/2"]	2	3 3/4"	7.5
1/4"	9/16"	2	4 3/4"	15
5/16"	11/16"	2	5 1/4"	30
3/8"	3/4"	2	6 1/2"	45
1/2"	7/8"	3	11 1/2"	65

* Turnback is length of the dead end tail <u>after</u> the thimble or loop

The above is drawn from the catalogs of the Crosby Group, Columbus-McKinnon and Chicago Hardware & Fixture

The only difference is in the wrench size for 3/16" clip (the less common size is in brackets)

Always check and follow manufacture instructions for any hardware Especially rigging hardware

LIGHTING C-CLAMP

Primary Locking Bolt
(1/2"-13 Square Head Set Screw)

1/2" Open End Wrench
1/2" 8-Point Socket*

Pan Locking Bolt
(5/16"-18 Square Head Set Screw)

5/16" Open End Wrench
5/16" 8-Point Socket*

Yoke Bolt
(1/2"-13 Hex Head Bolt)

3/4" Wrench or Socket

* 8-Point Sockets are much less common than 6-Point or 12-Point

These sizes are common but variation between brands does exist

Part 4 - Wrench Charts

PIPE* HARDWARE

Steel Cheeseborough** (aka Scaffolding Clamp)	7/8" Wrench or Socket
Aluminum Cheeseborough (with Aluminum Wing Nut***)	3/4" Open End Wrench
Rota Lock	9/16" Wrench or Socket
Slip-On Steel Pipe Fittings	5/16" Hex/Allen Wrench
Batten Clamp	9/16" Wrench or Socket

* All sizes are for US Customary hardware for 1 1/2 inch Schedule 40 or 1 1/4 inch Schedule 40 Pipe; <u>there are metric equivalents for all of the above</u>, as well as variation among the US customary sizes; all of the above are sized from common, reputable manufacturers

** Alternative spellings for "cheeseborough" include cheseborough, cheseboro, and cheeseburger

*** Manufactures may prohibit using wrenches on wing nut

MISCELLANEOUS HARDWARE

Coffin Lock (aka Roto Lock)	5/16" Hex/Allen Wrench
Truss Bolts (5/8"-11 Grade 8 Bolts)	15/16" Wrench or Socket

[THIS PAGE INTENTIONALLY BLANK]

Fastener Info

DRILL & TAP SIZE BY THREAD PITCH

Thread Size	Pitch	Decimal Inches	Drill Size	Closest Fractional
#4	-40	0.0890	43	3/32"
	-48	0.0935	42	3/32"
#5	-40	0.1015	38	3/32"
	-44	0.1040	37	7/64"
#6	-32	0.1065	36	7/64"
	-40	0.1130	33	7/64"
#8	-32	0.1360	29	9/64"
	-36	0.1360	29	9/64"
#10	-24	0.1495	25	5/32"
	-32	0.1590	21	5/32"
#12	-24	0.1770	16	11/64"
	-28	0.1820	14	3/16"
1/4"	-20	0.2010	7	13/64"
	-28	0.2130	3	7/32"
5/16"	-18	0.2570	F	1/4"
	-24	0.2720	I	17/64"
3/8"	-16	0.3125	5/16"	-
	-24	0.3320	Q	21/64"
7/16"	-14	0.3680	U	3/8"
	-20	0.3906	25/64"	-
1/2"	-13	0.4219	27/64"	-
	-20	0.4531	29/64"	-
9/16"	-12	0.4844	31/64"	-
	-18	0.5156	33/64"	-
5/8"	-11	0.5312	17/32"	-
	-18	0.5781	37/64"	-

4' × 8' Sheet Good Fastener Schedule

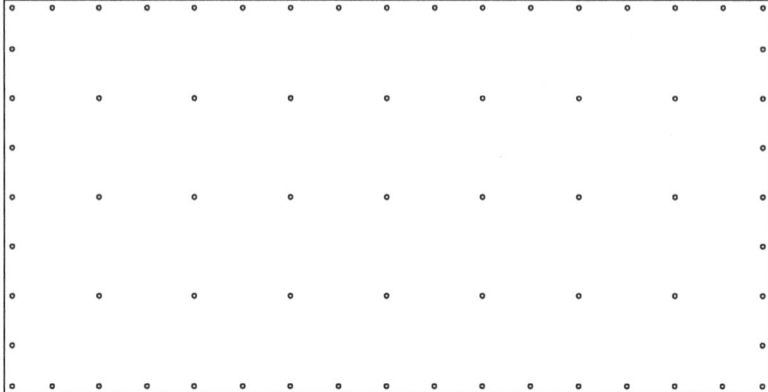

6" along Perimeter / 12" in the Field
48 Perimeter + 21 Field
69 Fasteners Total
(2.156 per sq ft)

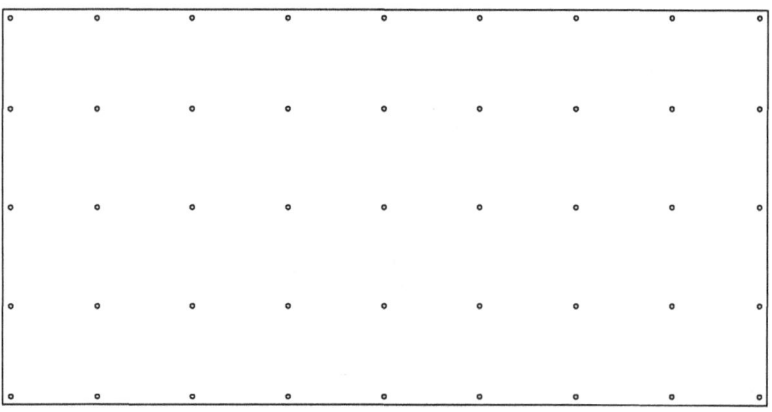

12" along Perimeter / 12" in the Field
24 Perimeter + 21 Field
45 Fasteners Total
(1.406 per sq ft)

Part 4 - Fastener Info

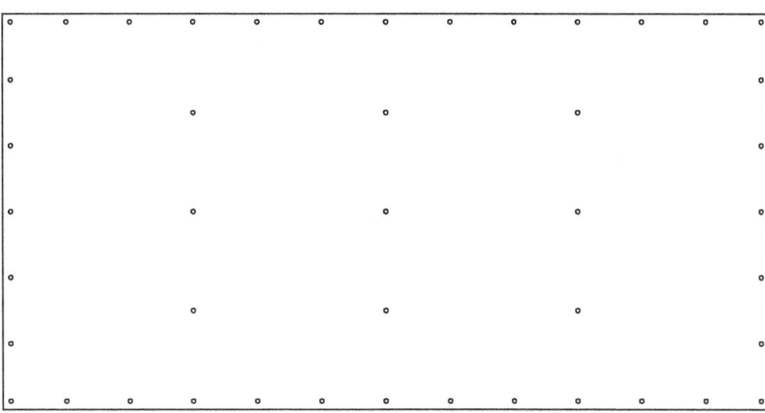

8" along Perimeter / 12" along Framing
Framing 24" O.C.
36 Perimeter + 9 Field
45 Fasteners Total
(1.406 per sq ft)

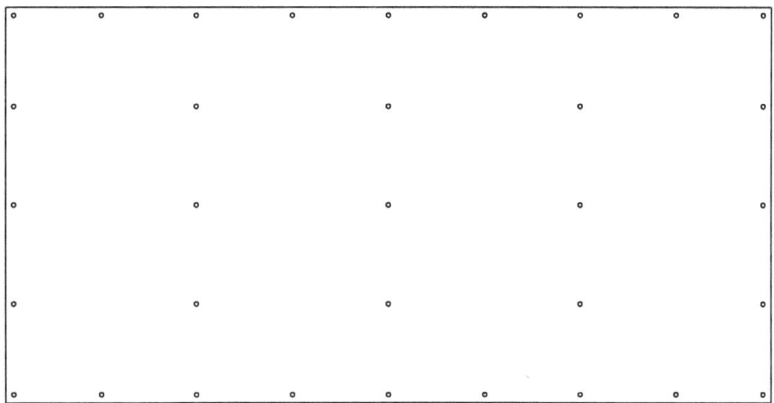

12" along Perimeter / 12" along Framing
Framing 24" O.C.
24 Perimeter + 9 Field
33 Fasteners Total
(1.031 per sq ft)

Drywall Screw Dimensions

Length	Screws per Pound*	Gauge Size	Head Clearance Hole	Thread Clearance Hole	Pilot Hole**
1"	335	#6	11/32"	5/32"	3/32"
1 1/4"	268				
1 5/8"	211				
2"	171	#6 or #7			
2 1/4"	153				
2 1/2"	117	#8	11/32"	3/16"	7/64"
3"	93				
3 1/2"	52	#10	3/8"	7/32"	1/8"
4"	47				

* Average based off several popular manufacturers

** Pilot Hole given is for Soft Wood (add 1/64" for Hard Woods)

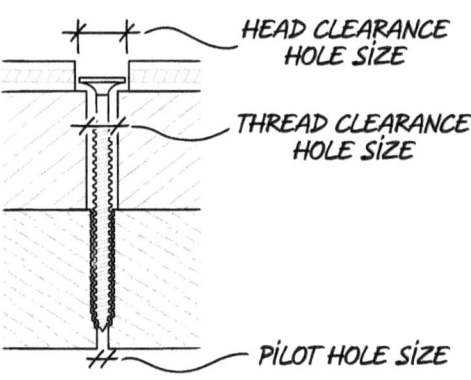

Estimating Fasteners Example

A 30 foot by 30 foot subdeck of OSB is going to get screwed down with 1 5/8" screws using the 12" perimeter / 12" field layout. How many pounds of screws are required?

$$30 \text{ ft width} \div 8 \text{ ft / sheet} = 3\frac{3}{4} \text{ sheets}$$

$$30 \text{ ft depth} \div 4 \text{ ft / sheet} = 7\frac{1}{2} \text{ sheets}$$

Deck will be 3 3/4 sheets wide by 7 1/2 sheets deep.

From the fastener schedule, we know the 12" perimeter / 12" field layout requires 45 fasteners per sheet.

$$\left(\frac{45 \text{ screws}}{\text{sheet}}\right)\left(3\frac{3}{4} \text{ sheets wide}\right)\left(7\frac{1}{2} \text{ sheets deep}\right) = 1266 \text{ screws}$$

From the drywall screw dimensions we know that, for 1 5/8" long screws, there are about 211 screws per pound.

$$(1266 \text{ screws}) \div (211 \text{ screws per pound}) = 6 \text{ pounds of screws}$$

If no screws are lost or have their heads stripped, and the manufacturer doesn't short the box, 6 pounds might be perfect.

Buy 7 pounds.

[THIS PAGE INTENTIONALLY BLANK]

Stage Weights and Arbors

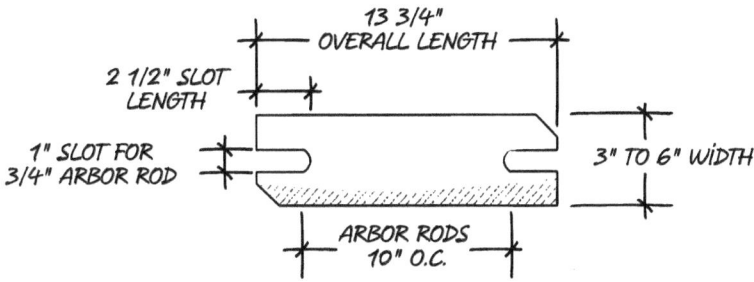

TYPICAL STAGE WEIGHT

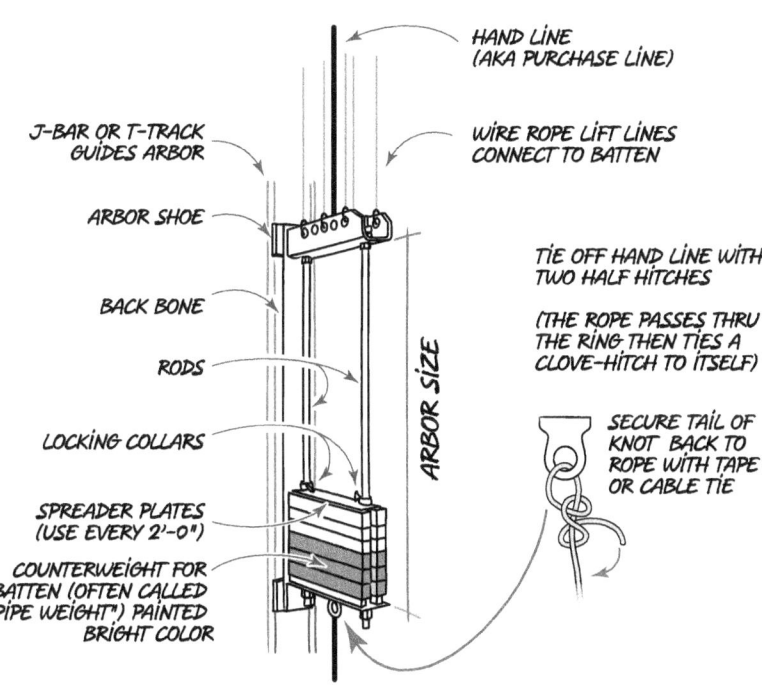

TYPICAL SIDE LOADING ARBOR

STEEL STAGE WEIGHTS
Approximate weight by size*

	3" Brick**	4" Brick	5" Brick**	6" Brick
1" Thick	10 lb (4.7 kg)	14 lb (6.4 kg)	18 lb (8.1 kg)	22 lb (9.8 kg)
1 1/2" Thick**	15 lb (7.0 kg)	21 lb (9.5 kg)	27 lb (12.1 kg)	33 lb (14.7 kg)
2" Thick	21 lb (9.3 kg)	28 lb (12.7 kg)	36 lb (16.1 kg)	43 lb (19.5 kg)

Note: small discrepancies are due to rounding

(For example: a 6" x 1" brick is actually a bit under 22 lb, so a 6" x 2" brick is less than 44 lb)

* All stage weights can vary in weight from this chart depending on the exact geometry and precision of the cut, loss to corrosion and wear, and the initial composition of the steel

** Bricks with these dimensions are less common

Different materials have been used over the years for stage weights (often called bricks). Lead and cast iron were both once common. Lead has well known health risks and is generally avoided today. Cast iron is also no longer preferred. All of the weights in this section will be for steel bricks. To convert between types of bricks, use the density chart on the next page.

Be warned: there is no dedicated stage weight factory, just some metal fabricators that flame cut bricks from time to time in addition to everything else they produce. Stage rigging manufacturers have long-term relationships and usually get consistent bricks, but they are not the only ones ordering. **For any given size, the actual weight can vary venue to venue, even from brick to brick.**

MATERIAL DENSITY CONVERSION

	Density (lb/in³)	Compared to Steel	
Steel	0.283	-	
Cast Iron	0.255	90	%
Lead	0.410	145	%
Aluminum	0.098	35	%
Concrete	0.085	30	%
Sand	0.052	18	%
Water	0.036	13	%
Wood	0.020	8	%

Other materials (based on variants commonly used in construction) are included for comparison

Actual products may vary depending on source and environmental conditions (this includes water). See *References* for more information

The Seesaw Analogy

The easiest way to explain to how a counterweight system works...

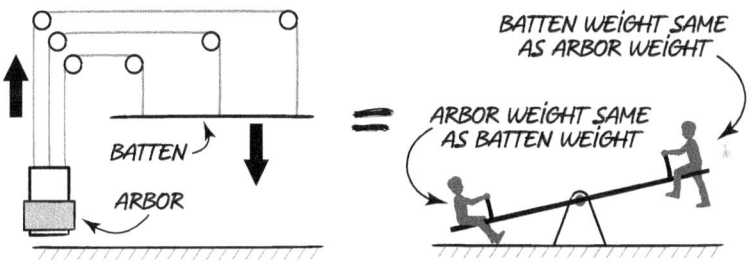

SINGLE PURCHASE SYSTEM

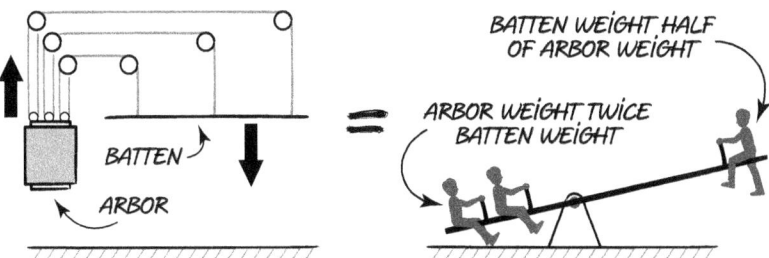

DOUBLE PURCHASE SYSTEM

Inches of Steel Weight for a Given Load (Approximate)

Load (lb)	3" Brick	4" Brick	5" Brick	6" Brick	Load (lb)	3" Brick	4" Brick	5" Brick	6" Brick
100	10"	7"	6"	5"	825	83"	59"	46"	38"
125	13"	9"	7"	6"	850	85"	61"	47"	39"
150	15"	11"	8"	7"	875	88"	63"	49"	40"
175	18"	13"	10"	8"	900	90"	64"	50"	41"
200	20"	14"	11"	9"	925	93"	66"	51"	42"
225	23"	16"	13"	10"	950	95"	68"	53"	43"
250	25"	18"	14"	11"	975	98"	70"	54"	44"
275	28"	20"	15"	13"	1000	100"	71"	56"	45"
300	30"	21"	17"	14"	1025	103"	73"	57"	47"
325	33"	23"	18"	15"	1050	105"	75"	58"	48"
350	35"	25"	19"	16"	1075	108"	77"	60"	49"
375	38"	27"	21"	17"	1100	110"	79"	61"	50"
400	40"	29"	22"	18"	1125	113"	80"	63"	51"
425	43"	30"	24"	19"	1150	115"	82"	64"	52"
450	45"	32"	25"	20"	1175	118"	84"	65"	53"
475	48"	34"	26"	22"	1200	120"	86"	67"	55"
500	50"	36"	28"	23"	1225	123"	88"	68"	56"
525	53"	38"	29"	24"	1250	125"	89"	69"	57"
550	55"	39"	31"	25"	1275	128"	91"	71"	58"
575	58"	41"	32"	26"	1300	130"	93"	72"	59"
600	60"	43"	33"	27"	1325	133"	95"	74"	60"
625	63"	45"	35"	28"	1350	135"	96"	75"	61"
650	65"	46"	36"	30"	1375	138"	98"	76"	63"
675	68"	48"	38"	31"	1400	140"	100"	78"	64"
700	70"	50"	39"	32"	1425	143"	102"	79"	65"
725	73"	52"	40"	33"	1450	145"	104"	81"	66"
750	75"	54"	42"	34"	1475	148"	105"	82"	67"
775	78"	55"	43"	35"	1500	150"	107"	83"	68"
800	80"	57"	44"	36"	1525	153"	109"	85"	69"

Part 4 - Stage Weights and Arbors

Load (lb)	3" Brick	4" Brick	5" Brick	6" Brick	Load (lb)	3" Brick	4" Brick	5" Brick	6" Brick
1550	155"	111"	86"	70"	2275	228"	163"	126"	103"
1575	58"	113"	88"	72"	2300	230"	164"	128"	105"
1600	160"	114"	89"	73"	2325	233"	166"	129"	106"
1625	163"	116"	90"	74"	2350	235"	168"	131"	107"
1650	165"	118"	92"	75"	2375	238"	170"	132"	108"
1675	168"	120"	93"	76"	2400	240"	171"	133"	109"
1700	170"	121"	94"	77"	2425	243"	173"	135"	110"
1725	173"	123"	96"	78"	2450	245"	175"	136"	111"
1750	175"	125"	97"	80"	2475	248"	177"	138"	113"
1775	178"	127"	99"	81"	2500	250"	179"	139"	114"
1800	180"	129"	100"	82"	2525	253"	180"	140"	115"
1825	183"	130"	101"	83"	2550	255"	182"	142"	116"
1850	185"	132"	103"	84"	2575	258"	184"	143"	117"
1875	188"	134"	104"	85"	2600	260"	186"	144"	118"
1900	190"	136"	106"	86"	2625	263"	188"	146"	119"
1925	193"	138"	107"	88"	2650	265"	189"	147"	120"
1950	195"	139"	108"	89"	2675	268"	191"	149"	122"
1975	198"	141"	110"	90"	2700	270"	193"	150"	123"
2000	200"	143"	111"	91"	2725	273"	195"	151"	124"
2025	203"	145"	113"	92"	2750	275"	196"	153"	125"
2050	205"	146"	114"	93"	2775	278"	198"	154"	126"
2075	208"	148"	115"	94"	2800	280"	200"	156"	127"
2100	210"	150"	117"	95"	2825	283"	202"	157"	128"
2125	213"	152"	118"	97"	2850	285"	204"	158"	130"
2150	215"	154"	119"	98"	2875	288"	205"	160"	131"
2175	218"	155"	121"	99"	2900	290"	207"	161"	132"
2200	220"	157"	122"	100"	2925	293"	209"	163"	133"
2225	223"	159"	124"	101"	2950	295"	211"	164"	134"
2250	225"	161"	125"	102"	2975	298"	213"	165"	135"

All values are approximate and for estimating only

The heavier the load, the more actual number of bricks may vary

Total Load by Inches of Steel Weights (Approximate load by pound)

	3" Brick	4" Brick	5" Brick	6" Brick		3" Brick	4" Brick	5" Brick	6" Brick
1"	10	14	18	22	30"	300	420	540	660
2"	20	28	36	44	31"	310	434	558	682
3"	30	42	54	66	32"	320	448	576	704
4"	40	56	72	88	33"	330	462	594	726
5"	40	70	90	110	34"	340	476	612	748
6"	60	84	108	132	35"	350	490	630	770
7"	70	98	126	154	36"	360	504	648	792
8"	80	112	144	176	37"	370	518	666	814
9"	90	126	162	198	38"	380	532	684	836
10"	100	140	180	220	39"	390	546	702	858
11"	110	154	198	242	40"	400	560	720	880
12"	120	168	216	264	41"	410	574	738	902
13"	130	182	234	286	42"	420	588	756	924
14"	140	196	252	308	43"	430	602	774	946
15"	150	210	270	330	44"	440	616	792	968
16"	160	224	288	352	45"	450	630	810	990
17"	170	238	306	374	46"	460	644	828	1012
18"	180	252	324	396	47"	470	658	846	1034
19"	190	266	342	418	48"	480	672	864	1056
20"	200	280	360	440	49"	490	686	882	1078
21"	210	294	378	462	50"	500	700	900	1100
22"	220	308	396	484	51"	510	714	918	1122
23"	230	322	414	506	52"	520	728	936	1144
24"	240	336	432	528	53"	530	742	954	1166
25"	250	350	450	550	54"	540	756	972	1188
26"	260	364	468	572	55"	550	770	990	1210
27"	270	378	486	594	56"	560	784	1008	1232
28"	280	392	504	616	57"	570	798	1026	1254
29"	290	406	522	638	58"	580	812	1044	1276

Part 4 - Stage Weights and Arbors

	3" Brick	4" Brick	5" Brick	6" Brick		3" Brick	4" Brick	5" Brick	6" Brick
59"	590	826	1062	1298	88"	880	1232	1584	1936
60"	600	840	1080	1320	89"	890	1246	1602	1958
61"	610	854	1098	1342	90"	990	1260	1620	1980
62"	620	868	1116	1364	91"	910	1274	1638	2002
63"	630	882	1134	1386	92"	920	1288	1656	2024
64"	640	896	1152	1408	93"	930	1302	1674	2046
65"	650	910	1170	1430	94"	940	1316	1692	2068
66"	660	924	1188	1452	95"	950	1330	1710	2090
67"	670	938	1206	1474	96"	960	1344	1728	2112
68"	680	952	1224	1496	97"	970	1358	1746	2134
69"	690	966	1242	1518	98"	980	1372	1764	2156
70"	700	980	1260	1540	99"	990	1386	1782	2178
71"	710	994	1278	1562	100"	1000	1400	1800	2200
72"	720	1008	1296	1584	101"	1010	1414	1818	2222
73"	730	1022	1314	1606	102"	1020	1428	1836	2244
74"	740	1036	1332	1628	103"	1030	1442	1854	2266
75"	750	1050	1350	1650	104"	1040	1456	1872	2288
76"	760	1064	1368	1672	105"	1050	1470	1890	2310
77"	770	1078	1386	1694	106"	1060	1484	1908	2332
78"	780	1092	1404	1716	107"	1070	1498	1926	2354
79"	790	1106	1422	1738	108"	1080	1512	1944	2376
80"	800	1120	1440	1760	109"	1090	1526	1962	2398
81"	810	1134	1458	1782	110"	1100	1540	1980	2420
82"	820	1148	1476	1804	111"	1110	1554	1998	2442
83"	830	1162	1494	1826	112"	1120	1568	2016	2464
84"	840	1176	1512	1848	113"	1130	1582	2034	2486
85"	850	1190	1530	1870	114"	1140	1596	2052	2508
86"	860	1204	1548	1892	115"	1150	1610	2070	2530
87"	870	1218	1566	1914	116"	1160	1624	2088	2552

All values are approximate and for estimating only

The taller the height of bricks, the more actual weight may vary

Arbor Weight

Traditional side-loading arbors are generally sized by their length in feet. An arbor cannot, however, be fully loaded with weights because there needs to be some room at the top to angle the weight in between the rods. (Front loading arbors do not have this issue, which is yet another benefit to using them.) To find the <u>approximate</u> maximum weight of an arbor, subtract one foot from the arbor length, multiply by twelve to convert to inches, then multiply by the weight of a one-inch brick; add this result to the self-weight of the arbor.

APPROXIMATE MAX. ARBOR WEIGHT

Arbor Length (ft)	Self-weight (lb)	Arbor + 3" Bricks (lb)	Arbor + 4" Bricks (lb)	Arbor + 5" Bricks (lb)	Arbor + 6" Bricks (lb)
4	56	416	560	704	848
5	67	546	739	931	1123
6	74	674	914	1154	1394
7	81	801	1089	1377	1665
8	89	929	1265	1601	1937
9	96	1056	1440	1824	2208
10	103	1183	1615	2047	2479
11	110	1310	1790	2270	2750
12	117	1437	1965	2493	3021
13	125	1565	2141	2717	3293
each additional foot	7	128	175	223	271

Pipe Weight Chart

APPROXIMATE BATTEN WEIGHT (lb) BY LENGTH

Batten Length (ft)	1 1/2 inch Sch. 40 Pipe (2.72 lb/ft)	Ladder Batten* (7 lb/ft)	12" × 12" Truss (5 ft = 36 lb) (10 ft = 61 lb)	20.5" × 20.5" Truss (5 ft = 56 lb) (10 ft = 85 lb)
10	27	74	61	85
15	41	111	97	141
20	54	148	122	170
25	68	185	158	226
30	82	222	183	255
35	95	259	219	311
40	109	296	244	340
45	122	333	280	396
50	136	370	305	425
55	150	407	341	481
60	163	444	366	510

Note: excludes weight of hardware and other rigging

* See *References* for details on construction

Cable Weight Chart (Lift Lines)

APPROXIMATE LOAD VARIATION* (lb) BETWEEN IN AND OUT TRIM

Batten Travel (ft)	Number of Lift Lines					
	2	3	4	5	6	7
10	2	3	4	6	7	8
20	4	7	9	11	13	15
30	7	10	13	17	20	23
40	9	13	18	22	26	31
50	11	17	22	28	33	39
60	13	20	26	33	40	46
70	15	23	31	39	46	54
80	18	26	35	44	53	62

* Based on 1/4" 7×19 Wire Rope Lift Lines (0.11 lb/ft)

Cable Weight Chart (Cable Swag)

APPROXIMATE WEIGHT (lb) TYPICAL STAGE CABLES

Cable Type	per foot	Length of Cable (ft)					
		10	20	30	40	50	60
12/3 SOOW (Stage Pin)	0.23	2	5	7	9	12	14
19 pin 2k (Socapex)	0.58	6	12	17	23	29	35
16/7 SEOOW (Fly Cable)	0.21	2	4	6	8	11	13
10/4 SOOW (with L15-20)	0.36	4	7	11	14	18	22
8/5 SOOW (with L21-30)	0.55	6	11	17	22	28	33
2/0 EISL (Feeder, per wire)	0.56	6	11	17	22	28	34
2/0 EISL (Feeder, 4 wire)	2.25	23	45	68	90	113	135
2/0 EISL (Feeder, 5 wire)	2.80	28	56	84	112	140	168
4/0 EISL (Feeder, per wire)	0.81	8	16	24	32	41	49
4/0 EISL (Feeder, 4 wire)	3.30	33	66	99	132	165	198
4/0 EISL (Feeder, 5 wire)	4.13	41	83	124	165	207	248

This chart shows common cable types, construction, and uses

Significant variation exists in manufacturing and application

For estimating only

Swaging

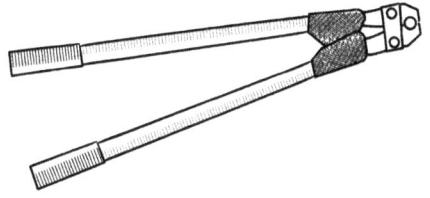

SINGLE GROOVE
SWAGING TOOL

MULTI-GROOVE
SWAGING TOOL

DIFFERENT STYLE
OF GO GAUGES

TYPICAL OVAL
SWAGE SLEEVE

Swage Sizes

The motivation for this section is that one drawer in the rigging cabinet which is a jumbled collection of swage sleeves and other hardware. Swage sleeves are excellent hardware but they need to be used correctly. The two most common types (but hardly the only types) are stop sleeves and oval sleeves. Plenty of reference books and manufacturer instructions cover how to use swage sleeves. The focus here is to examine the size of swage sleeves and how to differentiate them. Not to spoil the discussion that follows, but the conclusion is this: keep swages carefully organized and labeled by manufacturer part number as well as by cable size.

Military Standard MS51844E, among other things, outlines the manufacturing details of copper oval sleeves to be used with zinc or tin coated carbon steel cable. 7×19 Galvanized Aircraft Cable is a zinc-coated carbon steel cable. (And to apply to the standard we are discussing here, it needs to meet the MIL-DTL-83420 type I specification.) A table of the maximum dimensions for a sleeve is provided on the next page. The table includes sizes not recommended for use in the field by stagehands due to the risk of confusion; these sizes are indicated. It is important that the right size swage is used with the right size cable. In other words, don't dump all the swages into one big cup.

The two most common manufacturers for swage sleeves used by stagehands are Loos & Co, who use the name Lococo® for their rigging tools, and National Telephone Supply Company, who use the trademark Nicopress®. Both advertise their products as meeting the Military Specifications described above. In using the table on the next page, remember that all dimensions are for *maximum* allowable size. Actual swages are typically a bit less than the maximum. How much less varies based on the size of the sleeve and the manufacturer.

Part 4 - Swaging

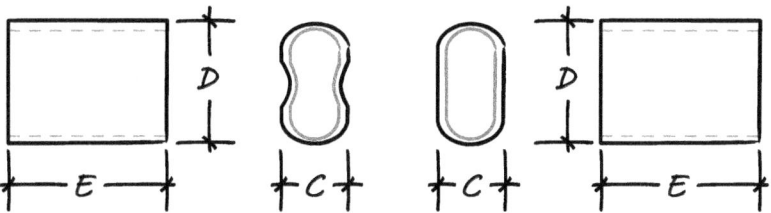

Cable Size (in)	Cable Construction	Nominal BS* (lb)	C Max. (in)	D Max. (in)	E Max. (in)
1/32	3×7	110	0.094	0.140	0.310
3/64**	7×7	270	0.140	0.206	0.440
1/16	7×7	480	0.180	0.270	0.440
	7×19	480	0.180	0.270	0.440
3/32**	7×7	920	0.240	0.380	0.440
	7×19	1000	0.240	0.380	0.440
1/8	7×19	2000	0.340	0.512	0.750
5/32**	7×19	2800	0.370	0.600	0.750
3/16	7×19	4200	0.450	0.710	1.000
7/32**	7×19	5600	0.480	0.740	0.940
1/4	7×19	7000	0.540	0.840	1.190

Note how the length *decreases* from 1/4 to 5/16

5/16	7×19	9800	0.680	1.030	1.125
3/8	7×19	14400	0.750	1.143	1.312

* Nominal breaking strength for MIL-DTL-86420, type I, zinc or tin coated carbon steel wire rope; termination may downgrade the actual breaking strength of cable assembly

** These sizes are not recommended due to potential for confusion

The smaller size swages are often all manufactured to the same length for both companies. Loos' ovals for 3/64" and 1/16" cables (part number SL2-1.5 and SL2-2) are both 3/8" long and vary by less than 1/16" in all other dimensions. Nicopress ovals for 3/64", 1/16", and 3/32" cable (part numbers 18-11-B4, 18-1-C, and 18-2-G) are all also 3/8" long. It is very difficult to sort these sizes if they get mixed together.

And here is another important difference in swage sleeve size: as the cable size increases, the length of the sleeve usually but not always increases too. For both Loos and Nicopress, the sleeve for 1/4" cable is actually longer than the sleeve for 5/16" cable. (Loos part numbers are SL2-8 and SL2-10; Nicopress part numbers are 18-10-F6 and 18-13-G9.) This is particularly problematic because length is the easiest dimension to reference in comparing sleeves.

If a stagehand is trying to make an eye in 1/4" cable and has both a 1/4" sleeve and a 5/16" sleeve, they would have two sleeves both of which will pass the 1/4" cable and one of which is shorter than the other. This shorter sleeve is the *wrong* sleeve. (The shorter sleeve is also fatter, which hopefully tips them off.)

All of the above measurements are for uncrimped sleeves. Once crimped, the dimensions change significantly as the sleeve deforms and a crimped sleeve can no longer be back-checked to these dimensions. Only a go gauge* can be used to confirm that the crimp is correct. Only the tool instructions can confirm that the correct number of crimps have been made. Only the user can confirm that they were made in the correct sequence.

---

* "Go Gauge" is the correct name. To learn more, see the "Swaging Tool Identification" tip in *Part 2* or go right to the source: Nicopress Technical Bulletin *TB-2*.

Swage Economics

	1/8" Cable	3/16" Cable	1/4" Cable
Cost per Swage Sleeve	$0.39	$1.08	$1.48
Swages Required	1	1	1
Cost per Swage Sleeve Termination	$0.39	$1.08	$1.48
Cost per Wire Rope Clip	$3.65	$3.75	$4.60
Wire Rope Clips Required	2	2	2
Cost per WR Clip Termination	$7.30	$7.50	$9.20
Cost Difference	$6.91	$6.42	$7.72
Cost per Swaging Tool	$171.20	$304.95	$455.80
Terminations to Offset Cost	**27**	**48**	**59**

All pricing from Rose Brand® (December 2020)

Wire rope swages are both efficient and economical. The relatively high cost of the swaging tool is offset by the economy of the hardware itself. Given that most cable assemblies have a termination at each end, a 1/4" swaging tool pays for itself with 30 cables and a 1/8" tools with less than 15.

Note: wire rope clips <u>might</u> be reusable if all the original parts stay together and if they are inspected to see if they meet the manufacturer's requirements for reuse. Some manufacturers may not allow reuse at all.

[THIS PAGE INTENTIONALLY BLANK]

PART 5

Computers & Calculators

[THIS PAGE INTENTIONALLY BLANK]

Part 5

193

An explanation...

If most of us did not walk around with a computer in our pocket, this part of the book probably wouldn't be here. But we do have easy access to computers and it's worth incorporating them into the set of tools we use on stage. So, here are some tips and tricks moving in that direction.

The first few pages of this part have some shortcuts for typing symbols. After that, three spreadsheet calculators are presented. This is what they do:

Advanced Two Tape Layout

    GOAL: Lay out points on stage by triangulating tape measures from two anchors

    ENTER: 1. Where you want the anchors for the tape measures
    2. How far points are from Center Line
    3. How far points are from Plaster / Setting Line

    GET: 1. Points' distance from down stage anchor
    2. Points' distance from up stage anchor

Bridle Geometry

    GOAL: Build a bridle to hit a point with a specific leg angle

    ENTER: 1. Where the legs hang from
    2. Where the point wants to be
    3. The bridle leg angle

Example: if you want the bridle apex as high as possible but do not want to exceed 90°, enter 90° into the calculator

    GET: Length of bridle legs required

Will it fit in the Elevator?

    GOAL: Get something thru a door on the diagonal

    ENTER: 1. Size of door
    2. Thickness of thing

Example: you know the thing will be a flat that is 2" thick

    GET: Maximum width of thing that will fit

When the background work is done, these calculators are simple and useful. They solve problems stagehands face all the time. But, be warned: like any good tool, what is simple on the outside can be quite complex on the inside. All a drill does is spin when you pull the trigger, but start taking one apart and you quickly appreciate just how sophisticated they are.

Every effort has been made to make both the use of spreadsheets and the math as accessible as possible. If you are a very novice user, that doesn't mean they will be easy, but if you stick with it you should come out successfully on the other side. If you've wanted to learn a bit more about trigonometry or programs such as Excel®, here's a chance to do it while also building some useful tools.

Typing Symbols

Some symbols are readily available on the keyboard. Holding down the **shift** key and hitting the **4** key will produce the **$** symbol. There is not enough room on the keyboard, however, for all of the symbols that are used in producing drawings, specifications, line set schedules and other documents. The following tables cull some of the most useful symbols from the Unicode tables.

Unicode, as the name suggests, is the universal set of symbols for electronic communication that includes everything from the basic 26 letters of the Latin alphabet to a full range of emoji.* Each symbol has its own number. Each number can be expressed as either a decimal number or a hexadecimal (hex) number. This is similar to how carpenters use 3/8 to describe the number 0.375. Same actual quantity, different notation. Just as fractional numbers are easier for carpenters, hex is easier for computer programmers.

Different programs and operating systems have shortcuts built in to access the Unicode. Some of these systems, such as used by Microsoft Office, actually predate Unicode and include some legacy codes. That is, for some symbols, you can either use the original number or the Unicode number. Adding to the complexity, when it comes to implementing Unicode, some programs default to using the decimal form while other use the hex form.

---

* Technically, Unicode is the name of the organization. The organization produces a number of different encodings, of which UTF-8 has been generally adopted and is what we are actually referring to when we say "Unicode".

Shortcut Chart

Symbol	Microsoft Alt Code	Mac Shortcut	Unicode (decimal)	Unicode (hex)	Name
π	227	⌥ p	0960	03C0	Lowercase Pi
μ	230	⌥ m	0956	03BC	Lowercase Mu ("myoo") (friction coefficient)
ϕ	232		0647	0278	Uppercase Phi ("fee") (electrical phase)
Ω	234	⌥ z	8486	2126	Uppercase Omega (ohm sign for resistance)
∞	236	⌥ 5	8734	221E	Infinity
±	241	⌥ shift =	0177	00B1	Plus-Minus (machining tolerance)
≥	242	⌥ .	8805	2265	Greater Than or Equal To
≤	243	⌥ ,	8804	2264	Less Than or Equal To
×			0215	00D7	Multiplication Sign
÷	246	⌥ /	0247	00F7	Division
≈	247	⌥ x	8776	2248	Almost Equal To
°	248	⌥ shift 8	0176	00B0	Degree
√	251	⌥ v	8730	221A	Square Root
²	253		0178	00B2	Superscript 2
³			0179	00B3	Superscript 3
™		⌥ 2	0153	2122	Trade Mark
©		⌥ g	0169	00A9	Copyright
®		⌥ r	0174	00AE	Registered Trade Mark
₡			8452	2104	Center Line
₤			8522	214A	Property Line (plaster line)
⌐			8735	221F	Right Angle
∠			8736	2220	Angle
∡			8737	2221	Measured Angle
Ø		⌥ shift o	8960	2300	Diameter Sign
✓			10003	2713	Check Mark

Part 5 - Typing Symbols   **197**

Microsoft®

To use special symbols in Microsoft, the original method was to use the alt keys: hold the alt key and then type the number that corresponds to the desired symbol. The first 255 symbols have remained relatively unchanged and work the same across most programs using the common fonts. Note from the table that, for any given symbol, the Alt Code number is different from the Unicode number. Most programs have some means of inserting Unicode, but the process varies by program and by release date. The exact method is beyond our scope here and well within the scope of a quick internet search.

Mac®

To use Unicode with the Mac OS, there are a number of shortcuts coded in for popular characters. All of these require holding the **option** (⌥) key and hitting another key. Some of them require holding **option** and **shift**, then hitting another key. For example, ≈ requires holding **option** and hitting **x**. To insert ±, hold **option** and **shift** and hit **=**. For symbols without a shortcut, Mac OS requires the hex form of the Unicode and the user has to modify keyboard preferences. See the internet for more information.

LightWright®

As of the summer of 2020, LightWright implements an older character encoding scheme by default: MacRoman. Apple used MacRoman in Classic Mac OS, up to the release of OSX. Apple's support of Classic Mac OS ended in 2002 but some programs, including LightWright, continue to use the legacy encoding. It is relatively simple to adjust LightWright to use Unicode (UTF-8), and doing so can help when exporting data between programs.

AutoCAD®

AutoCAD uses its own set of special inputs known as Control Codes, as well as the hex form of Unicode and also a version of the alt codes similar to Microsoft products. AutoCAD is an old program – older than Microsoft Office and significantly older than iWork – and this history matters: there are a lot of legacy options. What is shown on the chart are the few functions that should work with all common fonts and text objects. Other options are available.

AUTOCAD CONTROL CODES

Symbol	Control Code	Name
°	**%%d**	Degree Symbol
±	**%%p**	Plus/Minus Tolerance
∅	**%%c**	Diameter
\u+hhhh		Inserts Unicode character **hhhh** where **hhhh** is the hex number of the symbol. The backslash, the letter u and the plus sign are all typed out. Example: **\u+2126** produces Ω

Part 5 - Advanced Two Tape Layout **199**

Advanced Two Tape Layout

Back in the first part of this book, in the "Two Tape Layout" trick, we discussed how to lay out the two essential lines of a stage: Center Line and Plaster Line. We also discussed how to create a Setting Line that is different from Plaster Line. All layout begins with these basic techniques. An entire show can be laid out by using just these techniques. The same method for developing the Setting Line can be applied to any point. Often, these techniques are all that is needed. But for complicated shows, there are more advanced approaches that are worth knowing about.

Lasers that create 90° reference lines or dots are increasingly common. These lasers have become readily available and are useful for layout work, especially when there are a lot of points in a line perpendicular to Center Line. But lasers can be finicky to align and can become time consuming if the laser has to be moved around a lot.

Some shows have a lot of points all over the stage that need to land precisely and quickly. Here is a method to lay these out quickly, using two tape measures and a spreadsheet. This is a particularly useful approach when the show is both densely packed and geometrically irregular. Folks who do shows in non-traditional venues with a lot of scenery might do this sort of layout every load-in. Other folks who set up concerts in a house with a permanent rigging system may never need this technique.

This layout method builds on the initial layout steps. These are covered in *Part 1* of the book in "Two Tape Layout" and "Add a Setting Line". To proceed with the Advanced Two Tape Layout, we need to have established Plaster Line, Center Line, and – if it is being used – a separate Setting Line. (Some shows will use Plaster Line as the Setting Line.) These lines will define our 0,0 point. For a recap of this process, check out the flowchart on the next page.

Layout Flowchart

The Step-by-Step process of the Initial Layout

Define Two Points

in a typical theater, use the USL and USR Corners of the Proscenium Opening

↓

Establish Plaster Line

snap a line with a chalk box between the Two Points

↓

Find Center of Plaster Line

↓

Find Up Stage Center Point

measure an equal distance from the two ends of Plaster Line (the USL and USR corners of the Proscenium Opening) as far US as possible

↓

Establish Center Line

↓

Pick One of Two Options

↙   ↘

If Only Using **Plaster Line...**   If Using a **Setting Line...**

↓   ↓

0,0 is the Intersection of Plaster Line and Center Line   Offset a Setting Line from Plaster Line

↓

0,0 is the Intersection of Setting Line and Center Line

Part 5 - Advanced Two Tape Layout

Ok. We have the lines we need and a 0,0 point. How do we lay out the rest of the show? Well, it is worth mentioning again that there are a lot of different methods. Any single method could be the right choice for this show and the wrong choice for the next show. **This particular method, to be efficient, requires the use of a spreadsheet calculator.** That is why it is here, in the *Computers & Calculators* part of the book. Let's step thru the theory of how it works, then we will dive into how to build the spreadsheet.

A show starts as an idea in someone's head. This idea usually ends up being drawn on paper by a designer, first in a rough conceptual way, then more precisely as a scaled drawing. In this later form, all of the various equipment ends up drawn on a map of a venue, which we call the ground plan. The stagehand usually comes into the production process after the ground plan is created. We establish a single 0,0 point on the ground plan, then measure the distance of everything from this point. We end up with a list of points of where we need to put everything. Here is an example of such a list and the ground plan it was drawn from:

Point	Left / Right	Dist. From Center Line	Dist. From Setting Line
Main PA	CL	0' - 0"	NEG 0' - 6"
1st LX #1	SL	15' - 0"	1' - 8 1/2"
1st LX #2	SL	5' - 0"	1' - 8 1/2"
1st LX #3	SR	5' - 0"	1' - 8 1/2"
1st LX #4	SR	15' - 0"	1' - 8 1/2"
Show Banner #1	SR	16' - 2"	2' - 6"
Show Banner #2	SR	4' - 9 3/8"	4' - 8 1/4"
Proj Screen #1	SL	12' - 0"	3' - 0"
Proj Screen #2	SL	0' - 4 1/8"	5' - 0"
Audience Blinder	CL	0' - 0"	18' - 0"
Cable Pick	SL	1' - 0"	19' - 3"

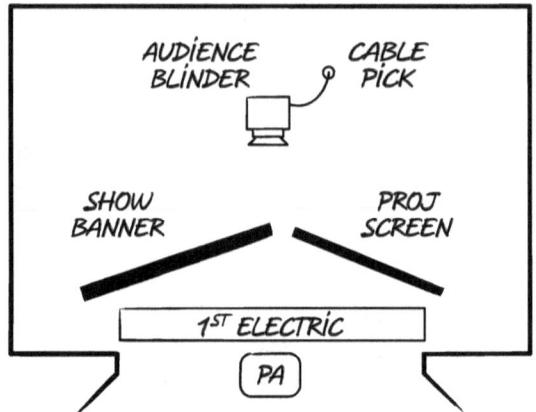

In this example from a made-up show, we have a big speaker, an electric hung on a pipe or truss, a banner, a projection screen, and an audience blinder light with a cable. Not a very big show, but we should notice a couple of complications. Let's start from the point furthest Down Stage and work Up Stage. The Main Public Address speaker ("Main PA") is going to be a big speaker hung right on center. Note that it is actually Down Stage of 0,0, which we indicated as a negative number. Next, the electric truss or pipe ("1st LX") is pretty straightforward: it hangs parallel to Setting Line and evenly splits Center Line. The banner and projection screen are a bit more complicated. Both of them are angled. In both cases, the ends further from Center Line are more Down Stage. The ends closer to Center Line are more Up Stage. This is a pretty typical way to angle things to make the stage picture a bit more interesting for the audience. Finally, we have a big light ("Audience Blinder") pointing at the audience from Up Stage Center. This light has a separate pick for its cable.

A real show could easily have ten times as many points as shown in the list here. The list for a real show would probably include both ground supported and rigged elements. It may even have points that will need to be transferred down into a trap room. But the basic process is the same, and so let us continue with our little made-up show.

Now, we have to move from the theoretical realm of the ground plan and a list of points to the real world of the stage floor itself. The first step is to establish **two anchor points at a specific distance from each other**. All of the show points will be located by measuring

Part 5 - Advanced Two Tape Layout   203

from the two anchor points. The <u>first anchor point</u> will be at 0,0. The <u>second anchor point</u> will be on the Center Line, at a specific distance Up Stage of 0,0. How do we choose this distance? It should be a whole number that is further Up Stage than our furthest point. In the example of the made-up show, 20' - 0" would be a good choice because the furthest Up Stage point is the cable pick at 19' - 3".

At this point, we have picked two anchor points and have created a list of points to be laid out. What happens next? The experienced user takes this information and plugs it into a spreadsheet, which they then use to layout the show. Because this is our first time, let's stop and show how we can layout a point, doing all of the work by hand.

We have laid out the CL and SL and picked our anchors. Now let's take a look at the Show Banner. Here is the relevant section from the list of points:

Point	Left / Right	Dist. From Center Line	Dist. From Setting Line
Show Banner #1	SR	16' - 2"	2' - 6"
Show Banner #2	SR	4' - 9 3/8"	4' - 8 1/4"

For each point, we need to find two numbers: the distance from the DS anchor to the point and the distance from the US anchor to the point. Let's work on "Show Banner #1". This drawing shows what we know about this point:

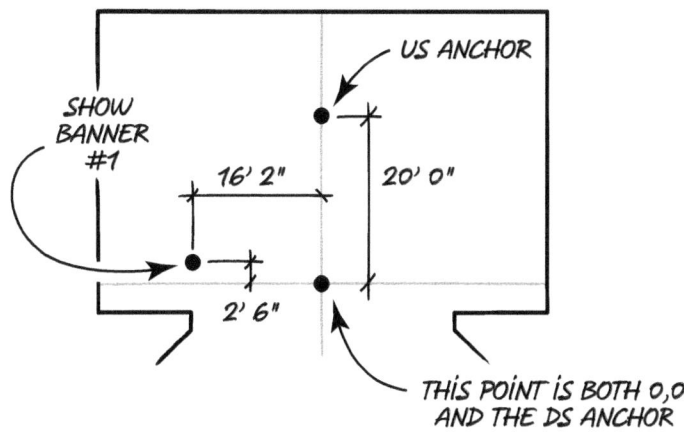

To find the distance from the point to each of the anchors, we draw triangles. These are going to be "right triangles". That is, one of the three angles will be a "right angle", which is 90°. This will allow us to use the Pythagorean Theorem, which is among the most useful tools in our mathematics work box. The next drawing shows the triangles.

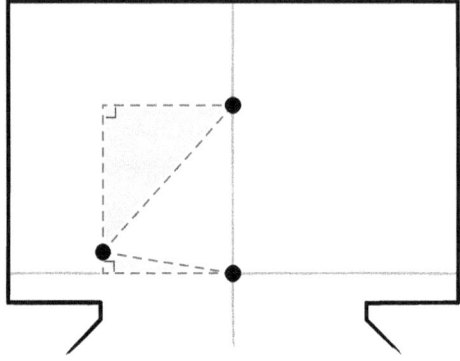

Generally, the Pythagorean Theorem tells us that, for a right triangle, the length of the long side will equal the square root of the sum of the squares of the two other sides. Here it is in equation form:

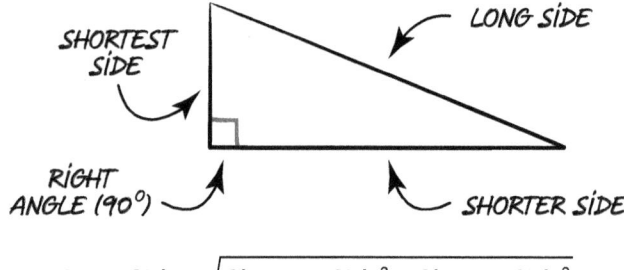

$$\text{Long Side} = \sqrt{\text{Shortest Side}^2 + \text{Shorter Side}^2}$$

The two shorter sides will always be joined by the right (90°) angle. The long side will always be the diagonal that connects the two shorter sides. (Hypotenuse is the technically accurate term for the diagonal.)

Applying the Pythagorean Theorem to this show, notice that in each of the triangles, the long side is the distance from the anchor to the "Show Banner #1" point. Let's start with the DS Anchor. We want to find the distance from anchor to point, and we know how far the point is from Setting Line and Center Line. For the sake of clarity, let's zoom in on our triangles and add some labels before jumping into the equations.

Part 5 - Advanced Two Tape Layout

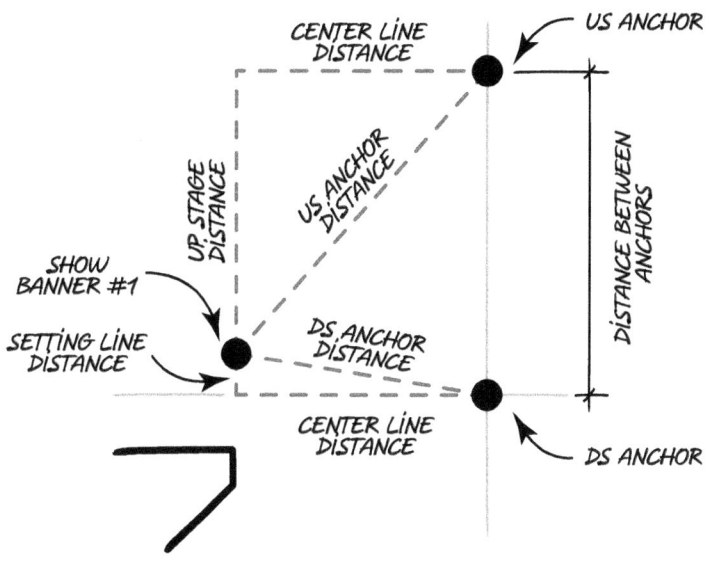

$$\text{DS Anchor Distance} = \sqrt{\text{Center Line Dist.}^2 + \text{Setting Line Dist.}^2}$$

Now we can plug in some real numbers. To make this easier, we are going to convert everything to inches. In fact, as a general approach during layout, this is a common practice, and a useful one for avoiding errors. (See the *References* for more information.) Generally, talking in "feet and inches" is better for a gut sense of how big or far something is whereas talking "inches only" is better for avoiding errors and simplifying the calculations.

Center Line Distance = 16'– 2" = 144 *inches*

Setting Line Distance = 2'– 6" = 30 *inches*

$$\text{Dist. to DS Anchor} = \sqrt{144^2 + 30^2}$$

Dist. to DS Anchor = 147.092

Now let's find the distance to the US Anchor. This is slightly more complicated. The Center Line Distance is the same as before. But for the other side of the triangle, we need to subtract the Setting Line Distance from the Distance Between Anchors. Let's call this the Up Stage Distance.

Up Stage Dist. = *Dist. Between Anchors* – *Setting Line Dist.*

Putting that into the equation gives us:

$$\text{Dist. to US Anchor} = \sqrt{\text{Center Line Dist.}^2 + \text{Up Stage Dist.}^2}$$

Now let's plug the numbers in. First, we convert the Distance Between Anchors and find the Up Stage Distance.

$$\text{Distance Between Anchors} = 20'-0" = 240 \text{ inches}$$

$$\text{Setting Line Distance} = 2'-6" = 30 \text{ inches}$$

$$\text{Up Stage Dist.} = 240 - 30 = 210$$

Now into the big equation:

$$\text{Dist. to US Anchor} = \sqrt{144^2 + 210^2}$$

$$\text{Dist. to US Anchor} = 254.629$$

And there it is. We now have the two numbers we need to lay out the Show Banner #1 point. Fast and easy, right? We just did a bunch of math, but remember that this is just to show folks new to the process what is happening. For the experienced user, all of this happens in a spreadsheet. Set up the equation once and you never have to do it again. The spreadsheet does all the work, as fast as you can type numbers into it.

Let's go on stage and actually lay out the point. Setting Line and Center Line have already been snapped with the chalk box. We've picked our anchors and have marked them on the floor.

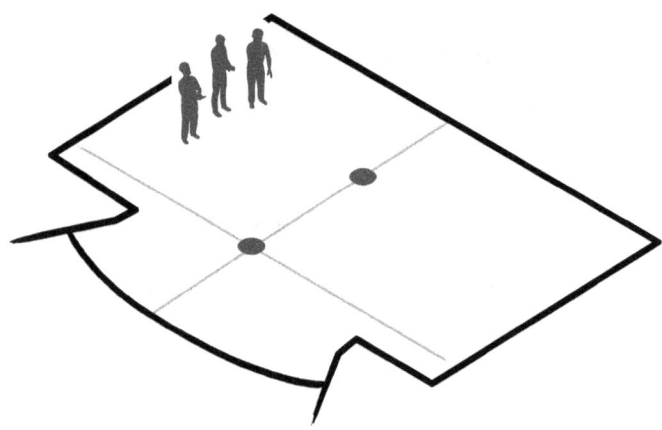

Part 5 - Advanced Two Tape Layout   **207**

We've done the math and we've found the two numbers:

Dist. to DS Anchor = 147.092

Dist. to US Anchor = 254.629

To locate the "Show Banner #1" point, we need **two tape measures and three stagehands**. One stagehand is at the DS Anchor and holds the end of first tape measure. Another stagehand is at the US Anchor and holds the end of the second tape measure. The third stagehand has both tape measures and walks across the stage, running them out, until the first tape measure matches the distance to the DS Anchor and the second tape measure matches the distance to the US Anchor.

That's it: the essential concept.

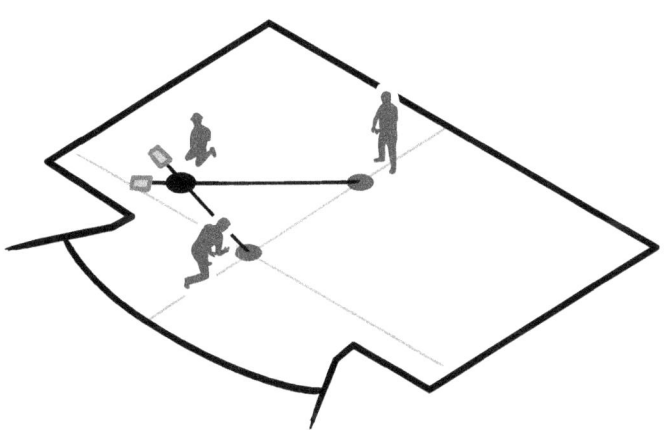

Ok, now some details. First, the tape measures have to be held straight and read correctly. (See the tips in the first part of this book for some traps when using tape measures.) Also, most tape measures read in fractional and not decimal inches. So the numbers 147.092 and 254.629 will have to be converted into the fractions used by the tape measure. With some work, this can be done automatically by the spreadsheet.

Another approach is to have the spreadsheet round the numbers to a precision picked by the user. This will limit the output to easily recognized decimals, like 0.500. If a stagehand only wants the measurement to the closest inch, they can select that on the spreadsheet. If they want it to the closest eighth of an inch, they can select that too. They can even select it to the closest 0.001 of an inch, though that level of precision is likely to be wasted effort on a stage. Let's get into how the spreadsheet works.

Part 5 - Advanced Two Tape Layout

Microsoft Excel® Syntax for Two Tape Layout

It is going to be easiest if we go directly into the specific syntax of a spreadsheet program to discuss how to build the spreadsheet. (Believe me, the first draft of this section attempted to do it generically and it was a mess.) We are going to use Microsoft Excel, but the concepts are easily applied to different programs. Please note that this is not an endorsement of Excel – there are plenty of other options. But Excel is a fine program, so please don't take the last sentence as any kind of condemnation either. Excel is a very functional program that is extremely popular. That is reason enough to select it. Onwards!

On the next page is an image of a completed spreadsheet. It is as basic as possible while still being functional. We will use one important trick: naming cells so that the equations are easier to read and understand. To do this, find the box to the left of where the formula is entered, enter a name for a given cell in this box and hit the enter key. (If using a different program or if Excel has changed where this box is since this was written, simply searching online for "name cell in excel" will bring up plenty of tutorials.) Before we begin with the preliminary information, we need to make one point very clear: **this spreadsheet works exclusively in inches**. All measurements will need to be converted from "feet and inches" into "inches only" measurements.

There are three pieces of preliminary information:

1. Distance Between Anchors
2. Offset
3. Precision

We are going to assume that the DS Anchor is located at 0,0 and that the US Anchor is also on Center Line. The **Distance Between Anchors**, as the name implies, will be the straight line distance between the two anchors.

					[CLIENT] [NAME OF PROJECT]				[SHOW DATE] [DOCUMENT DATE]	
Dist Between Anchors	240										
Offset	0.188										
Precision	0.25										
Point Name	SL/CL/SR	Dist of Point from Center Line	Dist of Point from Setting Line	DS Anchor: Raw	DS Anchor: +Offset	DS Anchor: Tape Reads	US Anchor: Raw	US Anchor: +Offset	US Anchor: Tape Reads
Main PA	CL	0.000	-6.000	6.000	6.188	6.250	246.000	246.188	246.250
1st LX #1	SL	180.000	20.500	181.164	181.352	181.250	283.867	284.055	284.000
1st LX #2	SL	60.000	20.500	63.405	63.593	63.500	227.553	227.741	227.750
1st LX #3	SR	60.000	20.500	63.405	63.593	63.500	227.553	227.741	227.750
1st LX #4	SR	180.000	20.500	181.164	181.352	181.250	283.867	284.055	284.000
Show Banner #1	SR	194.000	30.000	196.306	196.494	196.500	285.895	286.083	286.000
Show Banner #2	SR	57.375	56.250	80.349	80.537	80.500	192.499	192.687	192.750
Proj Screen #1	SL	144.000	36.000	148.432	148.620	148.500	249.704	249.892	250.000
Proj Screen #2	SL	4.125	60.000	60.142	60.330	60.250	180.047	180.235	180.250
Audience Blinder	CL	0.000	216.000	216.000	216.188	216.250	24.000	24.188	24.250
Cable Pick	SL	12.000	231.000	231.311	231.499	231.500	15.000	15.188	15.250

Part 5 - Advanced Two Tape Layout

The **Offset** is a useful tool for making sure the spreadsheet provides the user with the number that the tape measure will read. How can the "tape measure reads" number be different than the actual distance? One common way this happens is that the stagehands want to "burn a foot" on the tape measure. In this case, the Offset would be entered as 12. (See the "Burning a Foot?" tip in *Part 1* for more on this.) The Offset can also be useful when, for example, the stagehands drive drywall screws into the stage floor at the anchor points, then hook their tape measures to the head of the screw. This is a very efficient technique, but it does add an offset. This offset will vary, depending on the size of the screw and the design of the tape measure, but is usually somewhere between 1/8" and 1/2". In general, the Offset will be added to the actual distance to provide a "Tape Measure Reads" number.

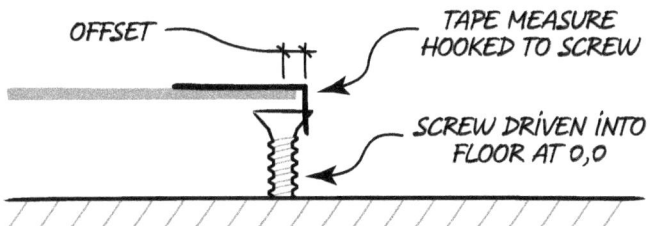

The **Precision** is where the user determines to what increment the spreadsheet will output results. For example, if the user is simply locating a bunch of tables for a catering event and only wants to work in whole numbers, they would enter a Precision of 1. If, on the other hand, they are locating a series of tightly fitting LED screens and want to work in eighths of an inch, they would enter a Precision of 0.125. The spreadsheet will take the actual calculated number and round it to the Precision increment indicated by the user. For example, let's say the raw calculated number is 8.639. The caterer's spreadsheet will round this actual number to 9 and the LED installer's spreadsheet will round this number to 8.625 (which is the decimal version of 8 5/8").*

---

* It is worth pointing out that the rounded number will never vary more than half the precision increment. The caterer will always be within 1/2" of the theoretical point and the LED installer will always be within 1/16".

Here is what to enter in the spreadsheet. Anything in this `font` should be typed in the actual cell. Each cell is defined by a column letter and a row number. Cell A1 is the top most, left most cell in Excel. For this spreadsheet, we are going to type out the contents indicated in the following table.

Cell	Cell Content	Note
A1	`Distance Between Anchors (inches)`	This is a Label
B1		Name this cell anchor_dist
A2	`Offset (inches)`	Label
B2		Name this cell offset
A3	`Precision (inches)`	Label
B3		Name this cell precision

Now we need to start feeding in the actual points. Each point should be its own row on the spreadsheet. Once one row is written and working correctly, it is a simple matter to copy it and create a sheet with as many points as you need. We will create one row of labels, then a row for an actual point.

Here is the row of labels:

Cell	Cell Content	Note
A5	`Point Name`	
B5	`SL / CL / SR`	
C5	`Dist of Point from Center Line`	
D5	`Dist of Point from Setting Line`	These are all labels
E5	`DS Anchor: Raw`	
F5	`DS Anchor: +Offset`	

Part 5 - Advanced Two Tape Layout

Cell	Cell Content
G5	DS Anchor: Tape Reads
H5	US Anchor: Raw
I5	US Anchor: +Offset
J5	US Anchor: Tape Reads

Next is a row for a point. This is where we are going to get into the actual Excel calculations, which can get long. Conceptually, the first two columns are simple labels where the user gives the name of the point and whether it is Stage Left, Stage Right or on top of Center Line. Next, the spreadsheet takes this number and calculates the distance between the point and the DS Anchor. We call this the "Raw" number. Next, the offset is added to the Raw number. Finally, the number is rounded to the closest Precision increment. The same happens for the US Anchor. The only geometric math happening is the Pythagorean Theorem discussed earlier. The rounding to the Precision increment separates the decimal from the whole number using the truncate function, then rounds this portion to the closest Precision increment.

Cell	Cell Content*	Note
A6		Blank for user input
B6		Blank for user input
C6		Blank for user input
D6		Blank for user input

* In Excel, everything typed into a cell will be on one line. Here, in this book, we don't have enough room to do that so it gets broken up onto different lines.

We can show how it will actually look in Excel by shrinking the font size. For example, here are the contents of G6:
=TRUNC(F6)+(ROUND((F6-TRUNC(F6))*(1/precision),0)*precision)

Cell	Formula	Description
E6	=SQRT(C6^2+D6^2)	Finds the actual distance to the DS Anchor
F6	=E6+offset	Adds the offset
G6	=TRUNC(F6)+(ROUND((F6-TRUNC(F6))*(1/precision),0)* precision)	Rounds to the specified precision
H6	=SQRT(C6^2+(anchor_dist-D6)^2)	Finds the actual distance to the US Anchor
I6	=H6+offset	Adds the offset
J6	=TRUNC(I6)+(ROUND((I6-TRUNC(I6))*(1/precision),0)*precision	Rounds to the specified precision

> **Note:**
> For any point that is further Down Stage than the Setting Line, enter the distance from Setting Line as a Negative Number.

And that's it. Simply copy this same line as many times as necessary to fill out the spreadsheet. This can be done a few different ways, such as highlighting the row and doing the Edit→Copy command, then highlighting where you want the new line and doing the Edit→Paste command. It is also possible to highlight the row, then drag-and-fill. There are lots of free tutorials online that cover these techniques and everything else Excel.

We have created a simple, but perfectly functional spreadsheet. To check your own spreadsheet, take a look at the example spreadsheet shown earlier. You should be able to input the information from the light gray cells and get the same output as shown in the dark gray cells. This example spreadsheet is "lightly" formatted: basically a few cells were shaded in and some lines were added, which just makes it easier to read. At the top right corner, a **Text Box** was added where basic project information can be added. Text boxes are a convenient

Part 5 - Advanced Two Tape Layout

trick for adding information to a spreadsheet that does not need to be in the cells. Anytime you want to add notes, labels, or anything not directly part of the calculation, try a text box.

Just because a spreadsheet starts simply, does not mean it has to stay that way. As a spreadsheet gets used, try to think about ways to save time and increase accuracy. For example, this spreadsheet depends on everything being input in inches. But it can be modified to accept both feet and inches from the user. (It can also be modified to output feet and inches, though experience shows that sticking to "inches only" can help avoid errors.) Another possible modification is to allow the user to input a position for the DS Anchor and the US Anchor that are not on Center Line. The DS Anchor does not even have to be on 0,0. (This can be useful if the user knows there will be an obstruction of some kind along Center Line.) Here is one last idea that is very useful but a bit more complicated: add an auto-generating scatter plot. As points are put into the spreadsheet, this will create a graphic plot showing where these points are in relation to each other. This is a great way to double check that everything looks right, and also gives the user a map when they are laying out a whole bunch of numbers.

The next two pages show a more developed spreadsheet and its auto-generating scatter plot of points.

PROJECT: Some Show
DATE: ##/##/####

[Good place to write notes]

LAYOUT PLOT: Electrics

	Down Stage Anchor		Dist from CL			Dist from Setting Line	
		ft.	in.	SL/CL/SR	in. only	ft.	in.
Down Stage Anchor		0	0	CL	0	0	0
Up Stage Anchor		0	0	CL	0	25	6

Offset 0.125 in   Precision Increment 0.25 in.   Tolerance ± 0.125 in.

Name	SL/CL/SR	Dist from CL			Dist from Setting Line			Tape Reads from DS Anchor			Tape Reads from US Anchor		
		ft.	in.	in. only	ft.	in.	in. only	raw in.	+offset	in. only	raw in.	+offset	in. only
Light Bulbs 1	SL	20	6	246	10	2	122	274.591	274.716	274.5	307.2	307.325	307.25
Light Bulb 2	SL	10	6	126	10	2	122	175.385	175.51	175.5	223.007	223.132	223
Light Bulb 3	SR	10	6	-126	10	2	122	175.385	175.51	175.5	223.007	223.132	223
Light Bulb 4	SR	20	6	-246	10	2	122	274.591	274.716	274.5	307.2	307.325	307.25
#2 Electric 1	SL	25	0	300	8		96	314.986	315.111	315	366.197	366.322	366.25
#2 Electric 2	SL	12	0	144	8		96	173.066	173.191	173	254.629	254.754	254.75
#2 Electric 3	CL	0	0	0	8		96	96	96.125	96	210	210.125	210
#2 Electric 4	SR	12	0	-144	8		96	173.066	173.191	173	254.629	254.754	254.75
#2 Electric 5	SR	25	0	-300	8		96	314.986	315.111	315	366.197	366.322	366.25
Ballyhoo 1	SL	5	0	60	-2		-21	63.5689	63.6939	63.5	332.459	332.584	332.5
Ballyhoo 2	SR	5	0	-60	-2		-21	63.5689	63.6939	63.5	332.459	332.584	332.5
Audience Blinder	CL	0	0	0	30		360	360	360.125	360	54	54.125	54
Cable Pick	SR	1	4	-16	31	6	378	378.338	378.463	378.25	73.7564	73.8814	73.75
SL Angled LX #1	SL	10	0	120	22		264	289.993	290.118	290	127.138	127.263	127.25
SL Angled LX #2	SL	18	0	216	19		228	314.07	314.195	314	229.652	229.777	229.75
SL Angled LX #3	SL	26	0	312	16		192	366.344	366.469	366.25	332.175	332.3	332.25
SR Angled LX #1	SR	12	6	-150	17		204	253.211	253.336	253.25	181.395	181.52	181.5
SR Angled LX #2	SR	17	6	-210	16		192	284.542	284.667	284.5	238.948	239.073	239
SR Angled LX #3	SR	23	6	-282	15		180	334.55	334.675	334.5	308.869	308.994	308.75
SR Angled LX #4	SR	29	0	-348	14		168	386.43	386.555	386.5	374.363	374.488	374.25
SL Boom	SL	32	0	384	2	6	30	385.17	385.295	385.25	472.897	473.022	473
SR Boom	SR	32	0	-384	2	6	30	385.17	385.295	385.25	472.897	473.022	473
	CL	0	0	0	0		0	0	0.125	0	306	306.125	306

C:\This is a good place for a file path...

Page 1 of 2

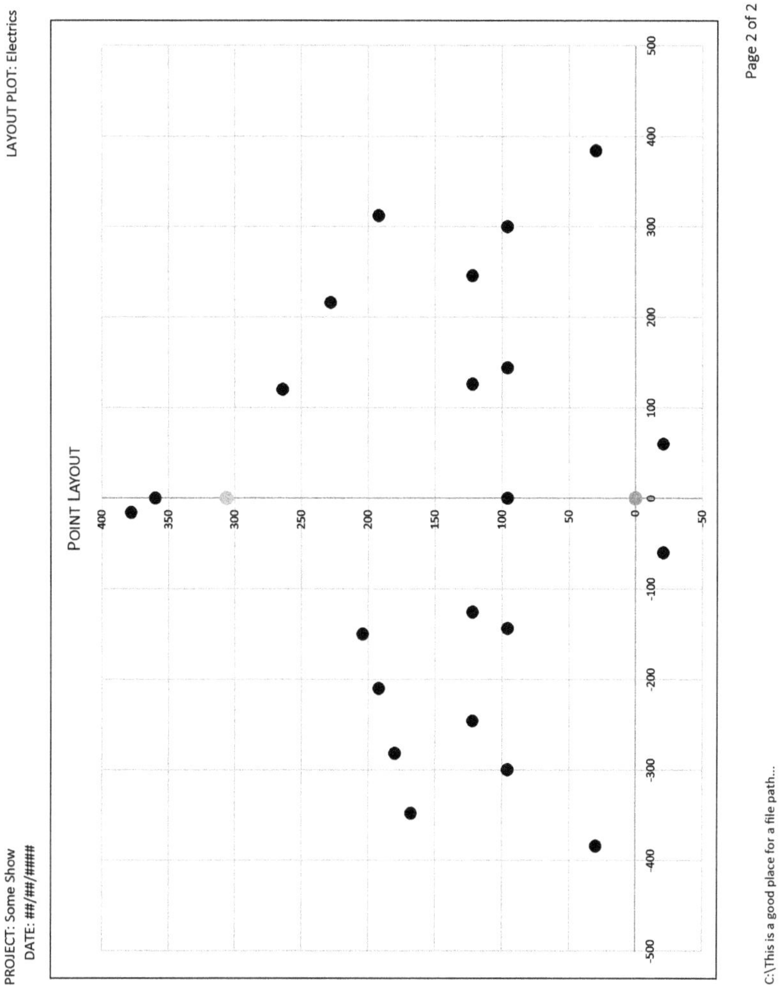

Part 5 - Advanced Two Tape Layout

Bridle Geometry

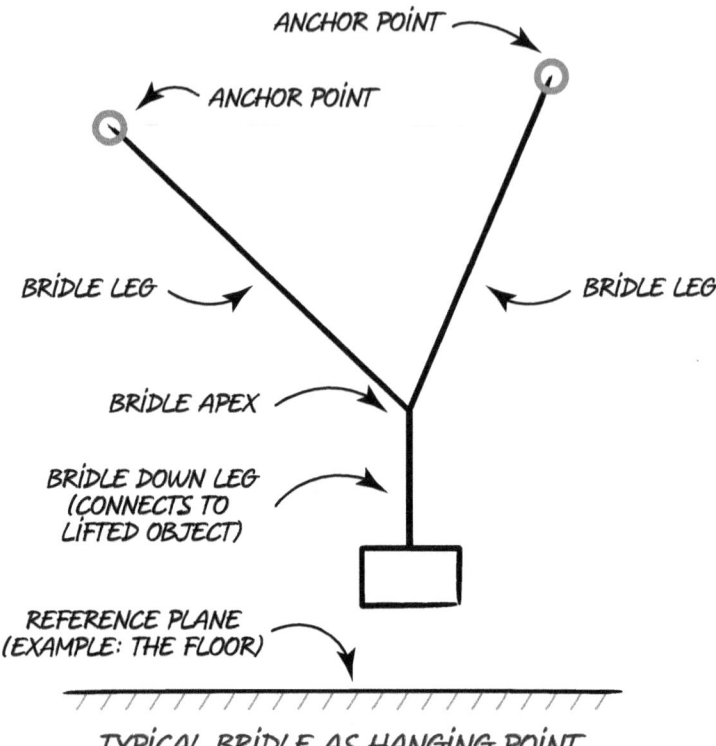

TYPICAL BRIDLE AS HANGING POINT

Two-leg bridles are a common solution to a range of rigging problems. When the hanging point does not land under an anchor point, or when the rigger wants to distribute a load rather than hang from a single anchor, a two-leg bridle is the go-to solution. (Another solution that is useful but less common in our world is to use a lifting bar.) By simply adjusting leg lengths, a bridle can hit any point between two anchors. Many riggers will immediately picture the roof steel in an arena when thinking about bridles. This is an "apex up" configuration. Just as useful is "apex down": inverting a bridle to help pick up an unusual shape.

Part 5 - Bridle Geometry **219**

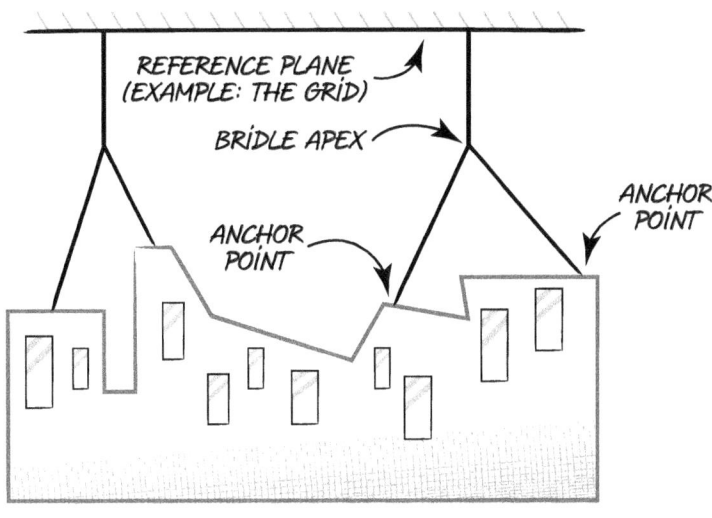

BRIDLES USED TO HANG
AN ASYMMETRICAL FLAT

As with all rigging, we need to make sure the total forces do not exceed the capacity of the rigging hardware or the anchorages. The weight of what we lift creates part of the total force. When using bridles, another force is created by the angle between the legs. As a bridle becomes flatter, the tension in the legs increases dramatically.

In this section, we will present a formula that can be used to design custom bridles. We often know where the anchorage points are and where we want the apex to be. We also frequently want to make the bridle as flat as possible, but without exceeding a critical angle between the legs. This formula takes all this information and determines the leg lengths required.

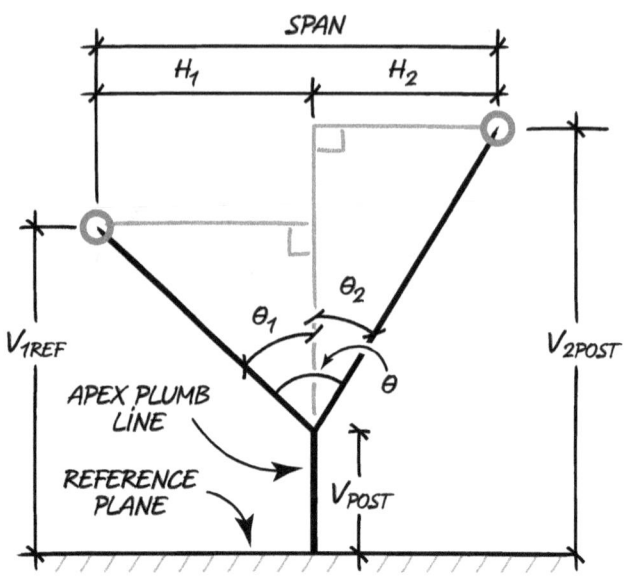

The basic approach is to find the total bridle angle by finding the angle from each leg to the apex plumb line. These angles θ_1 and θ_2 are then added together to find θ, the total bridle angle.

$$\theta = \theta_1 + \theta_2$$

$$\tan \theta_1 = \frac{h_1}{V_{1ref} - V_{point}} \qquad \tan \theta_2 = \frac{h_2}{V_{2ref} - V_{point}}$$

$$\theta = \arctan\left(\frac{h_1}{V_{1ref} - V_{point}}\right) + \arctan\left(\frac{h_2}{V_{2ref} - V_{point}}\right)$$

Note that the angles θ_1 and θ_2 depend on the vertical height of the point from the reference plane, v_{point}. The quantity we want to find is vpoint. Therefore, we have to rearrange the equations. We will use the trigonometric rule to add inverse tangents (written here as "arctan"). Here is the general form of the rule:

In this application, this works out to this:

$$\arctan(a) + \arctan(b) = \arctan\left(\frac{a+b}{1-ab}\right)$$

Part 5 - Bridle Geometry

In this application, this works out to this:

$$\theta = \arctan\left(\dfrac{\dfrac{h_1}{v_{1ref} - v_{point}} + \dfrac{h_2}{v_{2ref} - v_{point}}}{1 - \left(\dfrac{h_1}{v_{1ref} - v_{point}}\right)\left(\dfrac{h_2}{v_{2ref} - v_{point}}\right)}\right)$$

↑ Denominators in ↑
the denominator

Take a look at the denominators in the denominator. Notice how v_{point} will end up being multiplied by itself. This means we will need to use the quadratic formula to ultimately solve for v_{point}. The general form of this quadratic formula is this:

$$ax^2 + bx + c = 0$$

There are two values of x that will solve any quadratic. A simple example is the problem $x^2 = 9$. Both $x = 3$ and $x = -3$ are correct solutions. (Referring back to the general quadratic formula, in this simple example a = 1, b = 0, c = -9.) Thus, when we solve our equation for vpoint, we will end up with two possible answers. The two general solutions to the quadratic formula are:

$$x = \dfrac{-b + \sqrt{b^2 - 4ac}}{2a} \qquad x = \dfrac{-b - \sqrt{b^2 - 4ac}}{2a}$$

While our particular equation to find θ may look very different from the general form of the quadratic equation, it can ultimately be multiplied out and simplified to fit the quadratic equation. We are going to skip those steps here, but go for it if you're interested. Ultimately, after a bit of work, we will get these values for **a**, **b**, and **c**.

$$a = \tan\theta$$

$$b = h_1 + h_2 - \tan\theta\, v_{ref1} - \tan\theta\, v_{ref2}$$

$$c = \tan\theta\, v_{ref1} v_{ref2} - \tan\theta\, h_1 h_2 - h_1 v_{ref2} - h_2 v_{ref1}$$

We can then plug **a**, **b**, and **c** into the two solutions of the quadratic formula. (Note that the angle θ has to be greater than 0° and less than 180°.) How can there be two solutions to hanging a bridle? Well, this formula is actually just constructing a triangle between the two anchor points with the given angle θ and there are two solutions to the problem: one below the anchor points (closer to the reference plane) and one above the anchor points (away from the reference plane). Only the point closer to the reference plane is practical for a rigging system. This will always be the smaller of the two possible solutions.

While it is beyond the scope of this section, the user can easily integrate other bridle formulas that calculate the tension in the legs as well as vertical, and horizontal forces for a given load. Some good references for bridle math are provided at the end of the section. See also the "Bridle Tension" section of the *Fundamentals* in *Part 3*.

It is easy to check the geometry produced by this calculator to make sure the equations were put in correctly by drawing it in a CAD program, or very carefully on graph paper, then checking the bridle angle with a digital or an actual protractor. **Note: this is strictly a geometric formula. It is up to the user to understand the forces involved and select an appropriate geometry.** Forces generated by bridles increase exponentially as the geometry changes. It is also worth pointing out that some rigging hardware can only be loaded in a straight line and not used for bridles at all. Some hardware can be used for bridles but only within a limited angular range. The user needs to understand all of these limitations.

Part 5 - Bridle Geometry

Microsoft Excel® Syntax for Bridle Calculator

What follows is the exact syntax for entering the formulas into Excel. Anything in this font indicates what should be typed into each cell. The one trick used below is to name cells so that the equations read like real math rather than a spreadsheet. For a given cell, simply enter the name, such as h_1, in the box to the left of where the formula is entered. (There are plenty of simple tutorials online: search for "name cell in Excel".) The formatting choices are arbitrary and simple; once you have the spreadsheet working, modify as you like.

Cell	Cell Content*	Note
A1	Vertical Dist. from Reference Plane to Anchor 1 (feet)	This is a Label
B1		Name this cell v1ref
A2	Vertical Dist. from Reference Plane to Anchor 2 (feet)	Blank for user input
B2		Blank for user input
A3	Horizontal Distance from Apex to Anchor 1 (feet)	Finds the actual distance to the DS Anchor
B3		Name this cell h_1
A4	Horizontal Distance from Apex to Anchor 2 (feet)	Label
B4		Name this cell h_2
A5	Bridle Angle (degrees)	Label
B5		User inputs angles in degrees
A6	Bridle Angle in Radians	Label
B6	=RADIANS(B5)	Name this cell angle

The blank spaces above are for user input. All the calculations occur below. Excel uses radians rather than degrees (just like fractional versus decimal inches, these are two different ways of talking about the same amount) which is why the Bridle Angle gets converted.

| A7 | =Intermediate Variable "a" | Label |

Cell	Content	Note
B7	`=TAN(angle)`	Name this cell a
A8	Intermediate Variable "b"	Label
B8	`=h_1+h_2-TAN(angle)*v1ref-TAN(angle)*v2ref`	Name this cell b
A9	Intermediate Variable "c"	Label
B9	`=TAN(angle)*v1ref*v2ref-TAN(angle)*h_1*h_2-h_1*v2ref-h_2*v1ref`	Name this cell cee

Excel reserves "c" for other purposes so we have to use "cee"

Cell	Content	Note
A10	Quadratic Result 1	Label
B10	`=(-b+SQRT(b^2-4*a*cee))/(2*a)`	Name this cell x_1
A11	Quadratic Result 2	Label
B11	`=(-b-SQRT(b^2-4*a*cee))/(2*a)`	Name this cell x_2
A12	Maximum Vertical Distance from Reference Plane to Apex (feet)	Label
B12	`=MIN(x_1,x_2)`	Name this cell v_max
A13	Length of Leg 1 (feet only)	Label
B13	`=SQRT(h_1^2+(v1ref-v_max)^2)`	Calculate Length of Bridle Leg 1
A14	Length of Leg 2 (feet only)	Label
B14	`=SQRT(H_2^2+(V2ref-v_max)^2)`	Calculate Length of Bridle Leg 2

*In Excel, the content of a cell will all be on one line.

Part 5 - Bridle Geometry

To validate your own spreadsheet, the following inputs should produce the following outputs. If the graphic solution is implemented (see below), then your charts should match the charts illustrated.

V_{1ref}	10	ft		θ	1.40	rad
V_{2ref}	15	ft		V_{point}	3.01	ft
h_1	17.5	ft	→	L1	18.84	ft
h_2	2.5	ft		L2	12.25	ft
θ	80	deg				

All of the above creates a functional calculator. All we need to actually solve the problem is available in the calculator. So we can stop here. But, we can always improve on the work we've done, especially with calculators like this. The next few pages discuss some modifications that can make the calculator more user friendly.

From "Decimal Feet Only" to "Feet and Decimal Inch"

If you want to change the decimal feet result to feet and inches, the following formulas can be used. To begin, go back and name cell B13 `leg_1` and cell B14 `leg_2`.

Cell	Cell Content	Note
A16	`Bridle Leg 1 (feet)`	This is a Label
B16	`=TRUNC(leg_1)`	Whole foot portion
A17	`Bridle Leg 1 (inches)`	This is a Label
B17	`=(leg_1-TRUNC(leg_1))*12`	Inch portion
A18	`Bridle Leg 2 (feet)`	This is a Label
B18	`=TRUNC(leg_2)`	Whole foot portion
A19	`Bridle Leg 2 (inches)`	This is a Label
B19	`=(leg_2-TRUNC(leg_2))*12`	Inch portion

Same inputs as before with the new outputs:

V_{1ref}	10	ft		θ	1.40	rad
V_{2ref}	15	ft		V_{point}	3.01	ft
h_1	17.5	ft	→	L1	18.84	ft
h_2	2.5	ft			10.14	in
θ	80	deg		L2	12	ft
					2.99	in

From "Feet and Decimal Inch" to "Feet and Fractional Inch"

If you want to change the decimal inch to fractional inch, first you must choose the smallest fraction you want to display. The formula will round the results to that fraction. Then, to get the fraction to display, you will have to change the format of the cell. To do this, launch the "Format Cell" window by either finding it on the ribbon or by holding **Ctrl** and hitting **1**. The correct format is the "Fraction" Category and the "Up to two digits (21/25)" Type. Below, we have chosen 16^{ths} as the smallest fraction and have changed the formatting of two fractional inches.

Cell	Cell Content	Note
A16	Bridle Leg 1 (feet)	This is a Label
B16	=TRUNC(leg_1)	
A17	Bridle Leg 1 (inches)	This is a Label
B17	=ROUND((leg_1-TRUNC(leg_1))*12***16**,0)/16	
A18	Bridle Leg 2 (feet)	This is a Label
B18	=TRUNC(leg_2)	
A19	Bridle Leg 2 (inches)	This is a Label
B19	=ROUND((leg_2-TRUNC(leg_2))*12***16**,0)/16	

Reformat Cells in Gray

Numbers in **bold** determine the size of the fraction

L1	18	ft		L1	18	ft
	10.08	in	→		10 1/8	in
L2	12	ft		L2	12	ft
	3	in			3	in

The Visual Solution

It's always useful to visualize a problem, and it's actually relatively simple to add a chart that will draw out the bridle. We need to create a set of coordinates that can be used to generate a scatter chart. We also need to create a square reference frame so that the chart's proportions stay consistent as values are modified. This will be clearer with some images at the end of the section, but for now we need to generate a frame reference variable. We do this by checking which is our largest dimension, then generating a value 10% larger than this.

Cell	Cell Content	Note
A21	Frame Reference Variable	This is a Label
B21	=IF((h_1+h_2)>MAX(v1ref, v2ref),(h_1+h_2)*1.1,MAX(v1ref,v2ref)*1.1)	Name this cell f_ref

We are going to insert these coordinates in their own section of the spreadsheet, to the right of everything we've done so far. We are also going to change our format here in the book just a bit, to make sure we are putting down the coordinates in the correct relationship.

	Column D	Column E	Note:
Row 1	0	=v1ref	
Row 2	=h_1	=v_max	This will draw the Bridle
Row 3	=h_1+h_2	=v2ref	
Row 4			This row blank
Row 5	0	0	
Row 6	=f_ref	0	This will draw the Square Reference Frame
Row 7	=f_ref	=f_ref	
Row 8	0	=f_ref	
Row 9	0	0	
Row 10			This row blank
Row 11	=h_1	0	This will draw the Plumb Line
Row 12	=h_1	=v_max	

The next step is to simply highlight everything from cell D1 to cell E12 (upper left to lower right corner), then insert a scatter chart with straight lines. Exact steps will vary by version of Excel, but on one version, go to the "Insert" tab, then in the "Charts" section of the ribbon, there should be a drop-down option for "Scatter with Straight Lines". The goal is to produce a graph that looks like this:

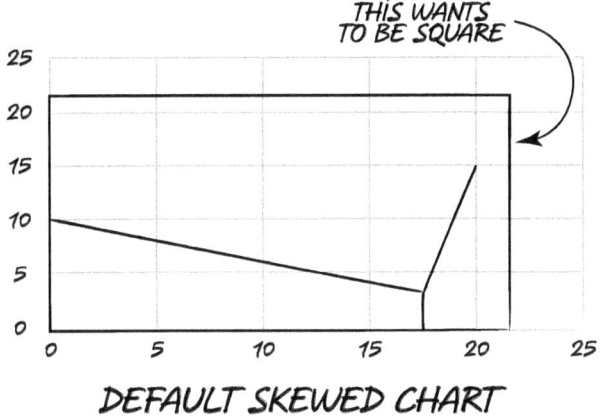

DEFAULT SKEWED CHART

The larger outside rectangle is actually meant to be a square. The proportions of the chart should be adjusted, usually by dragging a corner of the chart with the cursor, until the square reference frame looks square. Once the chart is adjusted, it will live update based on any new dimensions fed into it, but will maintain a square perspective. This allows us to visualize the bridle more accurately.

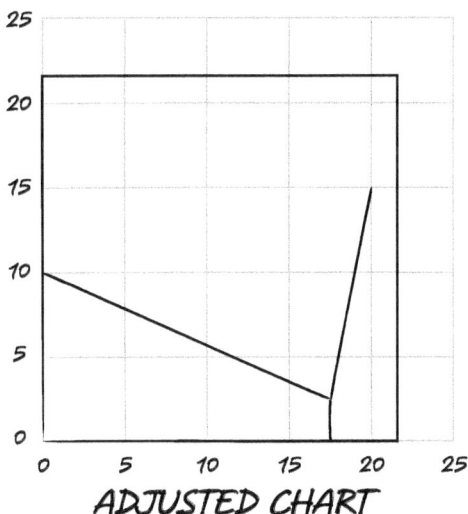

ADJUSTED CHART

Spreadsheets can be dangerous. If something gets changed unintentionally, the formulas can generate results that are dangerously wrong but look reasonable enough that the user does not notice. Having the spreadsheet generate a graphic chart is a great help in detecting this sort of error.

Bridle Math References

There are a lot of factors that go into the proper design of a bridle and the math presented here is but one small supplement to those factors. As mentioned earlier, a spreadsheet built from this section can be easily expanded to incorporate additional calculations. Here are three excellent sources for information on bridles as used by stagehands:

Harry Donovan, *Entertainment Rigging* (Seattle: Rigging Seminars, 2002), Chapters 20 to 23.

Jay O. Glerum, *Stage Rigging Handbook*, 3rd ed. (Carbondale, IL: Southern Illinois University Press, 2007), pages 17-20.

Fred Breitfelder, *Bridle Dynamics for Production Riggers* eBook available at: www.bridledynamics.com

Building Custom Bridle Legs

One final note is in order here. Many stagehands are accustomed to only using rigging hardware with stock lengths. A bridle leg calculated to a fraction of an inch may not seem so useful when the smallest adjustment is the 3 3/4" link of a STAC chain. In these circumstances, the calculated bridle can be used as a minimum length check: as long as both legs are built longer than the calculated value, the angle will not be exceeded.

It is entirely within the wheelhouse of stagehands to build custom rigging – including a bridle leg – which is accurate to within a fraction of an inch. The most important step here is to understand the effective length of each and every component in the system down to a fraction of an inch. With a simple **pick length calculator**, the rigging can be nailed. Every time.

For a good discussion of this, see:

Andrew James Gitchel, "Pick-Length Calculator: A Quick Reference", *Technical Design Solutions for Theatre, volume 3* (New York: Focal Press, 2013), pages 137-138.

[THIS PAGE INTENTIONALLY BLANK]

Will it fit in the elevator?

In theory, scenery is designed to fit the director's imagined world. In practice, scenery is designed to fit whatever dimension is the limiting factor on the path from shop to stage.

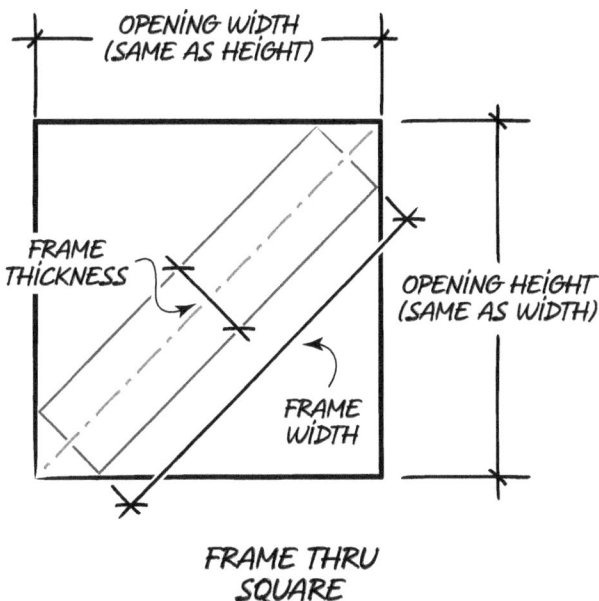

FRAME THRU SQUARE

The largest rectangle that can fit through a square opening is a simple geometric problem. For a given opening and a given thickness, the maximum width of a frame that can fit through a square hole is:

$$\text{Max. Width of Frame} = \frac{\text{Opening Width}}{\text{Sin } 45°} - \text{Frame Thickness}$$

It is also worth noting that once the frame reaches a certain thickness, there stops being any advantage to taking it diagonally thru a square opening. This limiting factor, in terms of the opening size, is:

$$\text{Thickness Limit} = \text{Opening Width} \times \sqrt{2} - \text{Opening Width}$$

For frames of thickness greater than this limit, there is no advantage to an angled approach and the opening width is the limit for the frame width.

Take, for example, a grid hatch that has a 48" × 48" opening. What is the longest piece of grid pipe that can be brought up? Because this grid has 3" gaps between slats (the channels that make up the floor of the grid), we'll use 3 inch Schedule 40 pipe because its actual diameter is 3 1/2" and it can't fall thru the gap. We'll plan on hoisting the pipe up level, without tipping it, to reduce any risk of dropping it. In terms of setting up the problem, "width of frame" becomes "length of pipe" and "frame thickness" becomes "pipe diameter".

$$\text{Max. Length of Pipe} = \frac{\text{Opening Width}}{\text{Sin } 45°} - \text{Pipe Diameter}$$

$$\text{Max. Length of Pipe} = \frac{48}{\text{Sin } 45°} - 3.5 = 64.382$$

Rounding down, 64.382" equates to a pipe that is 5'-4".

What happens if we want to bring pipe up four at a time? Now the diameter will be a bundle that is 7" wide.

$$\text{Max. Length of Pipe} = \frac{48}{\text{Sin } 45°} - 7$$

$$\text{Max. Length of Pipe} = 60.882$$

Five foot pipes sound like a good choice, and this is a fine use of the square opening equation. Of course, most openings are rectangles and not squares...

Part 5 - Will it fit in the elevator?   **235**

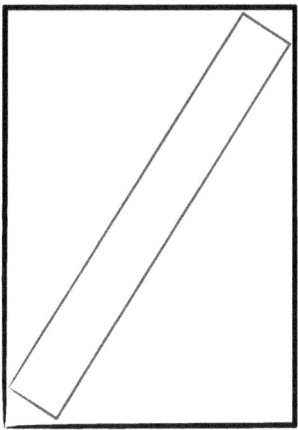

**FRAME THRU
RECTANGLE**

For a frame of a given thickness, the greatest width that can pass through a rectangular opening is actually quite a complicated problem. But it has been solved and this problem is common enough to the theater that the solution is worth developing here. **Be warned: there is quite a bit of math coming.** But if it is all wrangled into a spreadsheet, at the end of the day, all you will need to do is open the spreadsheet, type three numbers, and you will be able to instantly answer the "will it fit?" question.

In a geometric sense, we want to find a rectangle inscribed in another rectangle where we know the exterior rectangle dimensions and one of the interior rectangle dimensions. Visualize for a moment how the angle of the interior rectangle changes as its width changes.

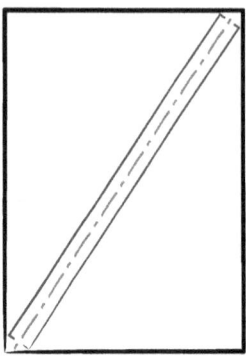 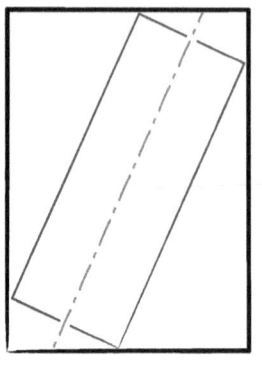 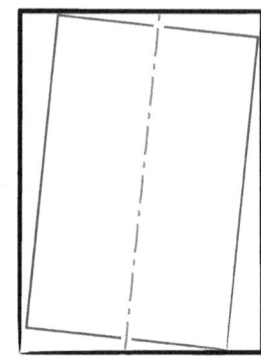

VARIOUS FITS

These shifting relationships end up being resolved through the use of a fourth order polynomial, whose general form is known as the Quartic Equation:

$$x^4 + 4ax^3 + 6bx^2 + 4cx + d = 0$$

You may recall that the equation $x^2 = 9$ has two solutions. The variable x can be either three or negative three and the equation works. (A negative number times a negative number gives a positive result.) Similarly, for a fourth order polynomial, there are four roots that can resolve the equation, though they may need imaginary numbers to do it. Yes, that's right, imaginary numbers. Here are the four general roots for the quartic.

$$x_1 = -a + \sqrt{u} + \sqrt{v + \sqrt{w}}$$

$$x_2 = -a + \sqrt{u} - \sqrt{v + \sqrt{w}}$$

$$x_3 = -a - \sqrt{u} + \sqrt{v + \sqrt{w}}$$

$$x_4 = -a - \sqrt{u} - \sqrt{v + \sqrt{w}}$$

Note that the variables u, v and w are intermediate variables that are based on the coefficients a, b, c and d. We'll get there in a moment. All of the above is the general form of the Quartic Equation.

Part 5 - Will it fit in the elevator?

Our particular problem with rectangles is solved with a version of this equation. We are going to step thru the entire process. **It is encouraged that no one ever do this math by hand and instead uses a spreadsheet program.**

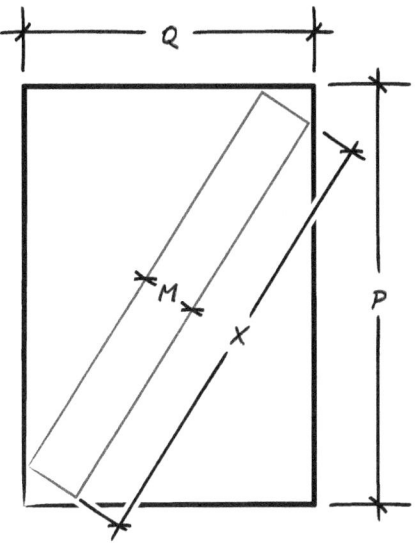

DIMENSIONAL DEFINITIONS

The opening in question is a rectangle with side *p* and side *q*. The thickness of the frame is *m*. We want to find the width of the frame *x*. Note that we are limiting these variables such that *p > m* and *q > m*. Here is the equation for how these variables interact:

$$x^4 - \left(p^2 + q^2 + 2m^2\right)x^2 + 4pqmx - \left(p^2 + q^2 - m^2\right)m^2 = 0$$

Note that there is no x^3 term in this equation. That means, referring back to the general quartic equation, that the coefficient of x^3 is equal to zero. Here is how it all breaks down:

$$a = 0$$
$$b = \frac{-(p^2 + q^2 + 2m^2)}{6}$$
$$c = \frac{4pqm}{4} = pqm$$
$$d = -(p^2 + q^2 - m^2)m^2$$

We now need to pass these variables **a, b, c,** and **d** through some intermediate equations before arriving at the four roots. We did mention not to try these problems by hand, yes? It is worth noting that **a** will always be zero, **b** will always be negative, **c** will always be positive, and **d** will always by negative. In solving quartics, whether terms are positive or negative determines whether or not the quartic can actually be solved. For the sake of brevity and clarity, we will focus on solving this particular form of quartic and ignore the theory. We aren't getting the full treatment of the general form, but we will get an equation that works to solve the "will it fit in the elevator?" problem. On to the next step:

Here are the first intermediate variables from the general quartic equation:

$$g = a^2 - b$$
$$h = b^3 + c^2 - 2abc + dg$$
$$k = \frac{4}{3}ac - b^3 - \frac{1}{3}d$$

Because **a = 0**, we can remove it and get:

Now, the next intermediate equation. Note that here we use a capital

$$g = -b$$
$$h = b^3 + c^2 + dg$$
$$k = -b^2 - \frac{1}{3}d$$

L whereas most authors use a lowercase **l**. Just because everyone does it, doesn't change the fact that lowercase **l** looks a lot like a 1.

Part 5 - Will it fit in the elevator?

$$L = \frac{1}{2}\left(h + \sqrt{h^2 + k^3}\right)^{\frac{1}{3}} + \frac{1}{2}\left(h - \sqrt{h^2 + k^3}\right)^{\frac{1}{3}}$$

We are now at the last set of intermediate equations before the root equations. We did suggest not attempting this by hand, right?

$$u = g + L$$
$$v = 2g - L$$
$$w = 4u2 + 3k - 12gL$$

Finally, we have arrived at the four roots for the quadratic equation. These are going to have some of their signs reversed when compared to the general form because of this relationship:

$$2a^3 - 3ab + c > 0$$

Which, for us, resolves to:

$$c > 0$$

Remember that for this particular problem, c will always be positive so we will never need to check this condition. We will always be reversing the signs on all of the terms except $\sqrt{w}$. We are also going to drop out *a* because we know it will always be zero. Again, we are not diving into the general theory but you deserve to know that this is happening. For this problem, here are the four roots:

$$x_1 = -\sqrt{u} - \sqrt{v + \sqrt{w}}$$

$$x_2 = -\sqrt{u} + \sqrt{v + \sqrt{w}}$$

$$x_3 = \sqrt{u} - \sqrt{v + \sqrt{w}}$$

$$x_4 = \sqrt{u} + \sqrt{v + \sqrt{w}}$$

Equation Road Map

The General Form of the Quartic Equation

$$ax^4 + bx^3 + cx^2 + dx + e = 0$$

A Useful Variation on the Quartic Equation for Optimization Problems.
The Merriman / Woodward Approach, based off the work of Euler and Legrange

$$x^4 + 4ax^3 + 6bx^2 + 4cx + d = 0$$

Working way back in the 18th century

First set of intermediate variables:
$$\begin{cases} g = a^2 - b \\ h = b^3 + c^3 - 2abc + dg \\ k = \frac{4}{3}ac - b^3 - \frac{1}{3}d \\ L = \frac{1}{2}\left(h + \sqrt{h^2 + k^3}\right)^{\frac{1}{3}} + \frac{1}{2}\left(h - \sqrt{h^2 + k^3}\right)^{\frac{1}{3}} \end{cases}$$

Plug the first set into the second set

Second set of intermediate variables:
$$\begin{cases} u = g + L \\ v = 2g - L \\ w = 4u^2 + 3k - 12gL \end{cases}$$

The roots are the solution to the problem

THE FOUR ROOTS OF THE QUARTIC

IF...

$$2a^3 - 3ab + c < 0$$

THEN...

$$x_1 = -a + \sqrt{u} + \sqrt{v + \sqrt{w}}$$
$$x_2 = -a + \sqrt{u} - \sqrt{v + \sqrt{w}}$$
$$x_3 = -a - \sqrt{u} + \sqrt{v + \sqrt{w}}$$
$$x_4 = -a - \sqrt{u} - \sqrt{v + \sqrt{w}}$$

IF...

$$2a^3 - 3ab + c > 0$$

THEN..

$$x_1 = a - \sqrt{u} - \sqrt{v + \sqrt{w}}$$
$$x_2 = a - \sqrt{u} + \sqrt{v + \sqrt{w}}$$
$$x_3 = a + \sqrt{u} - \sqrt{v + \sqrt{w}}$$
$$x_4 = a + \sqrt{u} + \sqrt{v + \sqrt{w}}$$

Our Particular Problem

$$x^4 - (p^2 + q^2 + 2m^2)x^2 + 4pqmx - (p^2 + q^2 - m^2)m^2 = 0$$

p, q, m are dimensions, *x* is the missing dimension — Worked out by some clever people a while ago

STEP 1

We need our equation (*above*) to look like the useful variation (*previous* page)

$$x^4 - \underline{(p^2 + q^2 + 2m^2)}x^2 + \underline{4pqm}x - \underline{(p^2 + q^2 - m^2)m^2} = 0$$

No x^3 term in our equation so: $4a = 0$

$$x^4 + 4\underline{a}x^3 + 6\underline{b}x^2 + 4\underline{c}x + \underline{d} = 0$$

STEP 2

Putting our dimensions into quartic terms

$a = 0$ (Because we have no x^3 term)

$-(p^2 + q^2 + 2m^2) = 6b$ Simplifying... $b = \dfrac{-(p^2 + q^2 + 2m^2)}{6}$

$4pqm = 4c$ $c = \dfrac{4pqm}{4} = pqm$

$-(p^2 + q^2 - m^2)m^2 = d$ $d = -(p^2 + q^2 - m^2)m^2$

STEP 3

Now put *a, b, c, d* into the intermediate variables...

First Set
$$\begin{cases} g = a^2 - b = -b \\ h = b^3 + c^3 - 2abc + dg = b^3 + c^3 + dg \\ k = \dfrac{4}{3}ac - b^3 - \dfrac{1}{3}d = -b^2 - \dfrac{1}{3}d \\ L = \dfrac{1}{2}\left(h + \sqrt{h^2 + k^3}\right)^{\frac{1}{3}} + \dfrac{1}{2}\left(h - \sqrt{h^2 + k^3}\right)^{\frac{1}{3}} \end{cases}$$

Second Set
$$\begin{cases} u = g + L \\ v = 2g - L \\ w = 4u2 + 3k - 12g \end{cases}$$

STEP 4

Now put *u, v, w* into the four roots...

Because...
$$2a^3 - 3ab + c > 0$$

$$\begin{cases} x_1 = a - \sqrt{u} - \sqrt{v + \sqrt{w}} \\ x_2 = a - \sqrt{u} + \sqrt{v + \sqrt{w}} \\ x_3 = a + \sqrt{u} - \sqrt{v + \sqrt{w}} \\ x_4 = a + \sqrt{u} + \sqrt{v + \sqrt{w}} \end{cases}$$

Our Answer

In the wonderful, ethereal world of numbers, a frame with thickness m and a width of x_1, x_2, x_3, or x_4 will fit through a doorway of height p and width q. When actual values for p, q and m are put into the equation, x_1 will be a negative number and both x_3 and x_4 will resolve to include $\sqrt{-1}$. The square root of negative one is the imaginary number i. In typical spreadsheet programs, a cell with an imaginary number will throw an error.

Of the four equations, only x_2 provides a dimension for a frame that we can build in a shop. We can use the following equation to determine the angle θ that the frame will sit relative to the ground in order to pass through the doorway. It is cleaner if we first establish z, the diagonal measurement of the frame of width x and thickness m.

$$z = \sqrt{x^2 + m^2}$$

$$\theta = 90° - \left(\arctan\left(\frac{x}{m}\right) - \arccos\left(\frac{q}{z}\right) \right)$$

We can also establish the dimensions **A, B, C,** and **D**. (Don't confuse these dimensions with the intermediate equation variables – we're running out of alphabet with this problem.) Dimensions **B** and **C** are useful if, for example, a cart is to be built to roll the frame through the doorway.

Part 5 - Will it fit in the elevator?

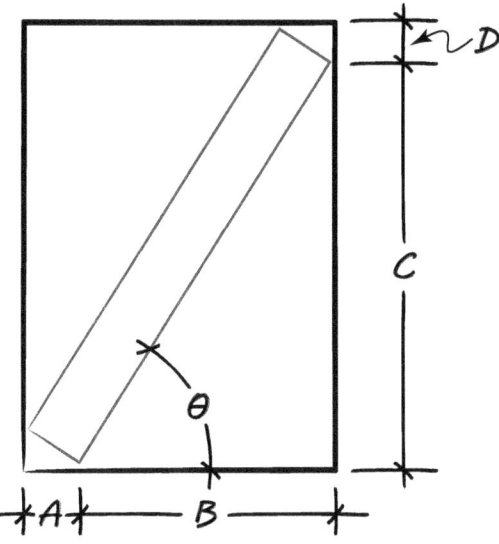

DIMENSIONAL DEFINITIONS

$$A = m \sin(\theta)$$

$$B = x \cos(\theta)$$

$$C = x \sin(\theta)$$

$$D = m \cos(\theta)$$

An important note here: this equation is to find a rectangle inscribed in another rectangle. At a certain point, as **m** increases for a given **p** and **q**, the resulting **x** will become less than the value of **p**. What does this mean? As the frame gets thicker, eventually it reaches a point where there is no advantage to angling the frame through the opening. At this thickness – and for any frame of greater thickness – the limiting factor for width is just **p** and there is no reason to take the frame on an angle. We saw this with the square opening as well.

Did we mention that it is best to put this all into a spreadsheet? Creating spreadsheet calculators allow for quick iterations. In this case, it can be handy to check any opening from trailers and shipping containers to grid hatches and trap plugs. Remember the garbage in/garbage out rule: if the exact opening is put into the spreadsheet and the resultant exact dimensions are used to build a frame, the stagehands are going to be scraping a lot of paint to get that frame through that doorway. A better approach is to measure the opening, then subtract an appropriate amount of clearance from each side. The vertical height usually wants more clearance than the horizontal width.

Where did all of this math come from? This is a classic if somewhat obscure problem that shows up every few decades in the recreational math magazines. Yes, recreational math. One of the best sources and the basis of much of the preceding, however, is an 1896 engineering text book called *Higher Mathematics* by Mansfield Merriman and Robert S. Woodward. The Quartic Equation appears on pages 19 through 21.* For an authoritative treatment of the math, see also John E. Wetzel's 2000 article in *Mathematics Magazine* "Rectangles in Rectangles". Regardless of whether you find the use of a nineteenth century textbook delightful or ridiculous, the nice thing is that the results can be immediately validated by drawing them in a CAD program (or very carefully on graph paper).

The following table provides validation data for your own spreadsheet. It also is a useful quick reference for some common openings. Please note that, except as indicated, no tolerance or additional clearance has been added. **Take your own measurements for your own applications.**

---

* Interesting aside: the authors of *Higher Mathematics* note that this equation was commonly used by civil engineers to calculate the dimensions of diagonals in trusses.

Common Door Opening Sizes

	Width	Height	Frame Thickness	Max. Frame Width
Typical Residential Door*	2'-11"	6'-6 1/2"	2"	7'-0.494"
			4"	6'-11.111"
			6"	6'-9.809"
Max. Width Commercial Door*	3'-11"	6'-6 1/2"	2"	7'-5.747"
			4"	7'-4.034"
			6"	7'-2.361
Min. Width Commercial Door*	2'-7"	6'-6 1/2"	2"	6'-11.072"
			4"	6'-9.832"
			6"	6'-8.688"
Typical-ish Passenger Elevator Door	3'-0"	7'-0"	2"	7'-5.974"
			4"	7'-4.629"
			6"	7'-3.364"
Typical 53 ft Trailer Door	8'-2"	9'-2"	2"	12'-1.337"
			4"	11'-11.352"
			6"	11'-9.368"

Here's a lesson a lot of us learn the hard way: Note the big difference in size between a 53 foot trailer's door and a rental truck's door

	Width	Height	Frame Thickness	Max. Frame Width
Typical-ish Rental Truck Door**	≈7'-4"	≈ 7'-4"	2"	10'-2.451"
			4"	10'-0.451"
			6"	9'-10.457"
Typical 40 ft Sea Cube	7'-8"	7'-5"	2"	10'-6.005"
			4"	10'-4.006"
			6"	10'-2.008"
Typical 40 ft High Cube	7'-8"	8'-5"	2"	11'-2.629"
			4"	11'-0.639"
			6"	10'-0.650"

*1" subtracted from width for stop strips and 1 ½" from height for stop strip and threshold (No Other Tolerances Added)

** For a square opening, use the "frame thru square" equation

Microsoft Excel® Syntax for Rectangle in Rectangle

The following is the exact formulas for using the above math in Excel. Anything in this `font` indicates what should be typed into each cell. The one trick used below is to name cells so that the equations read like real math rather than a spreadsheet. For a given cell, simply enter the name, such as `p`, in the box to the left of where the formula is entered. (There are plenty of simple tutorials online: search for "name cell in excel".) The formatting choices are arbitrary and simple; once you have the spreadsheet working, modify as you like.

Cell	Cell Content	Note
A1	`1st Opening Dimension (feet)`	This is a Label
B2		Name this cell `p`
A2	`2nd Opening Dimension (feet)`	Label
B2		Name this cell `q`
A3	`Thickness of Frame (feet)`	Label
B3		Name this cell `m`
	The blank cells above are for user input, all the calculations occur below	
A4	`1st Intermediate Variable`	Label
B4	`=0`	Name this cell `a`
A5	`2nd Intermediate Variable`	Label
B5	`=-(p^2+q^2+2*m^2)/6`	Name this cell `b`
A6	`3rd Intermediate Variable`	Label
B6	`=p*q*m`	Name this cell `cee`
	Excel reserves "c" for other purposes so we have to use "cee"	
A7	`4th Intermediate Variable`	Label
B7	`=-(p^2+q^2-m^2)*m^2`	Name this cell `d`
A8	`5th Intermediate Variable`	Label
B8	`=a^2-b`	Name this cell `g`
A9	`6th Intermediate Variable`	Label
B9	`=b^3+cee^2-2*a*b*cee+d*g`	Name this cell `h`

Part 5 - Will it fit in the elevator? 247

Cell	Content	Note
A10	7th Intermediate Variable	Label
B10	=4/3*a*cee-b^2-1/3*d	Name this cell k
A11	8th Intermediate Variable	Label
B11	=1/2*(h+SQRT(h^2+k^3))^(1/3)+1/2*(h-SQRT(h^2+k^3))^(1/3)	Name this cell L
A12	9th Intermediate Variable	Label
B12	=g+L	Name this cell u
A13	10th Intermediate Variable	Label
B13	=2*g-L	Name this cell v
A14	11th Intermediate Variable	Label
B14	=4*u^2+3*k-12*g*L	Name this cell w

Results are next, only Root 2 will be useful, but calculating the others is a good way to check that the sheet is working correctly

Cell	Content	Note
A15	Root 1	Label
B15	=a-SQRT(u)-SQRT(v+SQRT(w))	This should always return a negative number
A16	Root 2	Label
B16	=a-SQRT(u)+SQRT(v+SQRT(w))	This is the maximum width of the frame, name this cell root2
A17	Root 3	Label
B17	=a+SQRT(u)-SQRT(v-SQRT(w))	Label should return #NUM!
A18	Root 4	Label
B18	=a+SQRT(u)+SQRT(v-SQRT(w))	Label should return #NUM!

The following converts the Root 2 answer into feet and inches

Cell	Content	Note
A20	Max Frame Width	Label
A21	Feet	Label
B21	=TRUNC(root2)	The foot part of the answer
A22	Inches	Label

B22	=(root2-TRUNC(root2))*12	The inch part of the answer

The following finds the angle θ of the frame, where 0° or 180° would be the frame flat on the ground and 90° would be straight upward

A24	Diagonal Length of Frame	Label
B24	=SQRT(root2^2+m^2)	Name this cell z
A25	Angle of Frame	Label
B25	=90-(DEGREES(ATAN(root2/m)) -DEGREES(ACOS(q/z)))	Angle of Frame Name this cell theta

All of the above creates a functional calculator. All we need to actually solve the problem is available in the calculator. So we can stop here.

Part 5 - Will it fit in the elevator?

But it's always useful to visualize a problem, and it's relatively simple to add a chart that will actually draw out the rectangle-in-rectangle. To do this, we need to calculate the angle of the interior rectangle and the graphic dimensions a, b, c, and d. We are going to skip a few rows and continue with the graphic add-on to the calculator.

Cell	Cell Content	Note
A28	Dimension A	This is a Label
B28	=m*SIN(RADIANS(theta))	Name this cell dim_a
A29	Dimension B	Label
B29	=root2*COS(RADIANS(theta))	Name this cell dim_b
A30	Dimension C	Label
B30	=root2*SIN(RADIANS(theta))	Name this cell dim_c
A31	Dimension D	Label
B31	=m*COS(RADIANS(theta))	Label

These dimensions correspond with the dimensions shown in the image on page 241. The next step is to use these dimensions to create a set of coordinates that can be used to generate a scatter chart. We are going to insert these coordinates in their own section of the spreadsheet, to the right of everything we've done so far. We are also going to change the format just a bit, to make sure we are putting down the coordinates in the correct relationship.

	Column D	Column E	Note:
Row 1	0	0	
Row 2	=q	0	These are the coordinates for the exterior rectangle
Row 3	=q	=p	
Row 4	0	=p	
Row 5	0	0	
Row 6			This row blank
Row 7	=dim_a	0	

Row 8	=q	=dim_c	These are the coordinates for the interior rectangle
Row 9	=dim_b	=p	
Row 10	0	=dim_d	
Row 11	=dim_a	0	
Row 12			This row blank
Row 13	0	0	
Row 14	=MAX(p,q)*1.25	0	This section draws a square reference frame to keep proportions accurate
Row 15	=MAX(p,q)*1.25	=MAX(p,q)*1.25	
Row 16	0	=MAX(p,q)*1.25	
Row 17	0	0	

The next step is to simply highlight everything from cell D1 to cell E17, then insert a scatter chart with straight lines. Exact steps will vary by version of Excel, but on one version, go to the "Insert" tab, then in the "Charts" section of the ribbon, there should be a drop-down option for "Scatter with Straight Lines". The goal is to produce a graph that looks like this:

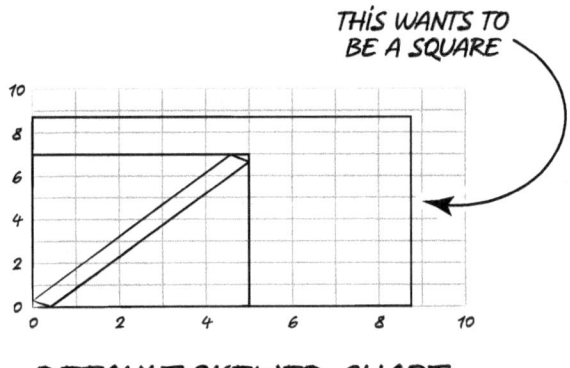

DEFAULT SKEWED CHART

The larger outside rectangle is actually meant to be a square. The proportions of the chart should be adjusted until this square reference frame looks square. Once the chart is adjusted, it will live update based on any new dimensions fed into it, but will maintain a square perspective. This allows us to visualize the opening and the object we are pushing thru it.

Part 5 - Will it fit in the elevator?

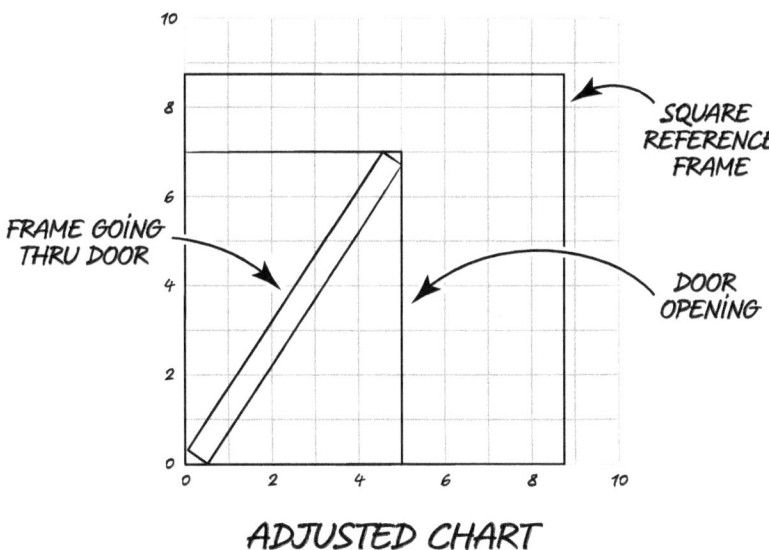

ADJUSTED CHART

[THIS PAGE INTENTIONALLY BLANK]

Acknowledgments

A book like this springs from working with conscientious folks who want to do the job right. When I sat down to write these acknowledgments, I started making a list of everyone who has gotten their hands dirty with me on a stage or in a shop. (Or in the alley behind the stage or shop, or at a freight yard, or on a boat, or in a television studio, or on the side of the road next to a broken-down truck…) Very quickly, the list became more than 200 names long. Using a small but still-legible font, this list filled a lot of pages. Worse, there were a number of folks who did not make the list. Some of the best stagehands I have worked with, I only knew by a first name or a nickname. And there are folks who taught me lessons I'll never forget whose names I never knew.

Writing a list like this lets you count some things about your career. For the last fifteen years, I have worked in over sixty venues across ten states – and I'm much more a shop or house stagehand than a touring one. Working for a range of theaters and shops, both as a staff member and on the bounce, I have been lucky enough to have worked with stagehands of all stripes, from more than fifteen countries. A piece of each one's ability and knowledge lives with me; I did my best to put it into these pages. So to each of you: my deepest thanks. Please know this book is a part of your legacy.

There are a few folks who were on that list that I need to thank again. Dan Carr, Tegan Condon, LT Gourzong, Will Hartley, Neil Mulligan, and Steph Waaser all read initial drafts of this book. Their specific comments on the manuscript were much like the many conversations we have had about the craft over the years: well-considered, insightful, and motivating.

This book also owes Jon Feustel a debt for convincing the author to get off his butt and go do it

[THIS PAGE INTENTIONALLY BLANK]

REFERENCES

LAYOUT

John Carroll, *Measuring, Marking & Layout: A Builder's Guide* (Newtown, CT: Taunton Press, 1998).

John Blurton, *Scenery: Drafting and Construction* (New York: Routledge, 2001), chapter 6.

KNOTS

Clifford Ashley, *The Ashley Book of Knots*, Corrected Edition (New York: Doubleday, 1993).

Philippe Petit, *Why Knot?* (New York: Abrams Image, 2013).

Jan Adkins, *Line: Tying it Up, Tying it Down* (Brooklin, ME: Wooden Boat Books, 2004).

PHYSICS

This may be the best book ever written in terms of making engineering concepts available to stagehands:

Alan Hendrickson with Colin Buckhurst, *Mechanical Design for the Stage* (New York: Focal Press, 2013).

A book purposefully and cleanly designed for teaching:

Verda Beth Martell and Eric C. Martell, *The Physics of Theatre: Mechanics* (North Charleston, SC: CreateSpace, 2016).

A book does not need to follow a strict textbook format to be extraordinarily useful. One of the greatest works on the challenges and solutions to material handling – full of genuinely useful ideas as well as relevant mathematics – is this delightful picture book:

Jan Adkins, *Moving Heavy Things* (New York: Macmillian, 1980).

PHYSICS: STACKING & FOOTING FLATS

For a statics textbook that provides a rigorous approach to these problems, see:

David J. McGill and Wilton W. King, *Engineering Mechanics: Statics*, 4th ed. (Bloomington, IN: Tichenor Publishing & Printing, 2003). Examples of "the ladder problem" can be found on pages 167 and 438.

Below is a diagram and the equations for calculating uplift. Both truss weights were selected from the same supplier; no hardware weight was included. Note that this text conservatively assumed that the footer would be resisting uplift by pushing down directly above the pivot point. For the sake of comparison, the equation for the corner is also provided.

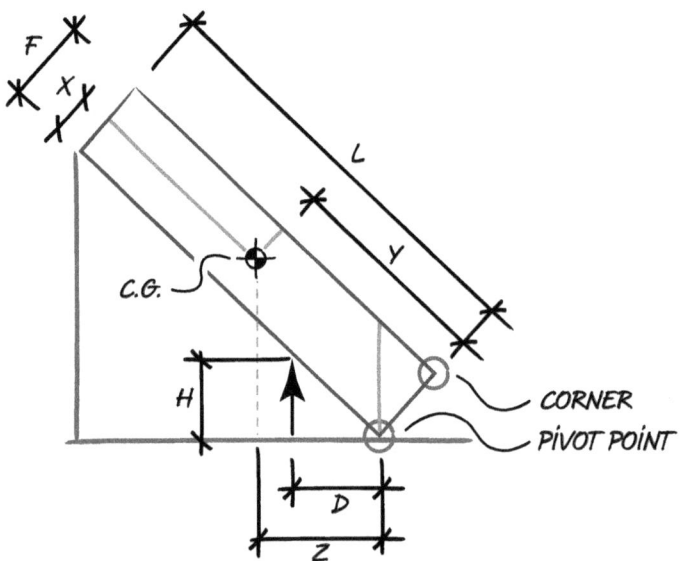

ASSUME:

Rectilinear cross section (side f is perpendicular to side L)
d = horizontal distance of lifter's grip from pivot point
h = vertical height of lifter's grip on object
w = weight of object with CG at datum point
x, y, z define location of CG datum point
$0 < d < z$

PLUMB LINE OF CG FROM PIVOT POINT:

$$z = \cos\left(\tan^{-1}\left(\frac{x}{y}\right) + \tan^{-1}\left(\frac{h}{d}\right)\right)\sqrt{x^2 + y^2}$$

UPLIFT ABOVE PIVOT POINT:

$$UPLIFT_{pivot} = w\left(\frac{z}{d} - 1\right)$$

UPLIFT AT CORNER:

$$UPLIFT_{corner} = w\left(\frac{z - d}{d + f\cos\left(90° - \tan^{-1}\left(\frac{h}{d}\right)\right)}\right)$$

HACKSAW WINDOW HOLD

It is tough to trace the original source on tips and tricks. But when a source can be found, it is worth noting the reference. John Blurton makes no claim to inventing the hacksaw trick, but he does give a good description of it in his book, which is a generally excellent text:

John Blurton, *Scenery: Drafting and Construction* (New York: Routledge, 2001), page 103.

If you know the origin of a tip or trick mentioned in this book, please let the author know (see contact information listed at beginning). Every effort has and will be made for giving credit where credit is due.

SPOTLIGHTS

Bert Morris, *Getting the Most from Your Followspot* (Washington DC: Theatrical Technicians Inc., 1990).

June Abernathy, *The Spotlight Operator's Handbook* (Johnson City, TN: Spring Knoll Press, 2019).

SOFT GOODS

Soft good information drawn from the *Backstage Handbook*. There is a general dearth of information on soft goods. Hanging a piece of fabric is simple; getting a stage drape to work well and look good is a nuanced, complex specialty. (It is worth noting that some of the most common and most sophisticated machinery used on stage is devoted to soft goods.) Currently, the most available resource is manufacturer catalogs. The best catalogs include comprehensive reference guides to types and finish of curtains. Some manufactures even break this information out into separate documents.

Paul Carter, *Backstage Handbook*, 3rd ed. (Louisville, KY: Broadway Press, 1994), page 283.

PNEUMATICS

For an in-depth exploration of the causes and costs of leaks:

Brian Elliott, *Compressed Air Operations Manual* (New York: McGraw-Hill, 2006), chapter 11.

For a theater-oriented perspective on pneumatics, see:

Eric Hart, *The Prop Effects Guidebook* (New York: Routledge, 2018), chapter 6.

Oxygen tanks are most likely to be encountered as part of oxygen-fuel gas welding and cutting rigs. Their proper use is covered by OSHA standard 1910.253. Among the many provisions, 1910.253(d)(5)(i) states that material used for testing oxygen lines shall be oil free and noncombustible. Soap, it is worth remembering, is usually made from either oils or hydrocarbons.

FAIL-SAFE

The concept of fail-safe is one part of a larger discussion of engineering structures and machines that are safe and efficient. There are other related and overlapping concepts, such as "Single Failure Proof", that are just as important. Perhaps the best umbrella term for all of these is "**Failure Modes and Effects Analysis**", often abbreviated as FMEA. This is a critical process that will only become more important as shows continue to get bigger, heavier, more complicated, and technologically more integrated. To learn more about these critical concepts specific to our business, check out the following resources.

Alan Hendrickson with Colin Buckhurst, *Mechanical Design for the Stage* (New York: Focal Press, 2013), pages 145-154, 313-314.

Gareth Conner with Loren Schreiber, *Scenic Automation Handbook* (New York: Routledge, 2018), pages 349-355.

Jim Shumway's book *Automated Peformer Flying*, in addition to useful technical insight, has a particularly good description of how to talk about safety with performers. In general, the human factor can be shockingly absent in engineering texts. Unfortunately, this trend has carried into many technical works in our own field.

Too little attention is paid to what we should tell a performer that has to stand under, on top of, or otherwise interact with the contraptions we bring on stage.

Jim Shumway, *Automated Performer Flying* (New York: Routledge, 2020), page 229.

There are a lot of general engineering books that cover these topics. NASA is a generally respected source of engineering information, and their standards are freely available. These standards define terms of art, such as "fail safe". Here is an example:

NASA-STD-5019, Fracture Control Requirements for Spaceflight Hardware (Washington, DC: National Aeronautics and Space Administration, 2008).

RIGHT TO WORK

Right to Work is an active political issue. As such, it does not seem possible to give a single, unbiased reference. So here are two:

AFL-CIO	National Right to Work Legal Defense Foundation
Information from a coalition of unions that includes many of the entertainment-focused unions.	Information from an issue-specific 501(c)(3) nonprofit organization that has been advocating since 1968.
aflcio.org/issues/right-work	www.nrtw.org

For information on the Federal Minimum Wage, see the Department of Labor's "History of Federal Minimum Wage Rates Under the Fair Labor Standards Act, 1938-2009". Here is a link, last accessed in the Fall of 2020:

www.dol.gov/sites/dolgov/files/WHD/legacy/files/chart.pdf

The Bureau of Labor Statistic's Consumer Price Index (CPI) Inflation Calculator was found here:

www.bls.gov/data/inflation_calculator.htm

How the CPI is calculated is explained here: www.bls.gov/cpi/

Montana's law relating to at-will workers is called the "Wrongful Discharge from Employment Act" (MCA, Title 39, Chapter 2, Part 9).

There are lots of sources floating around the internet that discuss it. You can read it for yourself here:

leg.mt.gov/bills/mca/title_0390/chapter_0020/part_0090/sections_index.html

(Website last updated September 2020, last accessed November 2020)

FUNDAMENTALS: STAGE DIRECTIONS

John Blurton, *Scenery: Drafting and Construction* (New York: Routledge, 2001), page 14.

References

FUNDAMENTALS: ELECTRICITY

The words we use when talking about electricity can be a fraught subject. There are parallel vocabularies. The terms that electricians use day-to-day running wire have alternative names in the NEC. There are also common terms that we use which are not the most technically accurate. What we call "voltage" is really a measure of electric potential difference or electromotive force. What we call "wattage" is really power. What we call "amperage" is really current. These terms act as mnemonics that help us connect the unit (volt, watt, or amp) to what they measure and are a convenient shorthand. We could say, "give me the measurement of electromotive force in volts" or we could ask "what's the voltage?" Working electricians have been using the shorthand terms since the 19th century, so we will continue to use them in this book.

The NEC is the standard across the industry. There is a handbook version that includes both the code and integrated narrative commentary to make the code more accessible.

NFPA 70: National Electrical Code Handbook (Quincy, MA: National Fire Protection Association, 2020).

Resources focused on show business:

Richard Cadena, *Electricity for the Entertainment Electrician & Technician,* 2nd ed. (New York: Focal Press, 2009).

Harry C. Box, *Set Lighting Technician's Handbook,* 5th ed. (New York: Routledge, 2020).

General reference:

Terrell Croft et al,. *American Electricians' Handbook*, 16th ed. (New York: McGraw-Hill, 2013).

Herbert P. Richter and Frederic P. Harwell, *Practical Electrical Wiring*, 21st ed. (New Richmond, WI: Park Publishing, 2011).

For information on electrical fires and worker deaths, see the following NFPA reports:

Richard Campbell, *Fatal Electrical Injuries at Work* (Quincy, MA: National Fire Protection Association, 2018).

Richard Campbell, *Home Electrical Fires* (Quincy, MA: National Fire Protection Association, 2019).

Available at:

www.nfpa.org/News-and-Research/Data-research-and-tools/Electrical/

For the earliest use of the shorthand terms, see Merriam-Webster.

Merriam-Webster.com Dictionary, s.v. "amperage," accessed December 8, 2020, https://www.merriam-webster.com/dictionary/amperage.

Merriam-Webster.com Dictionary, s.v. "voltage," accessed December 8, 2020, https://www.merriam-webster.com/dictionary/voltage.

FUNDAMENTALS: BRIDLE TENSION & RIGGING

More and more books are becoming available about rigging for stagehands, many of them quite good and interesting. But there are two stagehands who each wrote a book that are the foundation.

Jay O. Glerum, *Stage Rigging Handbook*, 3rd ed. (Carbondale, IL: Southern Illinois University Press, 2007).

Harry Donovan, *Entertainment Rigging* (Seattle: Rigging Seminars, 2002).

A free resource that is extraordinarily useful is available from the Prolyte Group. It's called the *Black Book*. If you want to learn more about truss and staging, this is a great place to start. Prolyte is a Dutch company and a lot of the book has a European focus and vocabulary. Fortunately, the fundamental principles of physics are the same worldwide.

www.prolyte.com/en/support/blackbooks

FUNDAMENTALS: POWER TRANSMISSION

Naval Education and Training Program Development Center, *Basic Machines and How They Work* (New York: Dover, 1997).

Joel Wiesen, *Mechanical Aptitude and Spatial Relations Test*, 2nd ed. (Hauppauge, NY: Barron's, 2009).

FUNDAMENTALS: ORTHOGRAPHIC PROJECTION

W. Oren Parker, *Sceno-Graphic Techniques,* 3rd ed. (Carbondale, IL: Southern Illinois University Press, 1987).

Joel Wiesen, *Mechanical Aptitude and Spatial Relations Test,* 2nd ed. (Hauppauge, NY: Barron's, 2009).

For two general references that complement each other, see:

David A. Madsen and David P. Madsen, *Engineering Drawing & Design,* 6th ed. (Boston: Cengage, 2017).

Alan Jefferis and David A. Madsen, *Architectural Drafting and Design,* 5th ed. (Clifton Park, NY: Thomson Delmar Learning, 2005).

For more on how our vision system works, see:

Donald D. Hoffman, *Visual Intelligence: How We Create What We See* (New York, Norton, 1998).

TRIVIA

All sources for trivia are at the end of the section.

HARDWARE: NUTS AND BOLTS

Bolted hardware information is drawn from several reference books and compared against the catalogs of prominent vendors for verification and to confirm availability. Vendors include McMaster-Carr, Fastenal, Bolt Depot, and MSC.

Erik Oberg, et al., *Machinery's Handbook,* 28th ed. (New York: Industrial Press, 2008).

Fastener Facts (Cleveland: Barnes Distribution, 2008).

US Customs and Border Protection, "Distinguishing Bolts from Screws," *Informed Compliance Publication* (July 2012). www.cbp.gov/sites/default/files/assets/documents/2020-Feb/icp013_3.pdf

HARDWARE: DRYWALL SCREWS

Drywall Screw information is drawn from popular vendors and the manufacturers that supply them, including Hilti, Hillman, Grip Rite, Good Screws, and Grabber.

www.hilti.com/c/CLS_FASTENER_7135/CLS_DRYWALL_SCREWS_7135/CLS_SCREWS_7135/r4640
www.hillmangroup.com/us/en/Fastening-Solutions/Construction-Fastener-Products/Screws/Drywall-Screws/Coarse-Thread-Phillips-Drywall-Screw/p/531DR8
www.grip-rite.com/product/drywall-screw-2/
www.goodscrews.com/submittals
www.grabberman.com/Media/TechnicalData/555.pdf

HARDWARE: PIPE FITTINGS

Information on pipe fittings was drawn from common manufacturers and distributors, including Rose Brand, Mutual Hardware, Flint's Hire & Supply, The Light Source, and Alvin Industrial.

www.rosebrand.com/downloads/cheeseboroughw1.pdf
www.mutualhardware.com/collections/rigging-hardwareshop.
flints.co.uk/Categories/pg_tubeclamps
www.thelightsource.com/products/
www.alvinindustrial.com/

TRUSS

References to truss in this work are drawn from a comparison of several different manufacturers, including Tomcat USA (part of Area 4), James Thomas Engineering (part of Area 4), XSF, Total Structures (part of EuroTruss), and Tyler Truss. All of these manufacturers, in addition to proprietary systems, produce industry standard box truss. Known as "generic" or "general purpose" or "utility" truss, all data is based on this type of common truss with plates that bolt together.

www.tomcatglobal.com/products/box-struss
www.jthomaseng.com/products/aa
www.xsftruss.com/box-truss/
www.totalstructures.com/products/generic
www.tylertruss.com/products

See also references for *Fundamentals: Bridle Tension & Rigging.*

References

STAGE WEIGHTS & ARBORS

For general reference, see:

Jay O. Glerum, *Stage Rigging Handbook,* 3rd ed. (Carbondale, IL: Southern Illinois University Press, 2007).

Bill Sapsis et al., *Entertainment Rigging for the 21st Century* (New York: Focal Press, 2015), chapter 6.

Dimensions and weights of arbors and stage weights drawn from the catalogs of J.R. Clancy, H&H Specialties, and Thern Stage Equipment.

www.jrclancy.com/j-guide-t-bar-single-purchase-arbors.php
www.hhspecialties.com/Cat11-rev1009.pdf
thernstage.com/counterweight-rigging/side-loading-arbors/

Densities of different material were drawn from *Machinery's Handbook*, *Desk Ref*, and *Structural Design for the Stage*, and checked against common suppliers.

Erik Oberg, et al., *Machinery's Handbook,* 28th ed. (New York: Industrial Press, 2008).

Thomas J. Glover and Richard A. Young, *Desk Ref,* 4th ed. (Anchorage: Sequoia Publishing, 2019).

Alys Holden, et al. *Structural Design for the Stage,* 2nd ed. (New York: Focal Press, 2015), page 561.

Weights of different types of batten were drawn from J.R. Clancy and Thern Stage Equipment, as well as the general weight of pipe and steel bar. For Truss used as batten, see Truss references. For weight of cable, see Wire Rope references.

www.jrclancy.com/battens-and-truss-battens.php
thernstage.com/wp-content/uploads/2019/12/C4900-ladder-batten-C4900.pdf

See also references for *Fundamentals: Bridle Tension & Rigging*.

WIRE ROPE & FITTINGS

ASME Standard B30.26-2015, "Rigging Hardware," ASME International, New York, NY, 2015.

Loos & Co., *2020 Catalog*
loosnaples.com/documents/LoosNaplesCatalog.pdf

Loos & Co., *Copper Oval Sleeves*, Dwg. No. SL2 CATALOG
loosnaples.com/files/PDF/SL2.pdf

National Telephone Supply Company, *Instruction No. 32 - Splicing Flexible Steel Cables with Nicopress® Sleeves and Tools*

National Telephone Supply Company, *Nicopress Part Nos. for Military Standard MS51844*, Dwg. No. 101-3159ADC

US DOD, Military Specification MS51844E, 2012

US DOD, Military Specification MIL-DTL-83420M, 2011

Wire Rope User's Manual, 4th ed. (Alexandria, VA: Wire Rope Technical Board, 2005).

For Wire Rope Clip Manufacturers, see the catalogs of the Crosby Group, Columbus-McKinnon, and Chicago Hardware & Fixture.

www.thecrosbygroup.com/products/wire-rope-clips/crosby-450-red-u-bolt-wire-rope-clips/
www.columbusmckinnon.com
www.chicagohardware.com/catalog/12_Fclips.pdf

See also references for *Fundamentals: Bridle Tension & Rigging*.

BRIDLE GEOMETRY

See references at the end of the tip. See also references for *Fundamentals: Bridle Tension & Rigging*.

WILL IT FIT IN THE ELEVATOR?

Mansfield Merriman and Robert S. Woodward, *Higher Mathematics*, 2nd ed. (New York: Wiley, 1898), pages 19-21.
archive.org/details/highermathematic00merruoft

John E. Wetzel, "Rectangles in Rectangles", *Mathematics Magazine*, volume 73, issue 3, 2000, pages 204-211.
doi.org/10.1080/0025570X.2000.11996836

Door sizes are drawn from a number of sources. For doors in buildings, the *International Building Code* is the ultimate reference that many states use. There is an interesting letter of interpretation that both lists common door sizes and draws a distinction between "a piece of equipment" occupied only for maintenance or service and "a building or structure intended for human occupancy".

International Code Council, IBC Interpretation No. 04-05, 2003 Edition, Issued: 12-12-2006, BU_03_04_05.
www3.iccsafe.org/cs/committeeArea/pdf_file/BU_03_04_05.pdf

For doors in vehicles and shipping containers, many trucking and shipping companies list interior dimensions on their websites. It is particularly important to check – and confirm – dimensions with truck rental companies. Surprising variation exists, from trailer to trailer. For resources from show business oriented companies, see:

clarktransfer.com/wp-content/uploads/2018/12/truckspecs.pdf
stagecall.com/resources/
www.rockitcargo.com/downloads/FreightGuide_Web_R5.1%20(1).pdf

Finding door openings on rental straight trucks is a hot mess. Best practice is to measure the door that you get. Good luck.

Index

0,0. See Zero, zero

A Chorus Line 150
Acrobatic 61
Adkins, Jan 25, 255
Aircraft cable. See Wire rope
Apron 10
Arbor 60-62, 75-77, 175-185, 265-270
Ashley Book of Knots 59, 255
Ashley, Clifford. See *Ashley Book of Knots*
At-will employment 103-105, 260
Automation 51, 58, 95, 259

Barn Dooring 39-40
Batten 59, 60-61, 95, 167, 183, 265
Blind Connection 36
Blurton, John 255, 260
Bolt 36, 37, 71, 72, 92, 263
  length 84-86
  purchasing 87
  versus screw 86
  wrench charts 161-167
Bowline 21, 24, 68, 152
Breitfelder, Fred 231
Bridle 125-127, 218-231, 262
Broom 54, 70
Buffer 5, 54, 115
Burning a Foot 6, 211

Cable 17, 66, 121-124, 184

coiling 67
weight 184
C-clamp 68, 166
Center Line 7-11, 12-15, 51, 196, 199-217
Center of gravity 34, 68
Chain motor 130
Chalk box 8, 10, 15, 200, 206
Cheek plate 23
Cheeseborough 161, 167
Chip brush 42
Clove hitch. See Knots
Coffin lock 99, 167
Cotton line 21
Counterweight line set 48, 60, 71, 130
Courtesy tab 5
Crescent Wrench. See C-wrench
Crow's foot 8, 15
Crush plates 85
C-wrench 114, 151, 152, 156

Decimal feet 94, 226
Deck track 51, 95, 98
Deck winches 128
Density 177
Dish dolly 41
Donovan, Harry 231, 262
Door hold 42
Door opening 245, 267
Down House 119
Draft angle 76
Drop cloth 82
Drop the mic 57, 151
Drywall screw 172, 264

Electrical safety 122-124

Employment law 103–105, 260
Environment 115
Epoxy 55
Etiquette 56, 57

Fail-safe 100, 258, 259
Fid 48, 49
Figure 8. See Knots
Fire curtain 12–13, 62
First clear line 12
Flats 26, 27–29, 30–32, 33–34, 37–38, 71, 72, 84–85, 219
Fleet angle 93, 94
Follow spot 46
Footing 30–32, 33–35, 256
Forklift 4, 124
Friction 21, 27, 43, 68, 88–89, 134, 196
Front of House 72, 116–118, 119

Gaff tape 5, 46, 66, 150
Galling 87
Gitchel, Andrew 231
Glerum, Jay 231, 262, 265
Glitter 52, 74
Glue 55, 62
Go gauge 96, 97, 188
Granny knot. See Knots
Grommet 90–91

Hacksaw 43, 257
Half-hitch. See Knots
Hammer 37–38
Hand line 47, 48–49, 56, 92, 130
Hotel 109

Impact driver 88, 98

Keeper 23
Knots
  Bowline 21, 24, 68, 152
  Clove hitch 20–21, 59
  Figure 8 22, 67, 83, 109
  Granny 18–19
  Half-hitch 18, 20–21, 59, 83
  Reef 18
  Square 18
  Timber hitch 20–22

Ladder 28, 72, 152, 256, 265
Ladder batten 183, 265
Last bolt 71
Layout 6, 7–11, 12–15, 16, 199–217, 255
Lens 41, 135
Load bar 44, 77
Lock rail 47
Lock washer 84, 87
Locoloc 95, 186

Main rag 4, 62
Mechanical Advantage 130
Mirror Matching 26
Monster Walk 25
Mop 52
Mopping 51, 52, 74
Musser, Tharon 150

Nail 70, 114
Name tag 109
National Electrical Code 121–124, 261

Offset distance 13–15
Off stage 12, 53, 60, 118
On stage 119

Over-under 67

PAR lights 41
Petit, Philippe 59, 255
Physics 27-29, 30-32, 33-35, 125-127, 128-129, 129-134
Pipe hardware 167, 264. See Rota lock
Pipe raising 20
Pipe sway brace clamp 99
Pipe weight 183
Plaster Line 7-11, 12-15, 196, 199-217
Pneumatic 101, 102, 130, 258
Punctuality 114
Pythagorean Theorem 204

Rake 117, 119
Reef Knot. See Knots
Right to work 103-105, 260
Robot 151, 156
Rope lock 47
Rota lock 99, 152, 156

Scene shift 58
Screw 37-38, 92, 211, 263-264
  burning in 88-90
  purchasing 87, 170-173
  self-driling/tapping 86
  versus bolt 86
Setting Line 7-11, 12-15, 199-217
Sheave 21, 23-24, 93, 94
Show blacks 56
Show stoppers 62
Slipped 18-19
Smoke pocket 12-14
Socket Head Screws 165
Soft good 53, 56, 90
Solder 49

Specialty cord 21, 95. See also Wire rope
Spike 46, 48, 50
Spotlight 46, 257
Spray duster 62
Spring clamp 75
Stage directions 7, 116-118, 119-120, 260
Stage weight 76, 175-184, 265
Swage sleeve 95, 185-189
Sweeping 51-52, 70, 74
Swing 60-61

Tape (adhesive) 5, 50, 53, 56, 66, 150
Tape measure 6, 7-11, 12-15, 16, 199-217
Tapped threads/hole 36, 86, 98
Tattoo 152
Teamsters 4
Tek® screw 37, 86
Tennis ball 54
Thru connection 36
Tie line 17, 59
Tony award 150-151, 155
Toothpick 55
Torque 128-129
Trade Show 109
Trailer. See Truck
Trap plug 39
Trash bag 53, 82
Trivia 149
Truck 4, 41, 44, 77, 126, 245, 267
Truss 33-34, 126-127, 167, 262, 264
  Batten weight 183
  Circle Truss Rule 36

Unbolting 72
Union 103-104, 260
Uplift force 30-32, 33-35,

256-257

Wagon brakes 101
Walking up a flat 30
Weld nuts 36
Wheel 73, 128
Whistling 151, 155
Window 43, 257
Wire guides 61
Wire rope 21-22, 23-24, 67, 127
  swages 95-96, 185-189
  weight 183
Wire rope clips 161, 166, 189, 266
Wood epoxy putty 55
Wrench 36, 128, 151-152
  size charts 161-167

Z-axis problem 37
Zero, zero 10-11, 13, 199-217

[THIS PAGE INTENTIONALLY BLANK]

An old joke for the road...

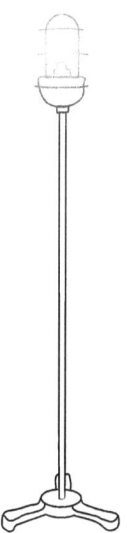

A stagehand walks into a bar and sits down. Everyone else gets up and moves to the other end of the room. The bartender, having a job to do, takes a deep breath and walks over to the stagehand.

The bartender asks, "What's with the smell, Sam?"

"Ah, well, the circus is in town and I got stuck cleaning up the elephant stall."

"Last week it was dragging feeder thru the mud, now it's shoveling elephant dung. Look, my cousin tells me their office is hiring. You're a hard worker, I could put in a word for you."

Sam looks up at the bartender, outraged.

"What? And leave show business?"

www.ingramcontent.com/pod-product-compliance
Lightning Source LLC
Chambersburg PA
CBHW071000160426
43193CB00012B/1852